P9-CMS-996

Enid Blyton and the Mystery of Children's Literature

Also by David Rudd

A COMMUNICATION STUDIES APPROACH TO CHILDREN'S LITERATURE

THE FAMOUS FIVE: A Guide to the Characters Appearing in Enid Blyton's Series

Enid Blyton and the Mystery of Children's Literature

David Rudd

First published in Great Britain 2000 by
MACMILLAN PRESS LTD
Houndmills, Basingstoke, Hampshire RG21 6XS and London
Companies and representatives throughout the world

A catalogue record for this book is available from the British Library.

ISBN 0–333–74718–6

First published in the United States of America 2000 by
ST. MARTIN'S PRESS, INC.,
Scholarly and Reference Division,
175 Fifth Avenue, New York, N.Y. 10010

ISBN 0–312–23212–8

Library of Congress Cataloging-in-Publication Data
Rudd, David, 1950–
Enid Blyton and the mystery of children's literature / David Rudd.
p. cm.
Includes bibliographical references and index.
ISBN 0–312–23212–8
1. Blyton, Enid—Criticism and interpretation—History. 2. Children's stories, English—History and criticism—Theory, etc. 3. Women and literature—England—History—20th century. 4. Children—Books and reading. I. Title.

PR6003.L8457 Z79 2000
823'.912—dc21

99–059251

This book is printed on paper suitable for recycling and made from fully managed and sustained forest sources.

10 9 8 7 6 5 4 3 2 1
09 08 07 06 05 04 03 02 01 00

Printed and bound in Great Britain by
Antony Rowe Ltd, Chippenham, Wiltshire

To my mother, the memory of my father, who only saw the beginning, my acquired mum and dad Rendle, and to Sheena, Duncan and Sophie

Contents

'The phenomenon of Enid Blyton is surely worth a Ph. D. thesis'
Ernest Moss, *The Times Literary Supplement*, 1970

DEEPING: Enid! We haven't toasted Enid!
BLYTON: Please don't worry about *me*.
WINN: We'd forgotten about you!
BLYTON: I'm quite used to being ignored. . . .

SKINNER (*raises glass*): To Enid!
OMNES: Enid!
BLYTON: This is quite absurd.
Michael Frayn (1987) *Balmoral*, pp. 71–2

'Only now, as a generation nurtured on Noddy achieves maturity without either having gone blind or weak in the head, are attitudes beginning to change.' (Charles Sarland, 1983a)

'[traditionally] sociologists have been going about their study of children mainly like colonial administrators who might be expected to write scientifically objective reports of the local populace in order to increase their understanding of native culture, and who do so by ideologically formulating only those research problems that pertain to native behaviours coming under the regulation of colonial authority.' (Matthew Speier, 1976, p. 99)

'What it [genealogical approach] really does is to entertain the claims to attention of local, discontinuous, disqualified, illegitimate knowledges against the claims of a unitary body of theory which would filter, hierarchise and order them in the name of some true knowledge. . . .' (Foucault, 1980, p. 83)

Acknowledgements

To Roger Chapman, Patricia Glennon, Richard Walker and others for finding me so many old Blyton books; also, to sisters Lynn and Debbie Atkinson (now Massey and Parkinson, respectively), for the loan of their original 'Noddy' collection; to Sheila Ray, for her unstinting help – access to one of the best children's literature libraries in the country, expert help on all my queries, a lifetime of contacts, plus excellent hospitality (and thanks to Colin Ray and the late Puss-Cat for their part, too); to Sheffield Hallam University and Bolton Institute Libraries, and all my colleagues at the latter, and to the rest of the Learning Support Services; to other libraries, too: the Bodleian, John Rylands and Manchester Metropolitan, plus Bolton Schools Library Service; to my PhD supervisors, Rosalind Brunt and Martin Jordin, for giving me much needed 'space', but always being there when required, with intelligent comment; to Michael Rouse and other intrepid 'Blytoneers': Norman Wright and Tony Summerfield for their expert help, encyclopaedic knowledge, and for granting me access to some of their Blyton rarities; to Stephanie Main and Mason Willey, likewise; to Richard Walker, for letting me treat his extensive Blyton collection like a public library; to Geoff Phillips, for supplying a copy of the illustration in Chapter 5; to Gillian Baverstock, Imogen Smallwood, Barbara Stoney, Robert Tyndall and Pam Ally, for their enviable insider knowledge; to John King, for first introducing me to the Internet and the power and speed of e-mail, as opposed to snail-mail, also to his general expertise, bailing me out on many occasions when things 'crashed', metaphorically and literally; to colleagues Lucie Armitt, Jon Glover, John Peacocke, Tom Phillips, Pauline and David Ward, Barry Wood and others for their support and stimulating conversation; likewise to BALCL colleagues, Children's Literature and Girlsown discussion lists; to Albert P., Ann B., Sarah B., Diane O., Gill S., Jacquie M., John B., Pat H., Penney C. – you know who you are! – many thanks; and to all my 'Children's Literature' students, past and present, for their general support and helpful comments, cuttings, etc. (especially John Briggs, Jackie Kerr and Gill Smith; and to Ina Elsagir, for her German translations); to the Division of Humanities and LSS for generously allowing me a semester's sabbatical; to Hugh Crago, Peter Hunt and Jan Nederveen Pieterse, for being so responsive to my requests; to Pete Johnson, Paul Jones, Andy Kershaw, Humphrey

Lyttleton and John Peel, for playing music that kept me sane. But, most appreciatively, to Sheena for her forbearance, as I curled up in bed once again with Enid Blyton, and for her general help, support, intelligent comment and disagreement; to Duncan and Sophie, likewise – Sophie, a special thanks for housing the Blyton collection till, several years on, it clashed with the heavy-metal iconography.

My thanks also to *Green Hedges Magazine, The Enid Blyton Book & Ephemera Collectors Society Newsletter, The Enid Blyton [Literary] Society Journal* and *Folly*, for first publishing some of the material herein, often in a rawer form. Likewise, the National Centre for Research in Children's Literature at Roehampton Institute provided a forum for two papers (subsequently published in *Enid Blyton: a Celebration and Reappraisal* edited by Nicholas Tucker and Kimberley Reynolds, NCRCL, 1997) which have been reworked herein.

I'd also like to thank the following for permission to use earlier versions of other material that first appeared elsewhere: part of Chapter 7 was published in *Children's Literature in Education* 26 (3) 1995, pp. 185–96; a chapter entitled 'Five on the Run: clearing a discursive space for children's literature' (in *Critical Textwork: an Introduction to Varieties of Discourse and Analysis* by Ian Parker and the Bolton Discourse Network, Open University Press, 1999). And finally, material from my own chapter 'Digging up the Family Plot: Secrets, Mystery and the Blytonesque' (in Adrienne E. Gavin and Christopher Routledge (eds) *Secrets and Solutions: Critical Encounters with Mystery in Children's Literature*, Macmillan, 2000).

My thanks to John Fuller for allowing me to quote a limerick from his father, Roy Fuller's, work (first published in *Seen Grandpa Lately?*, André Deutsch, 1972), on page 63. Also to Eyre Methuen, for allowing me to quote the lines from Michael Frayn's play *Balmoral* as an epigraph, and the lines from Joe Orton's *What the Butler Saw* on page 152. Finally, thanks to Charmian Hearne, my commissioning editor at Macmillan, for helping to see this book become a reality.

David Rudd

Note on Texts

Full titles of the key Blyton texts, together with their abbrevated titles, are given in the Reference section on pages 229–30. Where a new 1992 edition of Noddy has specifically been referred to, an asterisk has been appended to the number, as *N3**. Where both editions are being considered, I have added a solidus: *N3/**. The Macdonald Purnell second edition (1986) is not quoted specifically. Only the first eight of these are dated, and it seems that only twenty of the original twenty-four books were rewritten. They were all illustrated by Edgar Hodges.

1
Introduction

Enid Blyton was born in 1897, in *fin-de-siècle* England, just two years behind her fated contemporary, the golliwog. It was a time when the 'cult of the child' was pre-eminent and – with the invention of public cinema – a revolution in the media had just begun. But 1897 also saw the birth of *Dracula* and psychoanalysis (the term was coined the year before); in fact, Blyton and Freud share a final resting place, a crematorium at Golders Green. So, while there was a celebration of innocence and purity on the one hand, there was a recognition of darkness and instability on the other. This was the decade that produced many works that explored this ambivalence, such as Wilde's *The Picture of Dorian Gray* (1891) and Wells' *The Time Machine* (1895). The same ambivalence affected the country at large. Though Great Britain ruled the waves and much of the land, facts celebrated in Queen Victoria's diamond jubilee, there was a growing insecurity about its provenance. At home, there were increasing worries about anarchy (Kenneth Grahame was attacked by a gunman while at work in the Bank of England), growing unemployment and homelessness; abroad, among Great Britain's territories, unrest and war threatened. It is this backdrop which informs much of Blyton's life and work – work which seems to promulgate, long past the empire's sell-by date, a vision of a cosy, contented world, yet one where, beneath the surface, all is less tranquil.

The tension between sunny surface and welling undercurrent is one of the major paradoxes needing to be explored, but there are others. Why, it needs to be asked, has there been so little serious attention given to Blyton, the all-time bestselling children's author? Why, given her cosy middle-class ethos, do nineties streetwise children still find her so readable? Why, given her supposed Englishness, do children in so many countries find her so engaging? Why, given children's love of her work, have adults so systematically derogated her? And underlying these paradoxes is a more general concern about the role and status of children's literature.

These are questions intrinsic to the *materia* of children's literature, but there is also a more personal concern, one which I know many adults share: their own ambivalence towards Blyton. As a child who grew up on her, I also once found magic in her books. The controversial *Here Comes Noddy Again*! (*N4*)[1] was a present from a bookish aunt on my fourth birthday; it was the first book I can remember being explicitly given, and was, consequently, highly treasured. Later, I have a distinct memory of reading the 'Famous Five' books in bed at night, with suitable provisions hidden under my pillow ('Twiglets' being my favourite, each one slowly licked till all the savoury coating had been removed). I can also clearly remember when I stopped reading Blyton, at the age of 11, reading her *The Castle of Adventure* in a boarding school 'dorm' by torchlight. Although I was only about halfway through, I distinctly recall putting the book down and never going back to it. I remember thinking that I really didn't care what happened to Jack, Lucy-Ann, Dinah, Philip and Kiki. Blyton used to say that she wrote for the whole of childhood, 'till you are old enough to read adult books' (Blyton, 1952b, p. 96); she also said that if she was interrupted in the middle of writing a story, the spell was broken (Sykes, 1962, p. 21). Clearly, the spell can also break for readers in an equally dramatic fashion when they start to leave childhood behind.

Later, when I trained as a librarian, I became aware that her work was frowned upon and, though initially perplexed, I soon joined the chorus of disapproval (albeit, as a child, I can also remember being bewildered at this dismissive attitude on the part of librarians). It was only much later, in fact when my own children were born, that I returned to Blyton, having bought some of the old 'Five' hardbacks. Sadly, I found the magic lacking, while the simple vocabulary and the old-fashioned and often embarrassing attitudes obtruded woefully. Put simply, her world had become a closed book to me ever since I had shut that 'Adventure' story years before. My respondents have frequently made similar remarks:

> as a part-time adult student having had the option to re-read childrens books as part of a lit model [*sic*], I found EB to be nauseating and I'm at a loss to understand how or why I related to them as a child. (f)[2]
>
> I once started to read a FF [Famous Five] book when I was about 13–14 (I think I might have been reading out to my sister who is 5

> years younger than me, and who inherited my EB collection) and I couldn't believe how awful it was. I've never tried this again as I don't want to spoil my happy memories of hours spent riveted reading them all. (f)

> I found them [Secret Seven] incredibly dated, upperclass and was too embarrassed to read them aloud [to my children], but as a child in a working class background they did not seem like this. (f)

As Andrea Ashworth recalls, 'It was as if someone had come along and given the books a good shake until all the fizz had fallen out' (Ashworth, 1998, p. 113). Clearly, we as adults are left with empty words, whereas our children, like millions of others, are transported. For them, the words are the requisite incantation for the spell to begin its magic.

My intention here, then, is to explore this curious division between adult and child opinion – something that seems more powerful in Blyton than in almost any other children's author. This will involve crossing the adult/child divide erected and policed by society, with the consequent risk of being ridiculed. It will necessitate looking both outward and inward. *Out* towards a reified media figure, controlled by extensive marketing, the centre of multimedia tie-ins and spin-offs; and yet, away from the hype, it will also involve looking *in*, to the personal fantasies and psychic resonances that the Blyton industry can only tangentially control and over which it cannot surely be held accountable.

This book will explore the enduring popularity of Enid Blyton's work. Contrary to certain critics' predictions, her work has not 'gone away', although she herself died over 30 years ago. And, as John Rowe Townsend declares in his classic history of children's literature, 'Survival is a good test of a book', even if he chooses to ignore this in Blyton's case (Townsend, 1976, p. 13).

The question remains: why does a writer accused of being landlocked in an outmoded age, of being middle-class, snobbish, sexist, racist, colonialist, and so on, continue to fascinate in our multicultural world? To fascinate not only in France, Germany and Australia, but also in Malaysia, Russia and Japan, and in languages such as Catalan and Tamil. Various ideas have been put forward, generally in an offhand way, suggesting that to become too deeply involved in looking at the Blyton phenomenon is a mistake in itself. It might taint one, or even undermine one's credibility if one is seen trying to explain something that does not deserve such attention in the first place. So, although there are an immense number of references to Blyton, the majority of them turn out to be little more than one-liners: 'Valpolicella is to wine what Enid Blyton is to literature' (Gluck, 1991). Her name can signify cosy mediocrity, as here, but also nostalgia for a lost, safe world (epitomized in the Famous Five), the banal and facile (Noddy), or a more subversive 'child power'.

Clearly, the frequent recourse to Blyton's name, the use of her characters as cultural reference points, all demonstrate her significance. In fact, the intense media interest in anything to do with Blyton in itself warrants attention. On the one hand she is seen as trivial, not worth consideration, but on the other, the media seize every opportunity to do just that. Barbara Stoney's biography (Stoney, 1974; 1992), Sheila Ray's critical study (Ray, 1982) and the reminiscences of Imogen Smallwood (1989), Blyton's younger daughter, have all been extensively reviewed.

In this respect, Blyton shares the ambivalence that adults feel about other 'childish things' – Father Christmas, dolls, comics, and so on. Although they hold a central place in the adult mind, a nostalgic fantasy area that is sacred and closely guarded, there is also a defensive embarrassment about them, hence the dismissive belittling. Generally people like to keep their child and adult worlds separate, and there are powerful cultural taboos in existence to prevent any slippage (see Rose, 1984; Stainton Rogers and Stainton Rogers, 1992). But, as a consequence, real children are often excluded from discussions that are of central concern to them, especially where discussion is seen to involve issues that blur the child/adult divide – sexism and racism, for instance.

This study examines Blyton from three main angles, using whatever tools Cultural Studies can muster. The first is a textual analysis of Blyton's three most celebrated series: 'Noddy', the 'Famous Five', and 'Malory Towers'. Secondly, there is an analysis of what she means to her readers, both past and present, from those who read her first in Blyton's own magazines, to the multimedia children of today. The third approach involves an examination of Blyton as a cultural icon, something that was constructed partly by the writer herself, but also by the media, the critics, and her readership. Sometimes this authorial figure can be related to the texts she wrote, but at others, it seems a very different construct.

As the book unfolds, however, it will become clear that my three concerns, rather than strictly obeying this order, are more intermixed – for reasons that will become apparent in the chapter that follows. This is probably the weightiest chapter in the book in terms of the nuts and bolts of methodology, and those less interested in this aspect will find that they can skip some of it without losing the plot. I have divided the rest of the book as follows: first, a consideration of the previous writings on Blyton, to examine how the writer has been constructed – both by others, and by Blyton herself. Secondly, I focus on the chosen texts which, in turn, leads to a more extensive coverage of issues of sexism and racism. Finally, I suggest two, more productive readings of Blyton, one situating her in the oral tradition, the other seeking to explain her appeal in psychoanalytical terms. It is also to be hoped that in unveiling some of the mystery of Blyton's writing – partly due to the fact that so few have ever looked closely at it – some of the mystery surrounding children's literature as a whole will also be exposed.

2

Theory and Method: Literature, Discourse and the Constitution of the Child

Introduction

My methodological approach to this work has developed out of a more general concern with the way children's literature has been treated in the past. Many traditional approaches seem to me to be seriously inadequate, and for a number of reasons. First, many simply lack any methodological grounding, being prone to both whimsy and subjective judgement (what Hunt (1990, p. 5) calls 'pseudo-criticism'; see also Hunt, 1981). Second, even where more systematic investigations are undertaken, they are frequently too narrow, seeking to explore the topic through the lens of teacher training, librarianship, or as a byway of literary studies – all resulting in very partial analyses. Third, even if a wider perspective is adopted, and the analysis is systematic, studies which consider only the text still seem inadequate. As various commentators have indicated, this is one of the main weaknesses of cultural/media studies: that it rests on too narrow an empirical base (Morley, 1980; Hodge and Tripp, 1986; Buckingham, 1993). It is particularly the case with critics of Blyton, many of whom make their pronouncements with no thought of consulting the primary readership, something that is perfectly captured in Brian Alderson 's (1969) more general comment on 'the irrelevance of children to the children's book reviewer'.[1]

Thus there seems to be a certain hypocrisy in critics' complaining about Blyton's lack of research in writing her stories, when they also omit this practice. Here are two such examples. First, Derek Eales, who complains bitterly that writers like Blyton were to blame for the lack of attention given to such matters as the 1984–85 miners' strike and the growth in unemployment. Blyton, among other writers, he says, 'out-storied' such events:

> What must neither be neglected, nor denied, is the *power* of these writers to contribute to a blocking-out of certain cultural possibilities, to sustain and confirm certain basic concepts which ought to be far more strenuously and alertly resisted than they are.
>
> (Eales, 1989, p. 89)

His discourse is quite exclusionary here, though he himself excludes children's voices – especially those from the social groups he feels have been marginalized, those who might perhaps have found Blyton's escapism particularly satisfying (as some of my respondents certainly attest). Eales also neglects the fact that Blyton's works were themselves 'blocked-out' by an adult critical establishment. But, most damningly, he effectively asserts that it is a waste of time consulting readers, for it is the texts that hold the power, regardless of a reader's agenda or social background. A second example comes from Cadogan and Craig's book on the girls' school story, which, they say, is moribund; they argue, as Frith puts it, 'that such stories are no longer read by working-class girls in comprehensive schools' (Frith, 1985, p. 114). Once again, this is asserted rather than tested. However, working-class girls say different, as Frith's subsequent empirical work showed – and as, indeed, has my own.

In the light of the above criticisms, the methodology developed here tries to overcome such inadequacies by looking not only at texts, but at their production and consumption too; that is, at the *con*text and *sub*text of the text. It seeks to rise to Margaret Meek's injunction that an informed approach to children's literature must draw on the 'interactions of culture, history, language, literature, psychology, sociology . . . to say nothing of the children's reading autobiographies' (Meek, 1987, p. 100).

These elements will now be discussed in more detail, beginning with a theoretical section then moving on to the methods adopted.

Theory

Earlier approaches to children's literature

This section outlines three influential approaches, all of which have underpinned criticism of Blyton: the 'literary', the 'child-centred' and the 'reader-response'. Although they have been analytically separated here for the purposes of discussion, they closely overlap in the work of many practitioners.

The literary approach

In this the text is central, and can affect the reader either beneficially or malignantly. Implicit is the notion of a 'gold standard', the belief that some works transcend differences of class, race and gender and espouse universal truths and moral values. Such a view is enshrined in F.R. Leavis's 'great tradition', which lives on in many writers on children's literature, such as Fred Inglis, David Holbrook, Frank Whitehead and A.C. Capey. They readily endorse the notion of 'good' and 'bad' books. Inglis thus talks about a 'lesser great tradition' (1981, p. 101). In a similar way, Whitehead and Capey, in the influential Schools Council survey of children's reading, divide the books into 'quality' and 'non-quality' (Whitehead *et al.*, 1977).[2] Both Whitehead and Capey have also written negatively of Blyton, as has Holbrook. In a review of Ray (1982), for instance, Holbrook makes this immediately clear:

> The question is not whether Enid Blyton helps slow children to read, or whether her values are middle-class, or whether she is racist or sexist, or even whether she affects children's behaviour. It is simply that her work is bad art, in itself lacking in life and imagination.
>
> (Holbrook, 1982)

The emphasis on the work *per se* is clear; elsewhere Holbrook has elaborated on this, though still in rather nebulous terms:

> The worst failure in commercial popular culture is that it gives no help, offers no wisdom 'felt in the blood and felt along the heart', as 'culture of the feelings'. And so we suffer from inadequate holds on life, undernourished positives.
>
> (Holbrook, 1961, p. 52)

In setting up such a polarized view of texts, Blyton cannot help but be dismissed, or seen as a negative exemplar of literature – as in Margery Fisher's unrelenting claim that Blyton was 'slow poison'.[3] As Maslow put it, if the only weapon you have is a hammer, you treat every issue as though it were a nail, and this seems to be the approach of many literary critics to Blyton: quite simply, to 'hammer' her, concentrating exclusively on the text at the expense of what goes on around it.

The child-centred approach

This approach, usually influenced by the work of Piaget, would appear to be more open-minded, but in practice, it seldom is. It suggests that children of different ages will appreciate different things in literature, therefore critics should take account of these differences. However, because there is a pinnacle of development where these stages culminate, the pinnacle tends to be taken as the norm. And, although this norm is presented impartially as the ability to reason abstractly, it maps rather too neatly onto the contemporary figure of a mature, white, western male (Gilligan, 1982). Children are seen not in their own right, but according to how far short of this paragon they fall: the extent that they lack an ability to relate cause and effect, to see conceptual relations underlying surface features, and so on. Consequently, from the outset, children's literature is treated in a condescending manner, with only the greatest works being worthy of attention, and even then, such work is intrinsically second-rate: 'no children's literature could ever be a work of art in the same league as, say, Tolstoy, George Eliot or Dickens' (Tucker, 1976b, p. 18).[4] This is an interestingly phrased statement for, of course, two of these writers also wrote for children – although this work is obviously not seen to be fully part of their *oeuvre*.

A related criticism is that Piaget's model is almost exclusively concerned with cognitive development, to which moral and emotional factors are subsumed. More significantly, as a result of this model, where development is mapped out in stages, real children are often lost, and in their place we hear about 'non-conservers'; literary texts, likewise, become ciphers of particular developmental stages. Winnie-the-Pooh, for example, is seen clearly to be a non-conserver, fooled by the appearance of things, and animistic in his approach to the world, seeing inanimate objects like clouds as mindful (Singer, 1972); hence the books' appeal to children of a like-minded age. However, as Milne's books appeal to all ages, this scarcely explains anything.

Most importantly, the child-centred approach simply fails to take us much further: for particular books are meant to be popular because they have the qualities that are liked by children at a certain stage; for instance, 'Noddy' books are popular partly because they are animistic; thus, in *N21*, Mr. Plod's helmet blows off:

> 'Come back helmet!' But the helmet took no notice. It was having a lovely time, bumping and bouncing and rolling along. Ha – this was better than sitting still on Mr. Plod's head! (*N21*, p. 17)

The helmet is effortlessly animated, which at this stage of development, is something children supposedly like. Yet, presumably all books at this stage share this quality (by definition), so it still does not tell us why

Noddy in particular is so popular. The greatest irony, however, is that, though the Piagetian approach is frequently termed 'child-centred', children are rarely present. The approach, in presuming already to know the child, therefore decides to dispense with him or her in actuality.

The reader-response approach

This final, influential approach is often seen to stand midway between the above. It certainly seems to bring together text and reader, the latter being something that the others neglect. At its core it argues that the reader is an active maker of meaning, albeit guided by the text. Wolfgang Iser (1974, 1978; see also Chambers, 1985; Corcoran and Evans, 1987) argues that texts do not spell everything out; rather, they contain 'gaps' that readers must themselves fill, drawing on their own knowledge. This approach has lent itself admirably to classroom work, where the teacher can see how children actually make sense of texts. However, though laudable in its aims and, in the hands of certain teachers, genuinely giving recognition to the complexity of children's reading, all too frequently it tends to do the opposite: to marginalize individual responses. (Martin and Leather lament the fact that the National Curriculum for English, originally designed to respect personal meanings, ends up reducing 'the experience of reading to the level of the pub quiz' (1994, p. 5).) Meaning is seen to cohere round a particular centre, usually falling back on notions of the organic unity of a text, as created by some lone, gifted individual. The gaps in a text cease to be spaces that the individual reader can inhabit; rather, they become points to straddle, like sparkplug gaps, which, if set right, will ensure that the reader's mind successfully arcs across to complete a predetermined circuit, a unified reading. In other words, the reader is not really allowed a personal response; instead, he or she becomes a textual artefact, dutifully fulfilling textual instructions – as in the literary approach.[5]

Furthermore, not only are particular readings privileged, but the texts chosen for such work also tend to be predetermined; that is, those texts deemed to have the appropriate spaces where the imagination can do its work; whereas other texts are seen to have everything spelt out, with the reader being led by the hand. As Benton (1978, p. 30) puts it, 'A text with little indeterminacy is likely to bore the reader since it restricts his participation, a text with a large measure of indeterminacy . . . is likely to be exciting.' Blyton's texts, predictably, are seen to have minimal indeterminacy (Hunt, 1978; Chambers, 1985).

So each of the above approaches suffers a certain myopia, although each also has its useful elements, which can inform a broader perspective; one that, in Bergonzi's words, recognizes the 'personal, intellectual, literary, linguistic, [and] social . . . as constituent elements' (Bergonzi, 1978, p. 5). I have previously referred to this as a 'communication studies' approach (Rudd, 1992), but the term 'cultural studies' now seems more appropriate. It must be said, of course, that others in this field have also sought to distance themselves from the above orthodoxies, breaking down old disciplinary barriers. While it is impossible to typify this newer work, its concerns can be outlined. Certainly, a linguistic dimension is central (Hunt, 1991; Jones, 1991); it also takes account of historical, social and ideological factors (Avery, 1975; Leeson, 1985; Rose, 1984; Sarland, 1991); less commonly, psychoanalytical approaches feature (Rose, 1984; Jones, 1991); finally, it pays closer attention to narrative (Chambers, 1985; Hunt, 1991; Wall, 1991). Stephens (1992) is exemplary in presenting such a rounded approach. But let me move on to define my own version, which also seeks to keep language central.

A discourse approach

Barthes' notion of 'text as a field of force', to which Bergonzi alludes, is a helpful image to bear in mind. A key term that enables us to speak of this force-field, comprising text, context and readership, is 'discourse'. This allows us to recognize the textual dimension of everything, not just the literary text *per se*. It also helps break down the disciplinary barriers encountered above. However, there are drawbacks, the main one being that the term 'discourse' is itself so heavily overwritten with different uses. In this section I shall endeavour to spell out what I mean by the term, and the advantages of adopting such an approach.

It is Foucault's usage to which I am chiefly indebted, for it links ways of speaking about topics to sites of power. It is the latter dimension that is frequently neglected in other approaches (see Macdonell, 1986; Fairclough, 1992, for overviews), so that people talk about 'discourses' as if all had equal status. For Foucault, though, discourses are concerned with the authority with which people speak, what they can speak about, and in what manner. In conveying knowledge, discourses simultaneously embody power and, thereby, a set of social relations. So certain ways of talking about a subject, deriving from particular institutional sites, actually form that subject; not only this, but any one subject, being formulated in one way, is not thereby seen in another. Thus certain ways of speaking become naturalized and literally 'in-form' our thoughts, our way of addressing issues – as Foucault demonstrated in his own studies.

Children, of course, are also constructed in a certain way, usually as helpless, innocent beings – girls particularly so. This construction means that they can, thereby, be easily belittled and marginalized. It is a powerful discourse to the extent that children who in some way are perceived to be not 'innocent' are frequently described as not really being children. It is also self-perpetuating, so that it is very easy to argue that children should be protected from a wide range of inappropriate material – sexist, racist, classist, and so on. But in the very act of doing this, the discourse, in effect, underwrites its own truths. Put more simply, the very act of policing children confirms their minority status. So, on the one hand they are seen as pure and innocent – a fact that their literature strives to reflect – but on the other, they are not allowed to be anything else: they are thus removed from much that is considered the 'real' world – the world of adults.

Foucault doesn't write much about 'Literature', a powerful discourse in itself; rather, he treats literary texts as evidence, just like any other material. He is also as likely to draw on obscure as well-known texts – what he terms 'that everyday, transient writing that never acquires the status of an *oeuvre* . . . the interstices of the great discursive monuments' (Foucault, 1972, pp. 136–7).[6] This sounds like a ready-made entrée to children's literature, itself a neglected byway of literary studies, often trapped in the interstices of literature, education and librarianship, besides being aimed at an interstitial group. As for 'everyday, transient writing', this sounds specifically tailored to non-canonical writers such as Blyton. Moreover, in removing the value-laden literary tag and looking at texts in general, we have a chance to examine Blyton more openly.

Foucault's notion of discourse thus provides a *lingua franca* for discussing not only the works themselves, but their production and consumption. It allows us to read across from Blyton's texts to the texts of readers (questionnaires, interviews, criticism, newspaper stories), without prioritizing or essentializing either. More significantly, it recognizes that meaning and truth do not originate in the writer, the book, or the reader; rather, it sees these as the nexus points of particular discourses which we can then unpick. It also gets us round thorny issues like the 'intentional fallacy' by refusing to read a cause–effect relationship from signifiers to underlying referents; instead, it simply points to homologies amongst textual elements, be they 'biographical' or 'fictional'. However, although I am using a discourse approach I prefer to talk about 'discursive threads' rather than 'discourse' *per se*.[7] There are four reasons for this.

(1) The word 'discourse' now has many other associations, particularly in linguistics where it is commonly taken to refer to units of text longer than the sentence (Sinclair and Coulthard, 1975). In Foucauldian terms, one never sees a discourse 'whole' because most of it is simply not made explicit. It therefore resembles the proverbial iceberg, only 'referenced' or 'quoted' (the process of 'intertextuality' – see below). Hence there is no need to define it formally as larger than a sentence; it may well be, but it might just as easily be a single word or phrase; as Barthes puts it, 'A discourse is a long 'sentence' (the units of which are not necessarily sentences), just as a sentence, allowing for certain specifications, is a short 'discourse' (Barthes, 1977a, p. 83). The term 'discursive thread' seems to capture this more clearly.

(2) It foregrounds the metaphorical resonance of the word 'threads', suggesting the process of teasing out words used in a particular way of speaking – words which pre-exist and echo any particular utterance, but which, along with other threads, are ever being woven into new discourses. Texts thus have 'texture', being weaves of various threads – threads which people sometimes worry about 'losing'. There is also the panoply of terms associating *story* in particular with certain domestic arts: weaving a tale, spinning yarns, tying-up loose ends, and so on. These metaphorical links, in turn, connect with the textuality of life in general, reaching back to the three Greek Fates, Clotho, Lachesis and Atropos who, respectively, spun the thread of life, measured it, and cut it off at death – just as discursive threads help weave our identity, much of which is also beyond individual control, mapped out by our gender, class and ethnicity.

(3) The term is far more dynamic than 'discourse', suggesting a process rather than a thing, and is thus akin to Foucault's notion of 'discursive practices'. For discourses are not simply lumps of language; they are more like what Wittgenstein terms 'forms of life'. To use marxian terminology, they are not just 'superstructural' elements but are themselves materialistic, formulating tangible concerns constitutive of a particular social order. In Austin's (1962) famous phrase, we *do* things with words. To give an apposite illustration, if an adult tells off a child, the adult is not simply using these words to reprimand the child, but is also defining the child in the process; or, more exactly, is re-enacting and re-

invoking the relations of adult to child, where the latter is the powerless, the dependant.

This is fundamental to Foucault's conception of discourse as the embodiment of power relations. In particular, he was interested in the development of a new regime of power ('biopower') in which people began to regulate their own behaviour without the show of force (Foucault, 1979). The various ways of speaking that developed in the Industrial Revolution led people to see themselves as 'subjects' – individuals who could monitor and regulate their own behaviour through their 'consciences'. The vocabularies and explanatory frameworks that people used for this new understanding were those developed by institutions such as education and health. I use the word 'understanding', but this also should be seen as a form of 'self-regulation'. Foucault always talked of 'power-knowledge' as a single concept, to indicate how knowledge always has a controlling aspect, so that even self-knowledge involves a monitoring of one's actions (Foucault, 1979, 1980, 1981). Children, of course, are subject to just this discursive process, internalizing what it is to be a child who will later become an adult; and literature, especially literature for children, is ineluctably complicit in this.

This has serious implications, not only for looking at how children read but also at how we discuss their reading. We realize that there can never be an innocent interview in which truth is transparently revealed by the words spoken. Interviews are shaped by larger discursive elements, the interview itself being a recognized discursive practice. Thus there are differential power relations involved from the start (it is not a 'conversation'), which might be compounded by others (for example of race, gender, age). An instance, using gender, would be the girls' use of 'Georgina' rather than 'George' to refer to the tomboy in the Famous Five, though the *-ina* form was despised by the character. What the girls were doing was using the name strategically, to emphasize that they were talking about a *girl* doing these things. One has to be attentive to such minimal discursive threads, recognizing, as Foucault said, that 'there can be no statement that in one way or another does not reactualize others' (1972, p. 98).

It needs stressing, however, that discourses do not exist as some passive archive, but are being reformulated all the time. So, at any point, there is the possibility that a discourse will be differently fashioned. Obviously the weight of institutional power behind a discourse will tend to slant the outcome, but it is by no means inevitable. This is Foucault's key point about power not emerging from only one particular place in society, but being everywhere, and, in that very process, developing its own resistances:

> We must make allowance for the complex and unstable process whereby discourse can be both an instrument and an effect of power, but also a hindrance, a stumbling-block, a point of resistance and a starting point for an opposing strategy.
>
> (Foucault, 1981, p. 101)

It was for this reason that Foucault, to the annoyance of many marxists, avoided the term 'ideology' with its totalitarian and unidirectional implications. Instead, he preferred to explore more local issues, 'the microphysics of power', 'its capillary form of existence' (1980, p. 39). There are various examples of this throughout this book, both in the comments of readers, and in Blyton's own texts. To give an example from the latter, there is an interesting exchange in *FGOIC* (p. 198)[8] when Anne draws on her domestic role to enhance her power in the confrontation with patriarchy. Thus when Julian characteristically says they'll eat, 'Anne made them wash and tidy themselves first! . . . "I'll give you five minutes – then you can come"'.

The close relation of power and resistance is also shown in Foucault's notion of '"reverse" discourse' (Foucault, 1981, pp. 101–2). He gives the example of homosexuality, which despite being 'the love that dare not speak its name', actually became able to speak for itself as a result of the discourse developing around it – even though that discourse was derogatory. In a similar way, one can see how the concept of the child permits a challenging of more powerful voices. So, returning to my example above, where an adult is reprimanding a child, there is the option here for the child to use its inferior status to advantage. In other words, the process of defining children as incompetent, irresponsible, clumsy or whatever, actually gives the child a warrant to behave in this way, simultaneously empowering the child (the humour of Richmal Crompton's William Brown is built exactly on this (Crompton, 1922)).

(4) A final reason for using the term 'discursive threads' is its overt resemblance to 'signifying chains', but without the baggage associated with the latter. In particular, it avoids the atomism of the term 'signifiers', which, in my opinion, has permitted too freewheeling a response to many texts; for, despite the almost infinite creativity opened up, it is generally the case that signifiers come ready-packaged in larger units. In this way, 'discursive threads' seems to be pitched at a more suitable

level, between the rather monolithic notion of discourses proper, and the too atomistic signifiers. While the term captures the partiality, or 'quotedness' of all utterances, in that each thread is connected to and re-works earlier ones, it also recognizes that, for most of the time, the overall patterning of the threads reproduces the existing power relations of society. We can therefore continue to use terms like 'preferred readings' to indicate that some versions of events have the weight of traditional interpretation behind them, however contentious.

Although Foucault's notion of discourse is central in the above four points, the related work of Vološinov/Bakhtin also informs much of what follows, particularly his notion of the 'multi-accentedness' of signs (Vološinov, 1973).[9] He was one of the first to recognize that signs are 'a site of struggle'; in other words, that any particular word may be used differently by different groups to 'mean' in a particular direction (not, note, by individuals in some voluntaristic way). An obvious example would be the word 'gay', strategically used by the homosexual community to replace terms such as 'queer' and, equally, resisted by others. Bakhtin's more general approach is called 'dialogism', which is a recognition that what is spoken is always a response to earlier voices or texts (Bakhtin, 1981). This notion will prove particularly valuable when exploring the discursive threads from which Blyton wove her stories, drawing on both personal and social events; it will also help illuminate how these threads feed back into the culture, and help construct the 'Blytonesque'. However, rather than speak of 'dialogism' I have generally preferred to use Kristeva's associated term, 'intertextuality' – 'the insertion of history (society) into a text and of this text into history' (Kristeva, 1986, p. 39) – in that its meaning encompasses the *unthinking* reiteration of previous utterances.

Before moving on to some of the outstanding problems, let me reiterate three main issues about this discursive approach. First, a discourse approach, treating every trace as 'text', gives us a common currency to move across academic barriers, besides a useful way of 'levelling out' the various areas of analysis: primary texts, adaptations, criticism, media reaction, biographical and social elements. It also, building on the insights of Bakhtin, recognizes that these areas are intertextually related, later discourses responding to earlier ones, reconstituting and resituating them.

Second, though it levels things out for analytical purposes, it does not thereby make everything level – a criticism of much work in this area – losing sight of the fact that certain discourses carry more weight than others. In concrete terms this means probing why certain readings of

Blyton have been 'preferred', however contestable they might be. It also – precisely because of the way that discourses generate their own reversals – shows us how things might be read otherwise: we can explore a non-literary approach to her texts, for instance; or try listening to the voice of that usually muted group, children.

This brings me to the third issue, the involvement of children, who should be seen neither as the source of 'the truth' about Blyton (they simply provide an alternative reading), nor as simply mouthing 'adult' discourses. For a start, each person is obviously a different weave of constituent discursive threads (something we shall explore in terms of Blyton). Also, the child's very positioning means that it will use these discourses differently, producing hybrid forms, often mimicking and changing adult inflections (William Brown, again). Lastly, these threads will themselves be intermixed with a more resilient child culture (Opie and Opie, 1959).

Now to the problems. First, there is the question of *reliability*. I have been critical of studies that engage solely in textual analysis, ignoring how texts are actually consumed, so have sought to give an empirical base to my own study. I have also tried to use a variety of methods, some quantitative, others more qualitative.[10] While I am aware that 'triangulation' or 'multimethods' have their own problems, in that each method tends to produce its own truths according to its own ground-rules, I am confident that sufficient checks were carried out in the course of this work not to compromise its reliability.

The other side of this coin is that one can impose a false reliability: one gives 'to one voice a pervasive authorial function and to others the role of informants' (Clifford, 1986, p. 15), reducing others to adjuncts of one's overall truth. As the whole notion of Foucault's 'genealogical method' is to give expression to marginalized voices, entertaining 'the claims to attention of local, discontinuous, disqualified, illegitimate knowledges against the claims of a unitary body of theory which would filter, hierarchize and order them in the name of some true knowledge' (Foucault, 1980, p. 83), I would hope not to collapse these back into a new hierarchy. Certainly, I have suggested some overarching interpretations of Blyton, but without, I hope, submerging the voices that currently are muted.

The second main problem is that of *validity*, which brings in its wake considerations of relativism. I have already argued that Foucault's notion of discourse recognizes the ultimate arbitrariness of different versions of events while, historically, noting that certain discourses are undoubtedly privileged, or 'preferred', carrying more weight than others. This notion of power delimiting too freewheeling a reading of a text helps put the excesses of some relativists into perspective. Thus, literary critics can often turn out different interpretations almost on demand, 'doing' a Freudian, feminist, or structuralist reading (Easthope, 1985). Such readings can be sustained in *academia* but, like the particles created in bubble-chambers (Stanley Fish's (1980) 'interpretive communities'), outside this rarified atmosphere they are often seen to flounder.

This points to a perennial problem for anyone involved in this area: either to be accused of restating the obvious – hence of being trivial – or of being far-fetched in going beyond common-sense. Foucault's analysis is pitched between these extremes, I feel. He rejects any notion of ultimate truth as a chimera, but he also avoids an open relativism precisely by pointing to the sites of power that underwrite particular truths. Barthes makes a similar comment when he says that 'To interpret a text is not to give it a (more or less justified, more or less free) meaning, but on the contrary to appreciate what *plural* constitutes it' (Barthes, 1990, p. 5); in other words, instead of trying to study, for instance, racism *per se*, I have tried to examine how the discourse of racism is realized in Blyton's works, and how this discourse itself has a history and trajectory.

The whole study, then, was conducted in the postmodern recognition that the texts I was studying had no single voice, that Blyton herself is a nexus point of a variety of contending discourses – as are readers likewise, including that variety known as 'the critic'. We must then add to this the particular responses elicited by my intervention at a particular point in time (very different from what I might have received in the 1950s, or 1970s, for instance; and certainly very different from the reborn centenarian Blyton). Lastly, we must recognize my own positioning, itself mutable over the past eight years. Other studies are certainly no different, although some may try to adopt a false sense of unity.

Method

I have used four principal methods to generate the data for this study – textual analysis, questionnaires, interviews and other activities – each of which will now be discussed.

Textual analysis

Textual criticism

Blyton wrote over 700 books, and some 4000 short stories, so it is clearly impossible to look at them all. I have therefore sought to read as many as I could and to develop a general feel for her style and her concerns. I have then selected three series to examine in more detail, based on the age range she wrote for, the different genres she covered and, finally, the popularity of these works. Accordingly, 'Noddy', the 'Famous Five' and 'Malory Towers' were selected. I analysed this corpus of 51 texts, unpicking the various discursive threads, and seeking to relate them, where relevant, to the broader Blyton *oeuvre*.

Production

Textual analysis is not confined to the works themselves, however. My analysis also involves looking at the wider context of their production; that is, trying to tease out the discursive threads (the personal, social and cultural elements) that helped shape them, and, simultaneously, shaped the Blyton *persona*. This involves examining other works by Blyton, both fictional and non-fictional (autobiographical material, her comments on teaching and contemporary events), and the surrounding literary and cultural context.

My 'warrant' for this is based on my own 'cultural capital' – to use Bourdieu's (1993) useful term. I trade on the fact that I belonged to a society at least partially contemporaneous with Blyton (she was prolific throughout my childhood, only dropping her production rate at the time I grew out of her work).

Consumption

My own analysis of the texts, informed though I believe it is, is insufficient in that any thorough analysis should take account of the many other commentators on Blyton. I am interested not only in what they say about her texts but also in how they construct their version of the Blytonesque. It is particularly noteworthy that it is often culturally élitist voices that seek to pronounce authoritatively on her works, voices that are often least representative of its reception. Finally, I have tried to cast my net as widely as possible, drawing not only on 'literary criticism', but on other cultural references, however ephemeral, using newspaper and journal indexes and abstracts, CD-ROMs, the Internet, and on-line services such as *FT Profile*.

Questionnaires

Drawing on elements from my own reading, plus the observations of other commentators, I devised a questionnaire to explore people's experiences of Blyton: which books they had read, when, and what they thought of them (see Appendix I). The questionnaire had two main audiences: first, past readers of Blyton, now grown-up, stretching back to first generation readers (that is, those who were children in the twenties and thirties), and including international respondents. Second, contemporary readers, the *fin-de-siècle* kids of the nineties, a hundred years on from Blyton's own childhood.

The questionnaire itself was distributed in several ways: adult ones via personal contact, Blyton fanzines, librarians' professional publications, the media, and the Internet. All these proved productive, and frequently one enthusiast would put me in touch with another – what is known as 'snowball' sampling. This, of course, is not statistically representative, partly because the relevant population is unknown, but also because this would be inappropriate, given that my primary aim was to explore the views of those who had read and enjoyed Blyton – whatever they now felt. As Lincoln and Guba (1985, p. 202) say, in qualitative research 'sampling is terminated when no new information is forthcoming . . . thus *redundancy* is the primary criterion', the idea being to 'maximize information'.

There are no set rules in qualitative research regarding number of subjects, unlike those regarding significance in quantitative work. Consequently, numbers vary considerably across studies, something that is not always in line with qualitative depth. The literary critic usually constitutes the limit case in idiographic research, although even here, other critical voices are usually present. But if we look elsewhere, we find considerable variation in the empirical base: Fry (1985) draws on only six children; Sarland (1991) on 46, and Buckingham (1987) on 60. Ang (1985), in a study of adults' views of *Dallas*, depends on only 42 letters from Dutch fans, and provides no background information on them (she only became aware of them through a magazine ad). Christian-Smith's work (1990) is nearer in size to my own. She analyses 34 American teen romance stories and interviews 29 girls from three schools. It is also worth noting that the latter two studies draw on interested parties, Ang's being self-selecting, whereas Sarland – like Morley (1980) in his *Nationwide* study – asked individuals to examine texts of his choice, not their own.

My own subjects came from as wide a geographical, ethnic, class and gender base as possible. Aside from 385 adult responses, there were 490 children. I collected my questionnaires from contemporary children more systematically, selecting four schools on the basis of class, ethnic mix, and age-grouping (see Appendix II). Questionnaires were distributed in each, with either teachers or parents helping the younger children complete them. Although anonymous, many ignored or wrote 'N/A' against questions about parents' occupations and ethnicity (something that has been found to be problematic in other surveys).

The reluctance of minority groups to respond to the latter question is not unexpected. Another form to fill in was obviously viewed suspiciously, especially when it asked about employment status, coupled with the fact that, for many parents (some of them lacking English), the name Enid Blyton was meaningless anyway. At the other extreme, enthusiasm for Blyton among some white, middle-class parents led several to fill out the questionnaires themselves, bypassing their children!

Interviews

My interview schedule, cleared with the relevant authorities (Appendix II), stated my intention to discuss golliwogs, among other issues. However, for the actual interviews, I tried to make the atmosphere as much like a discussion as possible. I interviewed 170 children in groups, normally involving four individuals at a time. Generally these were of mixed sex, comprising two boys and two girls, but I also conducted some single-sex interviews with all-girl groups to counter the tendency of the boys to use what might be seen as patriarchal advantage (Spender, 1990; Cherland, 1994). Excluding boys, of course, does not thereby remove patriarchy, but it can lessen its interpersonal impact. This said, in mixed-sex groups the girls were usually more articulate and forthcoming. I also sought to mix whites and Asians in groups, although, again, I occasionally interviewed a group of all-Asian children – partly to redress the balance with the all-white groups in other schools, and partly to see if different issues might emerge when white peers were removed.

I, however – a middle-class, male, white adult – was present throughout, which was one of the main reasons for group interviews. In any adult/child dialogue, the power relations are skewed in favour of the former, so it was hoped that a *group* of children might minimize this; that a dialogue would occur within the group, with differences over texts, over male/female experience, and so on, emerging. Of course, the reverse is frequently argued: that in group interviews one loses the views of individuals; that there is 'interference' from a variety of social variables. However, as mentioned above, the whole notion of an individual response is problematic; for there is no way in which an individual stands alone; even if interviewed alone, traces of the social will still constitute their response (just as all-girl groups do not escape patriarchy). There is no way one can unproblematically tap a voice that resonates with some inner self, or, even if it were so, that one might be any more likely to tap it one-to-one rather than in a group (leaving aside the individual questionnaires, of course). Instead, the individual is more satisfactorily seen as the unique point of intersection of a variety of discourses, which are reworked and rewoven in particular contexts, including interviews.[11] Furthermore, the reading of texts can itself draw out different discursive threads, just as can watching TV:

> We are all, in our heads, several different audiences at once, and can be constituted as such by different programmes. We have the capacity to deploy different levels and modes of attention, to mobilise different competences in our viewing.
>
> (Hall, 1986, p. 10)

Other activities

Some other related activities were also conducted with pupils. However, in relying on the time and goodwill of a number of teachers in a variety of schools, these activities were not as methodical as I would have liked. Consequently, they are only referred to in passing. Briefly, they consisted of the following. The children were read two different but incomplete versions of a Five story, one favouring the boys, the other dividing tasks and action more evenly; they had to complete the story, indicating which version they preferred. (In the event, there was no determinable preference.) A second task required children to draw their favourite Blyton character or scene. This was mainly aimed at the younger children, to compensate for their lack of writing skills. However, many older children also enjoyed this task, producing some excellent artwork. Lastly, some of the children were involved in choosing both their favourite and least-liked Five illustrations from a selection by different artists. Again, this was not systematic, but results showed that today's children did not particularly prefer the style of any one artist. Rather, they went for what was represented: that is, for content rather than style.

Coda

The above has tried to emphasize the *-ology* side of methodology, for I have always felt that too many studies are driven rather mechanically by *method*. But without a keen awareness of why particular methods are deployed it is unlikely that any outcomes can be analysed meaningfully. This is especially the case with a discursive approach such as Foucault's where, drawing on the derivation of the word 'discourse', one is continually 'running in different directions', reflexively tacking back and forth. Given an awareness of how particular ways of probing, questioning, collating, categorizing, analysing and presenting results generate their own 'truth-effects', one has to be wary of whatever claims one makes. There is certainly variety in the range of methods used, but it is united in this discursive perspective.

In terms of presenting the results, I have sought to pursue the metaphor of a textual weave, incorporating responses from questionnaires and interviews within the main text, without being an interpreter who, 'Like a judge . . . "summons" others to appear, assigns to them their place and "cites" them before other judges' (de Certeau, quoted in Ahearne, 1995, pp. 20–1). It is for the same reason that it seemed apposite to have the discussion of methodology precede my review of Blyton's critics; for, in looking at the responses of previous writers to Blyton, textual analysis is already underway.

3
Person and Persona: the Construction of Blyton as Cultural Icon

Introduction

This chapter presents a general introduction to Blyton, her life and her status. It begins with a look at the known facts before moving on to examine how 'Enid Blyton' constructed her own *persona* – for public consumption, certainly, but with far more wide-reaching effects. From here I shall move on to look at the different constructions of Blyton over the years. Although people bandy her name as though it had a singular, uniform meaning, it has actually changed signification substantially. I shall outline four such moves, from her initial status as an educational writer, through popular children's writer, to reviled poisoner, and finally, to her present status as cultural icon, as respectable as Hammer Horror. For, despite the wishful-thinking predictions of earlier critics – 'it seems reasonable to suppose that the fabulous popularity will die a natural death', as Martin (1970, p. 26) put it – Blyton's popularity has actually increased, with cumulative sales now totalling over 500 million copies worldwide, and continuing sales of over eight million a year. There is even an 'Enid Blyton Literary Society' (1996–, although it dropped the 'Literary' recently), publishing a triennial journal of Blyton studies.

The life

The biographical information is, in many respects, hard to detach from other material about Blyton. This is so for two reasons: first, Blyton herself was very careful in creating a particular *persona*, suppressing information that did not fit the image; secondly, and as a consequence, the public has been particularly fascinated by the disparity between this *persona* and the 'reality', once the 'secret' information was uncovered, first in Stoney's (1974; 1992) discerning biography, then, and partly as a result of this, in the moving account by Blyton's younger daughter, Imogen Smallwood (1989).[1] More recently, a Channel Four series, *Secret Lives* (1996), featured a programme on Blyton that pursued this 'underside' relentlessly. As its title suggests, it was particularly interested in iconoclastic findings, which the press also covered extensively.[2]

But let me begin with the facts. Enid Mary Blyton was born 11 August 1897 at a small flat above a shop in East Dulwich, London. She was the first-born child of lower-middle class parents who had moved down to London from Sheffield. Her father, Thomas Carey Blyton, a cutlery salesman, was an artistic, self-educated man, teaching himself languages, shorthand, astronomy, music and painting, besides writing poetry, reading extensively and collecting books. Finances improved for the family when he went into business with his brothers, resulting in a move to Beckenham in Kent. Enid had two younger brothers: Hanly, born 1899 and Carey, born 1902.

Enid seems to have been very close to her father, who was also a keen gardener and naturalist. However, there seem to have been tensions with her mother, Theresa Mary Harrison, who found Enid uncongenial when it came to domestic chores, always preferring to be out with her father. Relations between the parents seem generally to have been strained, with many rows, ending in her father walking out shortly before Enid's thirteenth birthday. He had left Enid's mother for another woman – something concealed at the time, and which, Stoney suggests, set the pattern for Blyton's subsequent imaginative treatment of the truth. However, despite domestic upset, Enid did well at school, both academically and in games, becoming head girl at the local St Christopher's School for Girls. Relations with her mother eventually deteriorated to the extent that Enid left home, scarcely seeing her mother for the next 30 years.

At this time Enid was destined to become a concert pianist, but her heart was not in it, and she eventually sought her father's permission to go into teaching. She undertook Froebel training, then taught for several years before success in writing allowed her to give up the profession. By her own account, Blyton had 500 rejection slips 'before making any headway' (Blyton, 1951a, p. 4). At this time she was experimenting in a variety of forms – verse, humour, advertisements, greetings cards and adult fiction. Her first book was a collection of verse, *Child Whispers* in 1922.[3] Unfortunately her father was never to witness her success as a writer; he died suddenly in 1920. Enid, strangely, did not attend his funeral. In 1924 she married Hugh Pollock, an editor at the publishing house Newnes. After some initial trouble conceiving, the couple had two daughters, Gillian (b. 1931) and Imogen (b. 1935). Relations with her first husband deteriorated at the beginning of the war, and the couple divorced in 1942, Hugh considerately divorcing Enid, on condition that he had access to the children – something which Enid later denied him. In the following year she married Kenneth Darrell Waters, a surgeon, though the couple had been intimate a good while before this. As Imogen puts it, 'For a whole year, if my memories are correct, she carried on her lives [*sic*] with two different men, deceiving, or appearing to deceive, everyone who might have seriously criticized her' (Smallwood, 1989, p. 66). Strangely, four of Blyton's six books written under her 'Mary Pollock' pseudonym were published in 1943, when she had ceased to have any connection with the name. Enid and Kenneth Darrell Waters seem to have been very happy together until his death in 1967. She died the year after, on 28 November 1968. This said, her last few years were marred by mental deterioration, a condition which may have been Alzheimer's Disease.

These are the bald facts, but Stoney, who unearthed much material unknown to the daughters, has fashioned them into a convincing narrative that speaks of a woman who never really grew up, who had many dark fears that she managed to conceal until near the end. Stoney's reading is confirmed in Smallwood's memoir – of a woman who might have been mother to most of the world, but was not one for her (Smallwood, 1989, p. 12).

I shall return to these biographical constructions, but want now to consider Blyton's own autobiography, *The Story of My Life*, written expressly for children – a point she makes plain several times: 'I don't tell this sort of thing to grown-ups, of course, but you children will understand exactly how I felt' (1952b, p. 28). The very title hints at the notion of 'story' as fabrication, which is aided by the physical structure of the book. We have the sense of entering a fantasy realm, with the endpapers featuring an illustration of an idealized Green Hedges garden.[4] Having passed through this, we are then greeted at the door by Blyton herself, saying 'Welcome!' (ibid., p. 4). 'Dear Boys and Girls' (ibid., p. 5), she writes in a personal hand, and we are introduced to her story. At the end there is again the personal touch, with a salutation in Blyton's own hand, 'Your storyteller and friend/ Enid Blyton' (ibid., p. 124), before we are led out via the endpapers.

This notion of 'life-as-story' is furthered in the subject matter, in that almost half the book is about her writing (eight of the 19 chapters). Indeed, chapters are sometimes not what one might expect; 'How I began' is really about how she became a writer, not a person, as though she didn't exist until she had created herself thus. (In an early article she has a similarly ambiguous line, 'I love pretending myself' (quoted in Stoney, 1974, p. 189).) Another chapter begins, 'One of the questions you so often ask me is about my childhood. . . . You quite naturally want to know what mine was like' (1952b, p. 47); but she then proceeds to talk about the books she read. She thus runs life and imaginative experience together, and suggests, both here as elsewhere in the book, that everything an author writes is derivative, based on previously read or seen incidents. Consequently she recommends that prospective young writers stock their heads full of others' works. I shall return to this issue in Chapter 5, but let me note here a curious parallel with the one other autobiography I know called by this ambivalent title, *The Story of My Life*. It is that of Helen Keller (1903), the autistic, deaf and blind child, who records how she unwittingly plagiarized a short story, thinking it her own.[5] Apart from the fact that Keller's experience was a negative one, making her doubt her ability to distinguish imagination from reality, it is very similar to Blyton's in its depiction of writing and, of course, many of Blyton's stories certainly bear a resemblance to those of others. Blyton seems half-aware of confounding life and story, stating at one point that 'Writers cannot keep reality and imagination apart for long' (Blyton, 1952b, p. 124). I'd now like to pursue the implications of this in her discussion of three related themes: home, family, and gardens. Four chapters are devoted to her homes and gardens, and one explicitly to the family, though family photographs feature plentifully throughout the text. This said, a closer look reveals that the family is somewhat fractured.

Enid's two brothers are hardly differentiated, and they are certainly not named, though countless pets are. We have many pictures of the latter, yet none of her family (that is, of her parents and brothers). Her mother receives only seven mentions, whereas her father has over 100. Yet only once are they mentioned together (Blyton, 1952b, p. 101). Her father is quoted extensively, her mother but once, and that in a comment about her spouse (ibid., p. 78). Her mother also tends to be negatively referenced, whereas her father features predominantly in a positive light. In fact, the chapter 'My happiest times' is chiefly about things she did with her father. It is also of note that Blyton, in discussing her ambition, uses the following quotation:

> 'We fail!
> But screw your courage to the sticking-place,
> And we'll not fail!'

Though she does not give the source, these are, of course, Lady Macbeth's words, albeit the exclamation-marks are Blyton's. The context is ironic (leaving aside the fact that the discussion is about murdering a father figure) in that Lady Macbeth, as a mother, is trying to shut out her emotions, only later to find that she can no longer sustain this, and her actions return to haunt her. Blyton, of course, ignored her own mother for almost 30 years, not even attending her funeral. Then, towards the end of her own life, Blyton was often found trying to return to her non-existent parental home.

Her mother, notably, had died only the year before Blyton wrote this book, so Blyton's comments on a mother's responsibility for a child's character have a particular poignancy:

> It is the mother, always the mother, that makes the home. The father does his share, he holds the reins too – but it is the mother who makes a happy, contented home.
>
> (ibid., p. 118)[6]

Fathers are exonerated, but mothers are always to blame if they are not perfect, as Blyton clearly felt her own was not. Blyton gained ideological support for this from Froebel, who also saw any problems with a child as solely explainable through 'grave faults of handling in his first all-important years' (Isaacs, 1952, p. 194). However, in Smallwood's perception, her own mother fell short of this ideal:

> Her [Blyton's] feeling for her readers and for all children in the abstract was intense and loving; but as one of her two children who should have been the closest to her of all, I saw her only as a distant authority, a clever person, a strong and imaginative actress on the little stage of my life but never, or almost never, a mother.
>
> (1989a, p. 12)

Blyton, though, held fast to her story:

> As you can imagine, we are a happy little family. I could not possibly write a single good book for children if I were not happy with my family, or if I didn't put them first and foremost. How could I write good books for children if I didn't care about my own? You would-

n't like my books, if I were that kind of mother! They certainly wouldn't be the kind of books I always write for you.

(ibid.)

Her family, as she terms it, is her own, controllable construction, with much about her own parents and brothers omitted. She also erases her daughters' biological father; that is, her own first husband, despite a chapter on Old Thatch, where they had all lived. In his stead, Kenneth Darrell Waters stands at the centre of the text, replacing the real father with the adroitness of fairy-tale logic.[7]

A curious chapter, 'The little round pond', makes this point more clearly. Initially this struck me as a strange thing to give so much space to in a book about one's life. But, from Blyton's own words, it is clearly of great significance: 'I don't think I have ever enjoyed anything quite so much as my pond' (ibid., p. 44). And, in effect, this chapter could stand as the metaphoric core of the book, showing how reality and imagination are fused in a sunny, reflective surface, unruffled by anything untoward that might lurk beneath. She certainly liked to be photographed by ponds. Stoney (1974, facing p. 144) reproduces one from Elfin Cottage, where Blyton can be seen, Narcissus-like, locked in her imaginary *persona*. In her autobiography, Blyton is pictured by another pond, along with her reconstructed ideal family, reflecting an Imaginary wholeness.[8]

Talk of the pond neatly brings us on to Blyton's concern with gardens, which is not simply horticultural. Again, it links to her Froebel training. It is interesting that though Blyton talks of children at Green Hedges, they are curiously absent: the garden is empty of them. Yet the garden gives the impression of a protected realm, where children might desire to be, where they would have space to grow – as Blyton ambiguously declares: 'People are happy when they grow things, especially children' (Blyton, 1952b, p. 28). This association is Froebel's, the inventor of the kindergarten (literally, the 'children garden'), who has already been quoted on parenting. Froebel pointed to the split in society between mothering and working, arguing that women needed more support for the former. Hence the importance of trained 'child-gardeners' to support the child in its natural development into a social being, fully aware of its membership of a larger community. In that he saw women in this role, as trained teachers, Froebel was seen as subversive, and had his first kindergarten shut down. The notion of a 'garden' was not simply metaphorical, however, for he also laid great store on gardens as places for development and, indeed, on nature study in general: 'Teachers should scarcely let a week pass without taking to the country a part of their pupils . . . making them observe and admire the varied richness which nature displays to their eyes' (quoted in Lawrence, 1970, p. 252). Lastly, he advocated learning by doing, hence recommending gardening and looking after animals. For any but a fleeting reader of Blyton, these precepts provide some key ingredients in her stories.

So Blyton's autobiography, with its economic treatment of the truth, provides some revealing insights into the *persona* 'Enid Blyton'. Itself a fictional construct, 'Enid Blyton' freed her from patriarchal notions of being Mrs H. Pollock or Mrs K. Darrell Waters, allowing her to fashion her own ideal family tree, pruned and disentangled of unsightly roots. This reconstructed family centres on master-gardener Blyton herself, Froebel-trained, who knows how to grow (or story) her children.

This section has given a brief outline of Blyton's life but, more importantly, it has shown how her life has been mythologized, most capably by Blyton herself. With her carefully forged *persona* she managed to create a 'brand name' before most people knew what such a thing was – instantly identifiable from her famous signature, which she built into the title of many of her works.[9] Even those who could not yet read might recognize that familiar, rounded shape, and be set on the road to brand loyalty, to travel with her all the days of their childhood, 'from the very beginning . . . till you are old enough to read adult books' (Blyton, 1952b, p. 96).

Before leaving this section, though, there are two issues I'd like to draw particular attention to. First, Blyton's rebellion against the strict sexual division of labour at this time. Women were expected to stay in the home, although it was only men who had their own private space there: the study, whence they could escape. Girls were expected to help their mothers with domestic chores while boys were allowed to read and play. If boys worked anywhere, it was usually outside in the garden, whereas girls did the inside jobs (Dyhouse, 1981). Blyton, in not aligning herself with her mother, seems to have rejected this scheme of things – refusing the domestic role while simultaneously establishing here own private 'study', locking the door of her room and installing a doorknocker (Stoney, 1974, p. 21). Eventually, rather than submit to domestic servitude, Blyton opted to leave home.

The second issue is the claim that Blyton never grew up. The reason for her success as a children's writer is, reputedly, that 'she was a child, she thought as a child, and she wrote as a child' (Woods, 1968, p. 14; also Holbrook, 1961; Blishen, 1974; Stoney, 1992, p. 191). It sounds attractive, except that children generally do *not* write as Blyton did, although, once attuned to it, they can perform some creditable pastiches (see Clark, 1976). Secondly, I am suspicious because this is such a common explanation for the success of children's writers.[10] In other words – and thirdly – it is really a non-explanation, a tautology (Tucker, 1976, makes exactly this point). This said, others have pointed to additional evidence in Blyton's case, in that she is said to have had an underdeveloped womb, 'almost that of a young girl of 12 or 13', which Stoney convincingly relates to the departure of Blyton's father when Blyton reached puberty (Stoney, 1974, p. 79).[11]

This fact certainly adds weight to the 'child' explanation, but I am still suspicious in that this notion of the immature woman was itself a popular construct. Thus, the then famous psychologist, G. Stanley Hall, 'argued that women never really outgrew their adolescence – psychologically and emotionally they could best be understood as having had their growth arrested in the adolescent phase' (Dyhouse, 1981, p. 118). Even the diet of girls was designed to delay the onset of puberty (Avery, 1991, p. 316).

Status as a writer

Blyton the educationalist – the early years (1920s and 1930s)

As both Stoney and Ray have pointed out, Blyton's work was not subject to much criticism at all during her early years, and what little there was tended to be positive. Her name, as Ray says, is found in the company of works involving A.A. Milne, E.V. Rieu, and Lord Clark. When *Teachers World*[12] published a special issue on poetry in 1923, Blyton's poems appeared alongside others by established poets, including Kipling, de la Mare and Chesterton (Druce, 1992, p. 31). In an English retelling of the classic story of Babar by the French writer Jan de Brunhoff, it was Blyton who provided the text (Ray, 1982, p. 13). There was, in fact, very little negative criticism until after the Second World War, the majority still championing her work for being both readable and morally sound.

However, as Ray makes plain, professional critical awareness of children's literature was still relatively undeveloped in Britain till after the war, when things began to change. As an example of this, Trease quotes a librarian from the late 1940s bemoaning Blyton's 'intense mediocrity'

(1964, p. 118). Ray's point is well taken, but we should not forget that people had views on children's literature before this, the difference being that the critical divide between adult and children's books was not so well established. Thus Graham Greene could discuss Beatrix Potter (Greene, 1980) or Virginia Woolf 'Alice' (Dusinberre, 1987). Moreover, those that came into the developing field of children's literature after the war were heavily influenced by Leavis and American 'new criticism', which tended to foreground the literary text at the expense of the reader. Many of the criteria that were promulgated in the fifties were therefore actually detrimental to a more child-oriented and democratic approach to evaluation – an approach that has only comparatively recently allowed Blyton to be viewed in a less histrionic manner.

Nevertheless, I think there is more to explaining Blyton's status than simply to point to a lack of negative criticism. The fact is, she was highly regarded at this time in educational circles. She wrote in *Teachers World* from 1922 until 1945. For many educationalists, her work was influential, as a number of ex-teachers have informed me. She edited and contributed substantially to the following: a three-volume *The Teacher's Treasury* (1926); a six-volume *Modern Teaching* (1928b); a ten-volume *Pictorial Knowledge* (1930a); a four-volume *Modern Teaching in the Infant School* (1932) and *Two Years in the Infant School* (1936), aside from her many books on nature study, ancient history, religious studies, drama, and her class readers. The introduction to the first of these (Blyton, 1926) by Professor T.P. Nunn of London University, is glowing. So, for the first twenty-odd years of her career, Blyton was quite a respected figure.

Golden days: 1940s–1950s

Blyton's titles appeared in increasing numbers throughout the war, when many of her most well-known series appeared (including the first 'Famous Five', 'St. Clare's', 'Adventure', 'Naughtiest Girl' and 'Mary Mouse' books, plus *The Magic Faraway Tree*). Strangely, this was at a time when

> Shortage of paper and of time reduced the output of most writers, but not Enid Blyton. During the four years 1942–45, lean years generally, sixty-seven of her books were published.
>
> (Crouch, 1962, p. 92)

This might sound a lot, but current bibliographical research raises this total to 108 titles (Summerfield, 1998)! Ray explains that Blyton did so well out of this because of the diversity of publishing houses for which she wrote, which meant that the restrictions on paper affected her less. There was also the ingenious idea of using the offcuts from *Picture Post* to make miniature booklets, to which Blyton quickly responded with the character 'Mary Mouse'; the books were an instant success (Stoney, 1974, p. 129).[13] While the wartime situation favoured Blyton, it should not be seen as an explanation of her popularity – contrary to Blishen's comment that it was 'based on her sheer availability' (Blishen, 1967, p. 29). This is to have the tail wag the dog (and there will be more on tails anon), besides undermining children's ability to select what they like. After all, it was *Blyton* that publishers wanted. This is endorsed by the fact that the six books she wrote as Mary Pollock during the war years became popular in their own right, despite restrictions on promotion, and were subsequently re-issued under Blyton's own name (Stoney, 1974, p. 125).[14]

The reviews I have come across from this period are quite positive; for instance, *Circus Days Again* (1942a) and *Seven O'Clock Tales* (1943c) were both reviewed in *The Times Literary Supplement*, the latter being praised for its 'understanding of childish thought-processes and suitable language' (Anon, 1943).[15] The 'Adventure' series published by Macmillan probably received more positive attention than most, regarded, as Ray notes, as probably her best work. However, in 1948 came Eileen Colwell's frequently quoted (and often mis-quoted) comment on *The Sea of Adventure*: 'But what hope has a band of desperate men against four children?' (quoted in Ray, p. 52).[16]

By the 1950s, Blyton's *oeuvre* was substantial, the first 'Noddy' having appeared in 1949. In 1950 Darrell Waters Ltd was also formed, giving others some control over her affairs, which, though freeing Blyton from some onerous activities, might have abetted her subsequent overproduction (in the early 1950s, she was averaging over 50 titles a year). From this period on she began to top children's lists of favourite authors (Ray, 1982, p. 38). And with this popularity came the critical backlash, which, as Ray notes, was linked to the general growth in children's books as a defined market, and an increasing critical attention to its quality, especially by gatekeepers such as librarians and teachers.

However, there was still an ambivalence, especially in the early fifties when there was a worry about the invasion of American culture (horror comics, TV, rock music, teenage delinquency, Disney), against which Blyton was seen to stand. Her publicity endorses this, speaking of Noddy 'ousting the American creations of Walt Disney from our nurseries and homes' (Anon, n.d., p. 5). Consequently, it was only by the mid-fifties that any criticism of a substantive nature appeared, with Colin Welch calling Noddy an 'unnaturally priggish . . . sanctimonious . . . witless, spiritless, snivelling, sneaking doll' (Welch, 1958, pp. 21–2; see also Dohm, 1955; Woods, 1955). By this time Blyton was something of a Disney enterprise herself, especially thanks to the huge spin-offs from Noddy, in the form of theatre, TV, film and extensive merchandising.

Slow poison: the critical backlash, 1960s–1980s

In the sixties, a more consistently negative discourse was advanced, typified in Holbrook (1961), quoted earlier. Roy Nash sums up the mood of the times in an amusing article called 'Noddy-bashing', wherein Big-Ears comments, 'We're redundant in Toyland . . . Children want literature now. Literature with a capital L' (Nash, 1964). However, it was not the children who were making this claim; it was the cultural gatekeepers. The general public either maintained its silence, or occasionally rose to Blyton's defence. This was demonstrated when the journal *Where* asked the question 'Are your children addicted to Enid Blyton and what, if anything, do you do about it?' To their surprise, most respondents were positive about Blyton, with only six being 'firmly anti', this last group including the only teachers and librarians (Blishen, 1967, p. 28).

The moral panic reported by sensational newspaper stories seems to have been massively overplayed. Thompson's (1975) and Ray's assiduous coverage of the issues reveals that very few authorities actually banned Blyton, although the purchase of her books was controlled. Sheila Strauss, who worked at Nottingham City Libraries when the Blyton controversy began, has informed me that the whole event was orchestrated by the media.[17] When Cullingford (1979) wrote about Cumbria's complete banning of Blyton's works, the County Librarian promptly rebutted the claim (Ray, 1982, pp. 96–7).[18]

Following Blyton's death in 1968, Woods writes of a new tolerance towards Blyton emerging: 'it gives me a nice feeling to believe that the wind of change that blew fair for *Lolita* and *Lady Chatterly's* [*sic*] *Lover* (if not for *Fanny Hill*), has also blown with benefit on Julian, Dick, Ann [*sic*], George, as well as on a dog called Timmy' (Woods, 1974, p. 733). But I would query the extent to which things were any different. He had sent out 100 questionnaires to schools, to find that teachers generally approved of Blyton.

Unfortunately, Woods had conducted no earlier study, so he had no way of knowing whether there was really more tolerance towards her. Despite this, he might have drawn on what evidence there was, like the

Where survey (above), or the responses to *The Use of English*'s question to teachers, 'How does one wean 15-year-old girls from a diet of Enid Blyton?' (Anon, 1966a). Of the five replies received, none was particularly anti-Blyton, and three were very positive, including the following from D.W. Crompton, Head of English at Didsbury College of Education:

> 'How soon will we all be weaned from the idea that such "problems" really matter?' Or, to put it another way, 'How soon will we be reclaimed from that form of arrogance to which English teachers are particularly prone of believing that it is any part of our specific task to attempt to determine a child's spare-time reading . . . ?' . . . the short answer to the question as to how one weans 15-year-old girls from Enid Blyton ought to be that one doesn't.
>
> (Anon, 1966b, pp. 37–8)

He goes on to suggest that some of Blyton's books 'deserve almost unqualified praise'.

So I remain unconvinced that teachers were more anti-Blyton in the sixties. However, I am equally sceptical of what Woods calls a 'new tolerance', for in this same year Bob Dixon was publishing two, seminally damning articles (1974a; 1974b). Thus, what Woods calls his 'nice feeling' – a particularly Blytonesque phrase – seems to have been little more than that as far as the critics were concerned. What had changed, it seems, was the nature of the criticism. Whereas it had earlier been about her literary qualities, it now shifted to the social concerns of racism, sexism, and élitism, with Lena Jeger's attack on Blyton's *The Little Black Doll* being one of the first. This notorious story of a black doll disliked for his colour was seen as 'more insidiously dangerous' than the neo-fascist literature of the *British Independent* (Jeger, 1966). But, as John Attenborough of Hodder & Stoughton noted, though unpleasant, the criticisms and reputed 'banning' of Blyton's books were good for sales, resulting in children rushing out to buy their own copies of her works, and the publicity clearly made the most of this. Thompson (1988, p. 44) claims that Blyton's earnings 'soared' to over £100,000 *per annum* with her supposed banning.

The revolution in paperback publishing in the sixties aided this process. Children's paperbacks in particular had previously been the monopoly of Puffin, with its quality approach. In fact, Puffin's editor, Eleanor Graham, celebrated her antipathy to Blyton: 'I was, of course, frequently urged to get some Blyton on our list but I never did. It was not intended for *that kind of public*' (my emphasis; quoted in Ray, 1982, p. 28). Other publishers now produced junior paperback lists. Armada, a Mayfair Books imprint, was the first in 1962, its very first title being a Blyton (*The Adventurous Four*). By the end of 1963 it had 22 more of her works – over a third of its whole children's list. Dragon Books achieved a similar proportion between 1966–69.

Eleanor Graham's comment draws attention to one of the key ploys of Blyton's critics, which was simply to ignore her. After seeing the way that librarians had been mauled by the media, they were probably wise. However, over time, silence itself comes to look like a form of censorship. Thus Trease (1964) berates Dorothy Neale White for omitting Blyton from her critical study of children's books, and Townsend's standard history, *Written for Children*, has been similarly criticized (Ray, 1982, p. 62). This process continues. Hobson *et al.* (c1992), in a standard work on popular children's books for the 6–13-year-old, omit reference to her, though both Blume and Dahl are included. Kirsten Drotner's excellent work on the history of children's magazines omits any reference to *Sunny Stories*, despite the fact that her interest in the topic was initially sparked by Enid Blyton's 'serial excitements' (Drotner, 1988, p. ix). Even a work that explicitly aims to discuss popular culture in the twentieth century (Maltby, 1989) omits her – this on the one hand, is surprising, but, on the other, given the marginalization of children's culture, it is typical. Even in Blyton's centenary year – itself an unavoidable anniversary – a commemorative meeting of the Children's Books History Society was organized so as to discuss those authors 'obscured' by the 'Noddy-lady's fame' (Alderson, 1997, pp. 7–8).

Sunny Stories again: Blyton comes in from the cold

Readership studies

Since the 1980s, Roald Dahl's work has ousted Blyton from the most popular slot, but she still tends to hold second place according to most indicators. On 'Jackanory', the BBC's successful children's storytelling programme, Blyton's *The Circus of Adventure* was its second most popular reading ever, just behind Dahl (Wainwright, 1990). The final Assessment of Performance Unit (APU) report, published in 1991 after the Unit's demise, found Enid Blyton the second most popular author among junior children (Hughes, 1991). Likewise with more recent surveys: Wray and Lewis (1993), of 450 junior school children, the extensive 1994 W.H. Smith replication of the 1971 'Schools

Council' survey, Knowles and Malmkjaer's study (1995) of 246 10–12-year-olds, Millard's study of 255 11–12-year-olds (1997, p. 56) and, most recently, Roehampton Institute's survey of some 9000 7–16-year-olds (Reynolds, 1996). Lastly, the annual Public Lending Right figures, based on books borrowed from British public libraries, tell a similar story.

There are two points to note about Blyton's position, though. First, although she performs well as a popular author, she is less well known for any one distinctive title. Thus, a 1997 survey by Channel 4 and Waterstone's, contentiously looking for the top books of the century, had no one particular Blyton title that performed well, though she came first as the author with the most titles voted for, across some 44 books. Secondly, it is of note that Blyton not only performs well in the junior age range, as one might expect, but among older readers, too. In the APU survey mentioned above, Blyton was found to be very popular with 15-year-old girls, just as she was among Knowles and Malmkjaer's children of similar age. Even with older adolescents (16–18-year-olds), Blyton was equal fifth with Jan Mark (Knowles and Malmkjaer, 1995, pp. 38–9). Rosemary Auchmuty, looking particularly at the school story, had intended to ignore Blyton's contribution to this genre, but her popularity militated against it. Blyton's books, she found, 'were most frequently recalled from childhood reading. Some women, indeed, were reading them again in current paperback reprints, or even for the first time, in the 1990s' (Auchmuty, 1992, p. 45).

Intertextual Blytons

Blyton is no longer just an author. She is a cultural reference point, signifying a range of things. One of the earliest to use Blyton in this way was the 'Comic Strip' on the opening night of Channel 4 with their irreverent *Five Go Mad in Dorset* (1982).[19] This originated the apocryphal Blytonism, 'lashings of ginger beer', subsequently taken up in the 'lashings of Ambrosia Creamed Rice' advertisement. Other writers have also used Blyton's work as intertexts, such as Adèle Geras (1990–92) in her 'Egerton Hall' trilogy (*Malory Towers*), Jacqueline Wilson (1996) in *Double Act* (*St Clare's*) and Peter Hunt (1985) in *A Step off the Path* (*Famous Five*). More explicitly, there is Michaela Morgan's *The Not so Famous Four* (1994), while at the more oblique end, the crime writer Denise Danks has the liberated 'Georgina Powers' as her detecting heroine, inspired by George from the *Famous Five* (Danks, 1989). Finally, in *The Turkish Daily News*, one of the most talked about items is 'Noddy's Notes' – particularly popular with ex-pats.[20]

It is not only writers who have been influenced, though. A number of music bands reference Blyton – often explicitly, such as 'Current 93' (with their *Swastikas for Noddy* album), 'Noddy's Puncture', 'Die Funf Freunde'[21] and 'The Enid'; Carl Palmer, of *ELP*, used to picture Noddy on his drumkit; Herbie Flowers of *Sky* even dressed as Noddy. 'The Enid', founded in 1974 by Robert John Godfrey, were, in fact, originally known as 'The Famous Five', and give a subversive nuance to Blyton's name, which Godfrey plays up to:

> There have never been any fairies at the bottom of my garden apart from myself and the boy next door having fun behind the wood shed. Which one of us was Noddy or Big Ears is my secret.
>
> (Godfrey, 1996)[22]

An Irish singer-songwriter, Mickey MacConnell (c1993) has even recorded a song called 'Enid Blyton', which looks at how the Five might have matured into adults – a theme which has exercised a number of people (Mourby, 1994; 1998).

However, it is in the 'greyer' areas that the extent of Blyton's influence is more discernible. The Internet, for instance, has many revealing pages: discussions of the Five and Malory characters as grown-ups, how they'd perform at university, games based on Blyton's works, continuations of her stories, home pages from individuals named after Blyton characters, favourite quotations, such as 'Kiki-isms', recipes based on her books, and so on.

The media in general uses Blyton as a reference point for a number of discourses. There follows a very brief selection, starting with a reaction to Judy Blume's children's books: 'if . . . millions of readers really do crave pap on the lines of "The Mystery of the Vanishing Gro-Bra" or "Five Go Jacking Off Together" then the time has come to say "Come back, Enid, all is forgiven"' (Renshaw, 1980); pop music: 'most contemporary chart hits have words which make Enid Blyton read like Sartre' (Attila the Stockbroker, 1991); poverty: 'a study of contemporary poverty that makes Orwell's *The Road to Wigan Pier* read like Enid Blyton' (Morrison, 1993); and television adaptations:

> The frisson factor survives adaptation. Not so the charm: 'Oliver, what's that?' 'My cock.' 'But it's eenaaawmuss.' 'I've got an erection and I want to poke it into you.' This is Enid Blyton needing to wash her mouth out with carbolic: 'Five Talk Dirty in Cornwall.'
>
> (Pearson, 1992)

Here Blyton is not the poisoner of earlier years. Indeed, more recent moral panics – over high illiteracy rates, couch-potato TV consumption, video-nasties, child crime and violence, alco-pops replacing ginger-beer, lack of morality, child-abuse, incest, satanic rituals, and more – have made Blyton seem rather innocuous, standing, if anything, for an age of innocence and security and, in the fears over morality and illiteracy, to represent a possible answer.

When BBC2 screened *Sunny Stories*, a dramatic biography of Blyton, in Christmas 1992, it was interesting that Maureen Lipman played the author with intimations of Margaret Thatcher.[23] There are certainly parallels: externally the show of a mother-figure, but underneath, the fairly calculating businesswoman.[24] In fact, Thatcher was once called 'the Enid Blyton of economics' (Howard, 1987) and, in an amusing article entitled 'The life and times of the Famous One', Miles Kington takes the parallels further, rewriting Thatcher's life in Blyton vein. He sees her going off on holiday with her dog, Denis, having

> found some Spanish-speaking villains occupying some islands they didn't own (see The Famous One Goes to the Falklands) and had got them out. On another holiday she had found some valuable treasure belonging to the family and sold it all to help pay for things (see The Famous One Privatises Everything).
>
> (Kington, 1991)

John Major's version of society has also been likened to a Blyton story – especially his vision of an ideal nation given in his 1993 Mansion House speech: a 'country of long shadows on county grounds, warm beer, invincible green suburbs, dog lovers and pool fillers and – as George Orwell said – "old maids bicycling to holy communion through the morning mist"'. This vision was explicitly described by *The Independent* as 'the lost England of Enid Blyton's novels, where uncles were jolly, picnic hampers were overflowing and policemen rode bicycles – a private England whose citizens went harmlessly about voluntary and neighbourly activities, without bothering their heads over politics' (Anon, 1993a). Major certainly grew up during Blyton's writing heyday and objected to 'loony-left' councils banning her works: 'Big Brother versus Big Ears', he reportedly quipped (Aitken, 1991). However, for Noddy himself, Fleet Street had to wait for Tony Blair, with his 'tendency to nod and grin inanely', Mandelson being seen as his spin-doctor, Big-Ears (Wheen, 1997).

Blyton, then, is now everywhere. The discursive threads are there to link her to traditional values, to Thatcherite conservatism, but she can equally well be linked to new labour; however, her name has also been used more subversively, by bands and Internet groups. Up to now, though, the discussion has assumed that, although her image has changed, her texts have stood still. Yet despite Blyton's lifelong claim that 'Every word of every book that bears my name has been written by me. That goes without saying' (Blyton, 1951a, p. 3), since her death this is no longer the case. First came overseas rewrites; alongside apocryphal 'Secret Seven' and 'Mystery' tales, 22 'Famous Five' ('Le Club des Cinq') books were published in France from 1971 onwards using Blyton's logo signature on the covers (inside it said, 'a new adventure of the characters created by Enid Blyton' by Claude Voilier); and in Germany, again in the 1970s, there were a dozen anonymous sequels to 'Malory Towers' (see Chapter 7) and a similar number of 'St. Clare's' sequels. In this country, substantial rewrites did not occur till the 1980s, but have since gathered momentum. Noddy was the most substantially rewritten (see Chapter 5), but others were superficially altered, attending to sexist, racist, class and period references (clothing). For instance, in *The Secret Seven*, Peter's exchange with the girls:

> 'Can't we girls come too?' asked Pam.
> 'I don't want to!' said Barbara.
> 'Well, you *can't* come, anyhow', said Peter. 'That's absolutely certain. Boys only are in the performance to-night!'
>
> (Blyton, 1949b, pp. 77–8)

has been amended to:

> 'No,' said Peter. 'I am sorry but seven is too many. We'll have more chance of success if there are only four of us.'
>
> (Blyton, 1992, p. 62)

However, despite the rhetoric, the action remains a boys' only zone.

Recently, Blyton's texts have come to be regarded as more expendable. The chief scriptwriter of the filmed 'Adventure' series, for instance, was reported as saying, with apparent insouciance, 'Not one word of Blyton's is in the script' (Brown, 1996). These scripts have since been turned back into 'screenplay novelisations' (for example, Robinson, 1997), which the *British National Bibliography* (25th March 1998) describes as 'New Zealand' fiction (the film's location). Gillian Baverstock has more extensively rewritten some of her mother's works –

including a new 'Riddle' series, based on six previously separate books (see Baverstock, 1998a, 1998b).[25] Other writers have been involved in rewrites, too; for instance, the original 'Adventurous Four' books have been revamped by Clive Dickinson (the characters Mary and Jill now, for some reason, have trendy 1990s names, Pippa and Zoe, though the books are still set in the 1940s) and Anne Digby has written four sequels to the 'Naughtiest Girl' stories.

Changes to Blyton's texts have been driven, of course, by economic factors. Earliest to experience these was Noddy, whose texts were first revised in 1986, with a view to breaking into the American market – unsuccessfully in the event. Noddy, as part of the Macdonald publishing group, also became involved in the downfall of the Maxwell Communication Corporation. Most of the writers found a new home with Little Brown, but Noddy himself was rejected (a recurring experience for the character). Fortunately, others were keen, and BBC Enterprises finally bought the rights – a hugely successful move, as it turned out.

The Cosgrove Hall animated series followed, with spin-offs in terms of videos, a magazine and over 300 licensed products, making it one of the BBC's biggest money-spinners. In the 1995–96 financial year it had an estimated value of £42 million in merchandising and brought in £3.5 million (Winder, 1995). The programmes were rapidly sold to 32 other countries (Cowe, 1996). However, rumours that the BBC were negotiating a full-length Hollywood film of Noddy (Anon, 1993b) were fanciful. In fact, until recently, America was one of the few markets to resist Blyton (except for a few titles).[26] The last problem was reputedly Big-Ears' name, and it was suggested that this be replaced with 'Whitebeard', albeit this is another physically descriptive name (as is 'Noddy', come to that). This would seem strange, however, from the country that has Goofy and Big-Foot as two of its star attractions.[27] With hindsight, it seems to have been mischief-making for, as I write, in the winter of 1998, there has been a more successful 'push' to get Noddy into the States, with Big-Ears intact; almost £5 million has been spent on an animated series, complete with transatlantic accents and vocabulary.[28] Noddy is now more popular in the States than Sesame Street.

The money for this venture, however, did not come from Darrell Waters Ltd, but from the new owners. The family had announced its intention of selling the copyright of Blyton's works by 1997, the centenary year. There were various bidders, but in January 1996 the Trocadero emerged as the winner, buying the rights for a figure variously estimated at £12–14 million. Blyton was described as 'Britain's Disney' by Trocadero representatives (Brown, 1996), and Nigel Wray, its multimillionaire owner, declared his ambition 'to Noddify the world' (Snoddy, 1996a), unwittingly bringing the dreaded 'denoddyfication centres' – more pessimistically envisaged by Blishen some 34 years earlier (Blishen, 1967, p. 28) – nearer to reality! (Beek himself, the character's original artist, admitted to seeing little Noddies crawling all over his desk after he had been working too hard.)

David Lane, Gillian Baverstock's son-in-law, then managing director of the new Trocadero subsidiary 'Enid Blyton Ltd', reputedly inherited some 7500 publishers' contracts. One of the first things the new company did was renegotiate royalties, pushing them back up to Blyton's own illustrious 15 per cent. In May 1996, Enid Blyton Ltd also re-established its rights to Noddy with the BBC, the former accusing the latter of exceeding its prerogative, and threatening legal action. Enid Blyton Ltd now handle all the Noddy books not owned by the BBC (rights having been bought by HarperCollins), and license the extensive merchandising. Interactive CD-ROM versions of Famous Five and Noddy were also marketed by SIRS – the first, *Five on a Treasure Island*, appearing in October 1996, though only a few titles ever appeared. CD-ROM versions of the Five might have seemed to provide an excellent opportunity for discussing changes in language and attitudes over the years. However, when I spoke to a representative of SIRS, she was nonplussed. She had hoped to do this, she said, but was surprised at how little had changed. It turned out that she had been working from revised editions, and was unaware of the originals, although she admitted to being perplexed at children wearing jeans in the 1940s!

Helen Cresswell also found, when she came to work on some Famous Five adaptations, that she had been working from updated texts, despite her wish to preserve the period feel (Anon, 1997). These were for a new TV series, produced at a cost of £2.7 million and shown nationally on ITV from July 1996. It had been shown regionally the year before, and nationally in Germany (ZDF helped fund the production, and it attracted record ratings in Germany). It was also sold to a number of other countries, including America, with a second series following in 1997.

Adaptations of the Famous Five preceded Blyton's centenary year (August 1996 to July 1997), in which a number of events occurred. A blue plaque was mounted at 'Southernay' (207 Hook Road, Surbiton) where Blyton had lived and established a small school in the 1920s. Commemorative stamps were issued, featuring Noddy, the Famous Five, Secret Seven, Malory Towers and the Faraway Tree. The Oxford Union held a debate on Blyton's ideological soundness, which was upheld.

There was also a conference at the Roehampton Institute, 'Enid Blyton: a celebration and reappraisal', which attracted considerable media interest. This said, it was nothing to the attention she received in Germany, where a four-and-a-half-hour TV special was shown.

Of course, Blyton's books were also extensively repackaged, including reissues of the original Soper illustrated Famous Fives, and other series. These were obviously aimed not so much at children as grown-ups. There was also a short-lived magazine, devoted to Blyton characters, published by Fleetway, entitled 'Mystery and Suspense'. Tim Quinn (1997), the editor, has recounted the less-than-helpful suggestions he received, such as giving George a 'Girl Power' tattoo, or making just one of the Five (they are related, remember), Black or Asian. There was also a very successful Five musical that toured extensively, and a number of other film projects, of which the 'Adventure' series, mentioned above, was the most extravagant. It was made by Cloud 9 at a cost of £6.2 million, taking 6 months to film in over 358 locations. As opposed to the parochial Famous Five, these characters were made more cosmopolitan with a James Bond flavour – action, gadgetry, even romance. The results were certainly successful, selling to some 45 countries. Other ventures came thick and fast. The 'Secret' series has also been filmed for TV, as has 'The Enchanted Land', a cartoon series based on the 'Magic Faraway Tree' and 'Wishing Chair' books. In the pipeline are 'The Adventurous Four', 'Amelia Jane', 'The Secret Seven' and a lavish version of 'Malory Towers', reputedly to feature Dawn French and Jennifer Saunders as the two French Mam'zelles, with Liz Hurley as the first form teacher, Miss Potts. However, the series is to be updated with an American twinning arrangement and some multiracial characters, so it will be interesting to see how much of Blyton's dialogue survives this adaptation (Ahmed, 1997).

It was also in 1997 that Butlin's (owned by Rank) announced a huge update of their holiday camps, using the Noddy characters (Wainwright and King, 1997). Some original Noddy drawings, meanwhile, were auctioned at Sotheby's in October 1997, with Beek's initial letter to Blyton fetching £37,500. However, some idea of the value of his work had come earlier, in 1993, when the BBC at Shepherd's Bush was broken into and Noddy artwork stolen.

Nevertheless, despite the high profile, Trocadero suffered problems in share prices, largely as a result of the franchised electronic amusement arcade, Sega world, at the Trocadero Centre, in Piccadilly, whose operating losses prompted free admission before the venture was finally sold. Accordingly, when this was sold, Trocadero then changed its name to

Chorion (March 1998). In June it then acquired a controlling share in Agatha Christie, whose two billion world-wide sales exceeded even Blyton's. Interestingly, the Englishness of much of Blyton's work was now being dispensed with – presumably to capture a more international audience – in contrast to that of Christie, which was quoted by Lane as having a 'quintessential Britishness' (Midgley, 1988).

Enid Blyton Ltd earned a Queen's Award for Export Achievement in 1998. It is striving to emulate the vertical integration of Disney, controlling all interests, from production to the resultant media spin-offs, through their own outlets. Blyton's work is now being packaged in three sub-brands. At the youngest end there is 'Toyland', including Noddy. For the 4–7-year-olds there is the 'Lands of Far Beyond'. Then, for the 8–10-year-olds, 'Mystery and Adventure', which includes all her mystery and adventure stories, plus the school series. The company is trying to develop markets worldwide, opening offices in New York, South America and South-East Asia. They hope that localized versions of the various series will be produced in the indigenous languages, starting with a Chinese Famous Five (Ashworth, 1998). However, a recent setback (October 1998) has been the resignation of Lane, though he subsequently put in a bid to buy the intellectual property rights of Blyton and Christie for a reputed £70 million.

Conclusion

As the above indicates, Blyton has become more rather than less popular, but with different resonances to her work. The notion of her being seen as a dangerous presence for children – except, perhaps, as an economic drain – now seems laughable to most people. But with the growth in economic muscle there has been a loss of the intimacy that Blyton tried to foster with her audience. The child-oriented *The Enid Blyton Newsletter*, which Darrell Waters Ltd used to produce, became little more than an advertising flyer before disappearing altogether. More worrying is the fairly free revision of her work, turning her into the very writing collective that she once fought a court case to refute. However, this policy might still backfire, for reasons that will be discussed as our story unfolds.

4
The Pied Piper among the Critics

Introduction

There have already been substantial reviews of the Blyton literature (especially Ray, 1982; Druce, 1992). So here I shall treat the literature thematically rather than chronologically, using it as a resource in which I seek to discern how various constructions and interpretations have gone to make up the 'Blyton phenomenon'.[1] It will involve looking not only at the more substantive studies, but also drawing on a rich vein of ephemera. Generally, I have used material that discusses the Famous Five and Noddy, not only because these are the focus of my own research, but because they are also the most talked about. I have grouped the material according to the two main approaches adopted by critics: literary and educational. More exclusively social readings are treated in more depth in later chapters.

Literary readings

A broad indication of the literary approach to children's literature, and its inadequacies, was given in Chapter 2. In looking at how literary critics have dealt with Blyton, I shall now concentrate on three main aspects of their critique: discussions of her language, characters and plotting.

Language

Criticism of Blyton's language has been an enduring one. For instance, the teachers mentioned by Woods (1974) found limited vocabulary to be her worst feature. Peter Hunt, in 'The cliché count' (1978), specifically uses Blyton's work to make his point, and estimates that almost

75 per cent of an extract of her work is cliché-ridden. Hollindale, though, disagrees, calling her style 'crisp and economical, and not over-packed with clichés – it is just very simple' (Hollindale, 1974, p. 154). Similarly, Wall claims:

> she wrote good, clear, straightforward and vigorous sentences. Her vocabulary, though simple and too often repetitive is not patronisingly limited. Unsubtle and unstimulating though it may be, Blyton's prose is direct and practical, neither cliché-ridden nor pretentious.
>
> (Wall, 1991, p. 190)

Let me make two points here, as they underpin much of the following criticism. First is the attempt by some critics to judge Blyton as a literary writer, something she herself never claimed to be. Second is the confused and contradictory nature of much of the criticism – as in the accusation (above) of her work being cliché-ridden. Margery Fisher (1961) illustrates both these points, contrasting Blyton with Beatrix Potter. Whereas the latter was not afraid to use unfamiliar words, 'Blyton and others think that children are taxed too much if they are confronted by so much as a polysyllable' (Fisher, 1961, p. 28), she writes. However, both Tucker (1976) and Wright (1980) have pointed to a variety of polysyllables in her work.[2] Dixon is also damning, calling her language 'colourless, dead and totally undemanding' (1974b, p. 54). Blishen, too, complains that 'This is not children's language, but rather the language used when talking to children by ill-informed aunts who suppose children must be wrapped in verbal wool' (Blishen 1967, p. 28).

Dyer, on the other hand, says it is just how children do talk: 'If anyone wants an idea . . . for a valuable thesis in the realm of children's language, they might do worse than take Blyton as if she were a child writing as a child would want to write if adults weren't around' (Dyer, 1969, p. 16). I wish I could say (for his sake) that Dyer was parodying the Blyton style here. He also says that her writing conforms to Bernstein's 'restricted code' – that is, highly predictable and unelaborated (ibid., p. 13). This is ironic, as Bernstein saw the restricted code as characteristic of the working-class; whereas, to quote Dixon again, 'In Enid Blyton, the language which which [*sic*] we are invited to identify is, sociologically, middle class based' (Dixon, 1974b, p. 54).

There is a key insight here, though Dyer seems unaware of it. Indeed, some of his own somewhat awkwardly turned sentences tacitly demonstrate my point. He writes: 'Few children can write in it for adults, don't respond to it; so it goes unnoticed or despised' (Dyer, 1969, p. 16). Along with the floating comma, we have here one of Bernstein's key points about the restricted code: that it is characteristic of environments where knowledge is shared, where reference points are held in common. In other words, it is linked to the oral tradition of storytelling, dependent on a close circle, on common bonds, on shared knowledge – but, equally, on knowledge to which outsiders are not privy because of its very restrictedness. And, if this is characteristic of Blyton's process of storytelling, it is even more true of the groups of children who feature in her books, who have their own closeness, their signs and coded words; to which the reader, especially the initiated reader of a number of her stories, becomes party.

This partly accounts for some of the contradictory statements about Blyton's writing: for while it is generally flat and limited in the manner of many oral tales, it also involves us being initiated into a few less than usual lexical choices, their usage usually being explained and reinforced – for example, 'ingot' is explained in the first Famous Five, then taken as read in the second. And though some critics have despised Blyton's condescending explanations of words, this is a fairly standard practice, to the extent that one finds critics unwittingly engaging in it: 'The Noddy books are not polysemic – they have no layers of meaning' (Bentley, quoted in Faulks, 1990). Dixon seems to forget the intimacy that Blyton fostered, even criticizing her banal choice of proper names when, of course, these frequently came from the children in the first place – as did, reputedly, 'Cherry Tree Farm' and 'Green Hedges'. Even here, though, we find contradiction; whereas Dixon criticizes her banality in names, Dyer objects to their being unusual (1969, p. 15)!

The predictability of Blyton's vocabulary is also objected to: her overuse of words such as 'nice', 'good', 'little', and, less acceptably today, 'queer' and 'gay'. Clearly, the connotations of the last two have changed, though they were once immensely popular. Commenting on Henry James' usage, Karl Miller notes that a character can be both 'gay' and 'queer', these being 'favoured adjectives of the Fin-de-Siècle and after' (Miller, 1987, p. 236). But these words make the point, for they do obtrude nowadays, whereas most of her vocabulary is so common as to be invisible: in no way does it impede access to the narrative.

A related issue is Blyton's lack of figurative language, something which has also been criticized. Thus Fisher bemoans the fact that Blyton's vocabulary has no resonance. When Blyton describes some rocks as 'a curious red colour', Fisher complains that that is all there is to it: their redness has no metaphorical association; it is irrelevant to the story (Fisher, 1986, pp. 386–7). One can only assume that she never read much of the book, otherwise she would know the colour's relevance: 'And now I know why it's red. It's coloured by the copper deposits still in the hills' – as one character enlightens us (*Island*, p. 198).[3] Dixon makes a point similar to Fisher's, complaining that the sea, which 'shone as blue as cornflowers' in one book, continues to do so 'twelve books in the series later' (Dixon, 1974b, p. 55). But while Dixon at least acknowledges the simile, Ruth Dodsworth declares that, 'In a search through many of her books I found not one metaphor or simile' (Dodsworth, 1982, p. 26)! One might query whether this writer knows what a simile is like (let alone a pun) – for Blyton uses them extensively. A cursory glance at *FGTST* brings forth the following:

> It [a tree] had cracked the roof of the house like an egg-shell.
> (*FGTST* p. 24)
>
> The rope-ladder . . . slipped like an uncoiling snake.
> (ibid., p. 60)
>
> [Block] wrapped up in the blanket like a caterpillar inside a cocoon.
> (ibid., p. 102)

Again, much of the criticism is not only contradictory, but inaccurate. It also persists in presenting Blyton as a literary writer, thence to be compared with more established figures. Clearly, this is a 'no contest', and one wonders why critics feel the need to stage it in order to 'rubbish' a writer they feel isn't worth discussing in the first place.[4]

To take just one instance in more detail, Elizabeth McQuire sets up 'a comparison of Enid Blyton's *The Magic Faraway Tree* and Kenneth Graham's [*sic*] *The Wind in the Willows*' (McQuire, 1975, p. 48). Although McQuire starts by declaring that 'home is basic to the structure of each book', she is soon contradicting herself, criticizing Blyton for not expressing 'a love of home' – it is 'just the place you hang your hat' – unlike Grahame's 'dulce domum'. After several pages, McQuire seems to realize this, and gives up: 'It becomes increasingly difficult to compare the two books, until it reaches a point where it is better to let Enid Blyton fade away'; among 'his great underlying themes' she has no place (ibid., p. 51). All well and good, but one wonders why she went through the academic exercise in the first place. If one wanted to construct a hierarchy of literary writers, Blyton would clearly not feature. However, if the criterion was storytelling ability, or readability (Hollindale calls her '"readable" to a point where readability becomes a sin', 1974, p. 153), the tables might be reversed. Notably, Hunt conducted a similar exercise on these two authors more recently, but concluded that Blyton's *FGDTS* is a 'rich text', both in 'literary' (his emphasis) and populist terms

(Hunt, 1995, p. 239). This is a striking contrast to his earlier work, where he describes writing such as hers as 'requiring no thought, disturbing no brain cells, and thus, one assumes, appealing to the lowest common denominator' (Hunt, 1978); 'I would as much consider including her in a study of children's literature as I would consider including, say, Mickey Spillane on a literature degree course' (Hunt, 1974, pp. 121–2).

This section has concentrated on the contradictions in what critics say about Blyton's language, and to the literary *cum* educational roots of their discourse. Against this I have hinted at a different construction of Blyton, which draws more on the oral tradition; in many ways it is a restricted as opposed to an elaborated style of writing, but one that, paradoxically, is more indeterminate. In Barthes' terminology it is, in certain respects, more 'writerly', giving the reader greater latitude in imagining events. In Chapter 9 this alternative reading will be developed in detail.

Character

Another common criticism of Blyton is that her characters are flat and 'unmemorable', to use Cadogan and Craig's (1976) word for Julian, Dick and Anne. Dixon makes similar comments, describing Anne as quite insignificant and, as for the boys, they are 'scarcely nonentities – it is a single nonentity split into two'; their 'literary destiny is, clearly, to figure in the stories of *Woman's Own*' (Dixon, 1974b, pp. 52–3) – implying that this is also the literary terminus of the young Blyton reader. However, once more, there is a lack of agreement, with some, like Hollindale (1974) and Wright (1980), finding her characters far more notable.

Whatever the differences over Julian, Dick and Anne, George and Timmy are seen to be in a different league. Cadogan and Craig describe George as having a 'fairly strong character', with 'fierceness, resentment, the wish to have been born a boy' (Cadogan and Craig, 1976, p. 338). For many readers George seems to have provided a powerful role model:

> Harum-scarum, tomboyish George still lives with me now. I despised feminine frills and flounces and longed for the freedom, which was the privilege of the boy. I admired George for the ability to escape the restrictions and dressed as a boy, to be accepted as their equal. . . .
>
> (Bentley, 1969, p. 7)

Even so, there is a lack of unanimity. Fisher, for instance, calls George 'the ultimate stereotype . . . the crudest representative of a huge class of tomboy heroines' (Fisher, 1986, p. 382). Dixon endorses this, throwing in some simple psychoanalysis. George is, 'perhaps (unless we exclude Noddy) Enid Blyton's most fortunate invention [*sic* – I presume Dixon must mean "*if* we exclude Noddy"]. She is a very bad case of that castration complex, or penis-envy . . .' (Dixon, 1974b, p. 53).

As for Timmy, Wright (1980) perceptively points out how the children can express their emotions through the animal, and how he in turn acts as an adult with all the best qualities. Discussion of Blyton is dominated by the Famous Five, as I noted earlier, and this extends beyond the protagonists to George's father. Tucker, for instance, confesses that Uncle Quentin gave him 'a far more fearsome object than any of the stop-at-nothing crooks' (Tucker, 1981, p. 109). Hildick, commending Blyton more generally for her perceptiveness in creating adult characters, endorses this, finding the depiction of Quentin's temper and his dislike of children 'refreshingly unusual enough, in a field where the heroes' and heroines' fathers are usually stereotyped as bluff hearties or mild eccentrics' (Hildick, 1970, p. 88). This said, Hildick's praise for Blyton's 'adults' is limited to a consideration of male characters.

Hildick, a notable children's writer himself, also illustrates a more general problem for adult criticism. He credits Blyton with having 'fully portrayed the nasty, snobby, cruel selfishness that most children are capable of when they collect in packs of this sort – a dark side to children that very, very few children's authors ever touch on' (ibid., p. 86); and he speculates that 'the inordinate venom with which Enid Blyton's name is mentioned by many librarians and teachers' might be due to 'the discomforting accuracy with which she reflects some of the nastier traits of children of the middle-classes to which they themselves belong' (ibid., p. 88). The problem is that this is certainly not a child's perception of its heroes; nor do I think it Blyton's. It is, in fact, Hildick's own.

Hildick's criticism demonstrates two things: first, the problem of the adult critic examining children's popular texts, and second, critics' inbuilt literary agenda, shown here in Hildick's view of characterization, which is seen as the motivating source of plot. In the oral tradition, however, this position is inverted: action does not develop out of the behaviour of rounded characters; rather, action produces character, requiring particular functionaries to perform it. As Inglis candidly recalls, he read Blyton's books as a child precisely because of 'the untaxing safety of their stereotypes . . . I was hardly troubled by the notion of "character" at all' (Inglis, 1981, p. 65).

This is a point Vladimir Propp (1968) makes in his seminal analysis of folk tales: that there are various types required to perform certain actions in a story; though what their characteristics beyond this might be are not relevant to the story, in spite of the fact that an individual reader might elaborate them in any particular way that he or she wishes. Blyton's characterization is spare in this regard, permitting particular readers to construct their own types from these fairly minimal 'semic elements', to use Barthes' term (1980).

Let us now move on to plotting, though the issue of character will recur in relation to the credibility of Blyton's stories – just as it will return when we discuss issues of sexism and racism.

Plotting

Most critics are kinder on this aspect of Blyton. After all, her popularity has to be accounted for in some way, so for many it rests on her narrative ability. Wall is generous, acknowledging Blyton's 'remarkable skill in the manipulation of events and the management of pace', which shows up would-be imitators. Blyton has a 'particular strength' says Wall (1991, p. 190), in 'the briskness and economy of her narrative manner'. Others are more guarded, but still acknowledge her facility. Thus Hincks-Edwards (1982) complains of contemporary books where 'The prose may be melodic and charming, but, in an endeavour not to have blacks and whites, the authors give us greys, and consequently no story or plot worth talking of at all'. Having recently reread the Noddy books to her 4-year-old, Hincks-Edwards was impressed with Blyton's stories, so thinks that a 'space-age' equivalent is needed; or, as a publisher put it to Robert Leeson, 'What we want . . . is a working-class Enid Blyton' (Leeson, 1985, p. 163).

However, the contradictory reactions are still present, with other critics being far more negative: 'Enid Blyton demonstrated that children are so hungry for *stories* that they will read the same story over and over, slightly disguised', Moss claims (1974, p. 336).[5] Yet if children were hungry simply for stories, then this would not explain why Blyton's were particularly favoured – unless they were hungry precisely for *Blyton* stories, as Hincks-Edwards suggests. Given Blyton's incredible output, it is certainly true that she repeated herself, but not algorithmically.

Dixon is also captious, using *FFIA* to show that 'flaws occur at almost every turn in the story' (Dixon, 1974b, p. 54). He gives instances of two cases of people being locked up, with the keys left in the locks on the outside, so that others can easily free them. 'If a wall has to be scaled ivy happens to be growing conveniently on it' (ibid.). These are not flaws, however; they are contrivances, for which one might just as readily reprove Thomas Hardy.[6] Dixon continues, 'It is a pity, indeed, that more "brain" was not brought to bear in her writing, or that she never felt it necessary to plan or prepare her stories'; for, to give children less in terms of details of story structure, 'is to treat them with something approaching contempt' (ibid.). Once again, I would suggest that the critic is approaching Blyton from an inappropriate angle. Given her immense popularity with children, to suggest as an adult that she treats her audience contemptuously, seems in itself to belittle children's faculties – especially considering the rapport that Blyton established with her readers.[7]

Dyer makes this adult-centred criticism even more explicit, criticizing the 'startling looseness' of her plots (Dyer, 1969, p. 17), using *The Castle of Adventure* as an example. In this, a spike moves a slab to reveal a hidden staircase but, when the children are inside, Dinah pulls another spike and the slab reseals, trapping the children. Dyer comments, '*I* had foreseen the possibility of the spike acting exactly contrary to the one upstairs. But children do not naturally project causation in this way' (ibid.). Dyer, though, is wrong in several respects. First, he is wrong to lump the children together; for clearly, some *do* feel superior (even readers – I am bound to say – like Dyer), which is why one of the children, Philip, goes on to say, 'You are an idiot, Dinah, messing about with things before you know what they do' (Blyton, 1946, p. 169). Secondly, Dyer's projection of causality is not natural at all: it is more tenable to argue that if a lever closes by moving it one way, it opens by moving it the other – as, indeed, most do – otherwise it would be impossible to retrace one's steps. The point is that Dyer is not 'naturally' projecting causality at all, but an awareness of genre convention – a contrivance of plot, rather than a looseness.

Tucker, commending Blyton's professional writing skills, seems closer to most readers' experience: 'although the excitement and happy endings . . . are always predictable, the details in between are not, and for a time can keep even an older reader guessing' (Tucker, 1981, p. 114). This is not only true of the plots, but of the characters as well: there are formulaic expectations, but Blyton manipulates them. Let me give two examples, drawing on some conventional signifiers of criminal tendency in the Blyton *oeuvre*.

Mr. Lenoir seems one of the most obvious candidates. He 'smiled all the time, but with his mouth, not his eyes', which are 'cold' (*FGTST*, pp. 50, 53). He also hates dogs and, more significantly, we are told that his name means 'black' in French; indeed, this point is laboured with reference to his son, Pierre, who is nicknamed 'Sooty' because 'He's awfully dark! Hair as black as soot, eyes like bits of coal, eye-brows that look as if they've been put in with charcoal. And his name means "The black one," doesn't it?' (ibid., p. 13). Pierre is also cheeky and 'climbs like a monkey' (ibid., p. 13). But, as it turns out, the Lenoirs are all quite innocent.

For a second example, let us follow Dixon's hunch that 'people of evil intent tend to be bearded or ill-shaven' (Dixon, 1974b, p. 56). Mr. Penruthlan certainly seems suspicious in this: toothless with 'shaggy eyebrows drawn over his deep-set eyes', and with a 'dense black beard!' (*FGDTS*, p. 175). Unfortunately, he is also on the side of good – as is the similarly hirsute Morgan Jones in *FGIF*, despite the fact that he, like his mother and several other respectable characters, is Welsh. For, in another remarkable generalization, Dixon lumps the Welsh with gypsies, circus people and foreigners, claiming that in Blyton, 'They are all rather less than human' (1974b, p. 55). Mr. Penruthlan, incidentally, is also 'as dark as a sunburnt Spaniard' (*FGDTS*, p. 26).

As others have suggested (Perkins, 1979), the whole notion of stereotypes needs rethinking, in that they often contain inconsistencies, frequently have an empirical basis and, moreover, are not necessarily negative. This last point is certainly true of Blyton's characters, *all* of which are stereotypes, whether they are absent-minded scientists, orally gratifying mothers, or tall, blond leaders. The fun of the story is how Blyton plays with this formula; as Propp put it, 'everything drawn into a tale from outside is subject to its norms and laws' (quoted in Barker, 1989, p. 127). Stereotypes are used accordingly.

In drawing this section to a close, we can note that Blyton's plotting is less contentious than her use of language and character, but there is still a lack of unanimity. Just as most of her vocabulary is simple, with occasional words of more difficulty thrown in, so her character and plots are generally – indeed, genre-ly – conventional, but can adeptly confound predictability.

In sum, the literary readings of Blyton have been shown to be remarkably contradictory in their judgements. It is also evident that expert opinion is often based on blatant misreading of her work and on criteria that have little applicability to it. Yet, it is this literary discourse that has powerfully shaped a commonly accepted construction of

Blyton as monosyllabic, threadbare and pedestrian. As mentioned earlier, the bareness of Blyton's texts is what makes them, paradoxically, more writerly – that is, more open to different interpretation. The vastly differing interpretations by critics would seem to endorse that this is true not only of child readers, but of adults too!

Educational readings: reading and child development

One of the key discursive threads in criticism of Blyton is the question of her effect on the developing child, of how she might help or hinder reading ability and, more significantly, what might be termed 'quality of life'. As I have mentioned elsewhere (Rudd, 1992), underlying most discussions in this area is the notion that certain books can help children's minds to grow – not in a mechanical sense, but in some enriching, organic way. Blyton's supposed failure to do this is repeatedly emphasized. Hence many critics' concern over the future of Blyton readers, though hardly any seem to have looked for empirical support for their prognoses.

First in this category are those who see reading Blyton as leading, ineluctably, to later, non-quality fiction: 'And then the girls tend to go straight from Enid Blyton to Mills and Boon. We have to try to get them to look at other books' (a librarian, quoted by Ray, 1982, p. 96; see also Capey and Maskell, 1980). Alderson (c1982), reviewing Ray, makes a similar comment: 'there is little . . . to suggest that the Famous Five and the Girls of Malory Towers will carry their readers to any future but the wonder world of pulp romance'. Curiously, the books are here regarded as for girls only (note Dixon's earlier comment on the Five characters ending up in *Woman's Own*) – which, one might say, is already a move to typify them as second-class. So to demean the world of romance seems doubly to undermine them, whereas it may well be, as researchers like Radway (1987), Modleski (1988) and Christian-Smith (1990) found, that many young women seek out this sort of literature to empower them in the first place, from an otherwise marginalized status.

Concern over the female reader goes deeper than this, though, since it sees girls as more susceptible. Will they, like Madame Bovary or Catherine Morland, confuse reality with fantasy? Such tales are often recounted by the media, drawing attention to the dangerous consequences of reading Blyton. For example, one headline, 'Tragedy of the schoolgirl from Malory Towers', tells of a girl who committed suicide at a boarding school where she had been sent at her own request after being inspired by the Blyton series (Woodcock, 1993).

Mushram (1983), giving us a perspective from India (a place where, she says, 'English speaking children . . . read almost *only* Enid Blyton's books'), also speaks of a depressing progression, from Blyton to the Hardy Boys, Nancy Drew and James Hadley Chase. She specifically exonerates the 'Noddy' books, however, whereas Gutteridge (1982) names them as the culprits: 'when the child who started on Noddy became the grown-up reader it would read tripe in the main library instead of Jane Austen or William Golding'. Welch, earlier, had commented, rather superfluously, that reading Blyton would not help you with the Cambridge English Tripos, adding, 'It certainly did not help poor Christopher Craig, of whom, at his trial for murder, it was stated that "the only books he knows anything about are the books of Enid Blyton"' (Welch, 1958, p. 20). This is even worse than Frederick Woods' prediction that a diet of Blyton would lead to a life of *Reveille* (regarded as a degraded weekly) and strip cartoons (Woods, 1995)!

In complete contrast, others have suggested the opposite, 'that those who now read adventure stories for adults did not read at all as children, and those who were hooked young on the Famous Five are now more likely to be reading Booker Prize winners or modern poetry' (Armstrong, 1982, p. 118). It seems that some such remark must have prompted Jan Mark's sarcastic comment that adult writers seldom admit to having read any children's books, with the 'alarmingly often' exception of Blyton's: 'I grew up on the Famous Five, never did me any harm, made me the Booker Prize Winner I am today' (Mark, 1992, pp. 101–2).

Her comment might also have been sparked by the surprisingly 'frequent mentions of Enid Blyton' that Antonia Fraser notes in *The Pleasure of Reading* (p. 11), where celebrities from the arts revealed their formative influences. She draws particular attention to the contribution of Ronald Harwood, for whom, 'as a child in Cape Town . . . her work represented the "magic world" of England' (Fraser, 1992, p. 11):

> Enid Blyton described the English rural scene so vividly that I carry to this day what I believe to be her images of tree-tunnels and green hillsides and well-kept careless gardens. I am told now it was a sugary, middle-class idyll she created (a criticism as meaningless to me now as it would have been then), romantic, idealized, nostalgic. The fascinating aspect of her power, however, is that when, many years later, I went to live in a Hampshire village and walked the footpaths and climbed the hangers, my memory was jolted by her descriptions of the England in which the capers of the Famous Five took place

> and seemed to me accurate. I cannot say she influenced my own writing but as a reader I owe her an enormous debt. . . .
>
> (Fraser, 1992, p. 121)

Similar comments are made by others in the volume: Sally Beauman, Melvyn Bragg, Wendy Cope, Carol Ann Duffy, Paul Sayer and Joan Smith; and elsewhere there are like-minded accounts from Janet Ahlberg (Foster, 1992), Jane Asher (Knowles, 1988), Eileen Atkins (Grove, 1989), Beryl Bainbridge (1974), Brian Blessed (Ewbank, 1990), Heather Brigstocke, Anne Fine (Palmer, 1997), Ken Follett (1994), Richard E. Grant (Moncrieff, 1998), Susan Hill (1982), Keri Hulme (Kemp, 1985), Hanif Kureishi (Lambert, 1993), Jan Leeming (1982), Ian McEwen (McAfee, 1994), Bernard MacLaverty (Mackenzie, 1998), Pat McLoughlin (Kirby, 1992), Christopher Milne (1979), Brian Patten (1995), Mike Read (Knowles, 1988), Polly Toynbee (1982) and Di Trevis.

Sally Beauman writes that 'Kipling's *Puck of Pook's Hill* and Blyton's *Malory Towers* were equally magical' for her. She candidly continues:

> I might like to think now that I could differentiate between the imaginative power, the prose style, of Carroll, Blyton or Conan Doyle, or to kid myself that I found the adventures of Alice more resonant than William Brown's run-ins with the housemaid or the perils experienced by those intrepid adventurers Philip, Jack, Dinah and Lucy-Anne (from Blyton's *Adventure* books) – but it would not be the truth. The truth is I was a little heathen and – true god or simulacrum – I loved them all.
>
> (Fraser, 1992, p. 186)

There are two observations to make of such declarations. First, it is apparent that Mills and Boon, or similar fate, is not the inevitable result of reading Blyton. Secondly, most children read both 'quality' and 'non-quality' material, often without making any distinction.

The first observation should really come as no surprise, as evidence has been available for some time. For example, in America, a similar fate was feared for readers of the popular Stratemeyer series books (Nancy Drew, Hardy Boys, and so on). But this was challenged in a 1930 study, where not only were these books the most popular, but when IQ scores were taken into account, it was found that 'about twice as many series were reported by the people with greater mental ability' (quoted in Soderbergh, 1980, p. 69). Similarly, Margaret Clark's research, which looked at the reading of children able to read proficiently by the time they started school, found that alongside books by Kipling, Lewis

Carroll and Swift, 'most of the children had an obvious love for a variety of books by Enid Blyton' (Clark, 1976, p. 77). Though Blishen derides the idea of progression, jokingly querying, 'From the Famous Five to the Three Musketeers in one leap?' (Blishen, 1977, p. 82), many readers recall exactly this: 'Ten and eleven were my Blyton years; by twelve I was into Daphne Du Maurier, Hugh Walpole, the Brontës and Dickens' (Richardson, 1980, p. 4). As Armstrong suggested earlier, it is quite likely that Blyton actually provides some of the basics to facilitate such progression. Carol Billman (1984) certainly credits the adventure story with teaching children the conventions of literature, of how suspense is constructed, and how good and bad characters are both depicted and detected (as instanced in the previous section). Sarland, looking specifically at Blyton and Dahl, substantiates this, arguing that:

> By the time they have read these two [authors] . . . readers will have been introduced to the basic 'grammar' of narrative stance and narrative function . . . virtually every technique that is available to adult authors may be found in embryo form here . . . technical expertise abounds . . . and is put to the service of moving the story on in such a way that children will continue to read it.
>
> (Sarland, 1983, p. 170)

Finally, from a reader's point of view, Hugh Crago is quite specific about how a particular Famous Five book 'scaffolded . . . [his] first attempts to "read" Dickens' classic'; without this, and other similar inputs, he says, 'I doubt I would ever have opened it until, as a young adult, I was forced to' (Crago, n.d., p. 5).[8]

On the second observation, it is apparent that most children simply read, whether comics or classics, 'from Biggles to D.H. Lawrence . . . from Blyton's *Famous Five* to John Steinbeck' as Melvyn Bragg puts it (Fraser, 1992, p. 169). The recent W.H. Smith survey also notes children's 'eclectic reading tastes. . . . One girl's reading in the previous month consisted of Enid Blyton's *The Naughtiest Girl in the School, Cinderella, Having a Baby*, and *A Beginner's Guide to Feminism*' (Hall and Coles, 1996, p. 4). So Chambers (1975) might be highly amused by a young reader speaking of the 'big step from Enid Blyton to Doetovsky (sic)', but it is not impossible for the same person to be reading both, exactly as the critic Alison Hennegan claims she was doing, aged 15 (Hennegan, 1988). Unfortunately, critics of children's literature too often assume a one-track notion of reading progression: 'each child should read books which challenge his growing powers of thought, feeling and imagination, and stimulate him to more ambitious sorties into the field of reading', as Leng puts it (1968, p. 12). We need to get away from such notions, I think, and explore the idea that people can derive differing pleasures from books.

However, critics who still think Blyton harmful might argue that I have only mentioned those readers who were already reading 'a varied diet', and for whom there is no problem. The issue is more with those who become addicted to Blyton exclusively. There are several references to this in the literature, but Lowe's is one of the most extensive. An Australian teacher, she begins her article, 'Once upon a time, there was a little girl named Kate', who fared quite well till she read Blyton, 'and now, poor child, she has joined the ranks of the Enid Blyton addicts' (Lowe, 1979, p. 107). Lowe persuades Kate to write a story, which is reproduced, and contends that Kate's style is 'blighted with Enid Blytonisms!' (ibid., p. 108). Unfortunately we have no idea of what her writing was like pre-Blyton, to see whether there really has been a deterioration or, *horribile dictu*, an improvement. Neither does Lowe comment on the extensive length of the narrative, nor the generally good quality of spelling and punctuation; rather, it is specifically its Englishness to which she objects.

Regrettably, Lowe's own knowledge of Blyton's books, and of cultural influences in general, seems limited. Thus, Kate is rebuked for numbering the police cars, which we are told 'is definitely not an Australian trait [*sic*]'. However, it was certainly not a British one, either. Lowe also picks up on the use of 'Mam'. Again, this might not be Australian, but neither is it a Blytonism. From this, it is certainly inappropriate to claim that 'Kate is so adulterated by the language in her favourite novels that a story would not be a story unless it occurred in front of an English backdrop' (ibid., p. 108), for the items I have mentioned show not an English influence, but an American one. Interestingly, Lowe does not draw attention to the phone number dialled in the story, which is not '999' – the English emergency code – but '000', the Australian equivalent. In other words, local knowledge, plus that of American films *and* of English books, is all interwoven in Kate's story.

Aside from Lowe's specific comments, it should be said that the entire story is not characteristic of 'the Blyton formula'. The children are not active agents; rather, they are at the mercy of the criminals, who tie them up. As a consequence, it is not the children who bring in the police (and are subsequently rescued by them), but their mother; lastly, the criminals escape in the end. All this is very unlike Blyton, where children are the heroes, outwitting adults. Kate's story reflects a more realistic stance, in which adults are still very much in control. If it shows anything, it is how Blyton has been refracted through a particular cultural lens.

It is a shame that Lowe was not aware of Clark's research, mentioned above, for Clark quotes extracts from a 7-year-old girl who also enjoyed telling and writing stories – 'mystery stories of twenty or thirty pages' (ibid., p. 86) – which, as Clark's extracts show, are far more Blytonesque than Lowe's. Clark notes that most of the stories tended to adopt the style of the author, which meant using a different vocabulary, a more elaborate syntax, inversion, and a variety of conjunctions, together with direct rather than reported speech. One might be grateful that Lowe did not oversee the first literary effort of Australasian Booker Prize winner, Keri Hulme, aged 7 – a 28-page Blyton pastiche called 'The Cave of Adventure' (Kemp, 1985)! Nevertheless, *pace* Jan Mark, it is remarkable how many of those praising Blyton have turned out to be writers.

Returning to the issue of the child who reads only Blyton, Christine Hindle's personal testimony in a letter to *The Guardian* (1982) sounds more serious. She found that she could not read anyone else after a solid diet of Blyton until rescued, by a headmistress, with Hardy and Dickens. It is interesting to link Hindle's experiences with those of the novelist, Sally Beauman, also quoted above. Beauman, a keen Blyton reader, also stopped reading for several years, though she later went on to read Literature at Cambridge. Ironically, Beauman blames not Blyton, but being introduced to 'literature'. Certainly, abandoning reading for a period in adolescence is not unusual – in fact Ray credits Blyton with being one of the first to write books for young teenage readers, a group not previously catered for – and Hindle's subsequent move from Blyton to Dickens 'in one leap', to borrow Blishen's phrase, would certainly be regarded by most as quite an achievement. Perhaps Blyton was developing her skills more than she realized, as Crago has articulated (above).

Against the statements that Blyton impedes reading, there are also many who speak of Blyton with gratitude, for turning their children into readers. Cadogan (1982), for example, writes that the 'Noddy books . . . turned my non-reading daughter overnight into an avid word devourer, and gave me – like thousands of other parents – cause to bless Enid Blyton'. An Australian researcher, who says that she 'became a reader overnight' when given a copy of *FGAA* at the age of 9, provides more systematic evidence (Phillips, 1992, p. 273). As a result of her experience she explored that of others', and found that the majority of students enrolled in a language and literature course named Enid Blyton as their favourite author, including five who had been unable to speak

English when they began school. Ken Watson records similar pleasures opened up for English undergraduates, following the challenging comment of one of them, 'If it weren't for Enid Blyton, I wouldn't be here!' (Watson, 1987, p. 209). Lastly, Hunt found among his literature undergraduates that *The Magic Faraway Tree* 'was by far the best-remembered book of their childhoods' (Hunt, 1994, p. 116).[9]

Fry, who gives detailed accounts of various children's reading experiences, also credits Blyton with establishing the habit in Karnail, 'as for millions of other readers' (Fry, 1985, p. 47). This said, Fry is nevertheless concerned about Karnail moving on from Blyton, which he thinks less easy, as do Chambers and Leng. One might have thought Chambers, in writing about reluctant readers, would value Blyton more, but he dismisses it as 'drug' literature – the 'Blyton neurosis . . . a symptom of arrested development' (Chambers, 1969, pp. 18, 22). Leng has a similar concern, giving the example of two contrasting readers, one of whom

> begins the year by borrowing Enid Blyton's *Mystery of the Hidden House*. Three months later, he is reading Enid Blyton's *Lucky Story Book*; three months later still, it is Blyton's *Sunny Story Book*, and at the end of the year he is back where he began, with Enid Blyton's *Mystery of the Hidden House*. In all he borrowed 74 books in the year, 38 of them by Blyton. In the following year, he borrowed none at all. It need not be doubted that he enjoyed his reading, but it got him nowhere, and so he gave it up. And this, perhaps, is not entirely to be regretted; others, less wise or less fortunate, fail to break the habit, but obsessively continue looking for they know not what, reading ever more futilely until at last they become incurably addicted to reading-matter of the most ephemeral kind.

The other

> begins the year in much the same way, with Enid Blyton's *Mystery of Tally-ho Cottage*. In the following five weeks, he runs through ten books by Enid Blyton in a row, and then moves on to other tales of mystery and adventure . . . reading altogether 43 books in the year, and finishing with *Biggles Takes the Case*, an adventure story with an adult hero, by W.E. Johns. The following year he rejoined the Library and took out a further 27 books. Whereas the first boy's reading was static or regressive, finally to be rejected as being of no value, this second boy had stumbled by some chance upon the secret of pro-

> gressive reading; his reading grew with him and played a part in the process of his growth.
>
> (ibid., p. 183)

This is a curious conclusion. For some reason Leng believes that the first boy will never return to books, unlike the cases quoted earlier. Leng also regards the second boy's reading as progressive because his first year finished with a 'Biggles', whereas the other returned to Blyton – presuming, of course, that this boy took the book out for himself the second time.[10] The favouring of Biggles over Blyton seems dated nowadays, Leng arguing that the former deals with adults and adult themes, including 'war . . . violent crime and death' (Leng, 1968, p. 141).

Yet his conclusion still seems strange. Does it depend on this single 'adult' book (which we don't know the boy actually read)? For we are not told what the boy's subsequent reading consisted of. The former boy had still borrowed more books overall when he abandoned reading – if indeed he did; for we don't know that he wasn't obtaining books elsewhere. Leng's comment that he is probably wise to give up the habit, rather than reading futilely, is a strangely value-laden judgement, presuming that reading is only about intellectual development. It ignores all the psychological pleasure that might be derived from reading. Thus he commends another young girl for reading certain material while condemning her continuation with Blyton, which 'could hinder the process of maturing' (ibid., p. 19), and he goes on to recommend career stories!

I have dealt with Leng at some length because his work typifies a general attitude to children's fiction: that it must 'stretch' the child, otherwise it is worthless. A great deal of the above is implicitly concerned with this issue. Blyton has been seen either to leave children where they are, or to move them sideways into equally worthless fiction, dead-end jobs and, generally, to a poor quality of life – girls especially. Even though many celebrities have shown otherwise, there persists the fear that 'weaker' children are more at risk (a less than helpful tautology): 'many children soon outgrow the Blyton cult leaving the backward or culturally deprived child to wallow in a sticky morass of Blytonese' (Martin, 1970, p. 26).

Conclusion

This chapter has been rather an involved one in terms of its argument, but so are responses to Blyton. In addition, I have not simply intended to present a literary review but an analysis of a critical corpus: the discursive threads that have been woven round Blyton's name and work. Having tried to summarize each section as I have progressed, let me here return to the major issues. One of the most enduring findings has been the contradictory opinion held about Blyton, found in all areas: whether on her general reputation, her language, her characters, plots, influence on reading and personal development, or, as we shall see later, her sexism and racism. The one constant that unites a great proportion of the critics is that they are anti-Blyton, despite the different grounds of that claim. The more I examine their statements, which are sometimes blatantly contradictory, the more it seems that this dislike is an *a priori* one, to which reasons are later attached. Statements like Dohm's, which compares Blyton with quality books, help sustain such a view: 'no one who has known or seen the difference between a child's shining response to that and the empty clamour (like teen-agers for a crooner) accorded the formula book can doubt which is really "just what the children want"' (Dohm, 1955, p. 361).

It is not only apparent in the contradictory statements critics make, but in the loaded way that they are phrased (taking Dohm's as one example). Even in the contentious area of corporal punishment Blyton seems to have been singled out, whereas it occurs just as much in the work of her contemporaries (in some, such as C.S. Lewis, more so) and is also to be found, unremarked, in more recent work for children (for instance, in *Pingu*, BBC, 1994). Equally, Blyton's depiction of a cosy, bucolic middle-class world is not exceptional for its time, and occurs even now – as in the Ahlbergs' celebrated books (for example, Ahlberg and Ahlberg, 1991). These are all matters which will be discussed further.

5
Noddy: Discursive Threads and Intertextuality

Why do elephants have big ears?
Because Noddy won't pay the ransom.

Though Shakespeare's our national bard
His poetry's terribly hard.
It would benefit those
Who were sitting their 'O's
If in *Lear* it was Noddy who starred.

– Roy Fuller (1976, p. 10)

Introduction

The Noddy books are the bane of any Blyton researcher's work. Blyton was herself referred to in 'Noddy' terms, this character metonymically taking over in newspaper stories, and anyone else who becomes involved is automatically 'noddified'. Noddy was first launched on the world in 1949, and, over 50 years later, is her best-selling creation, not only in terms of books, but also merchandising; Noddy material is even the most valuable for Blyton collectors – a leading collection of some 1900 items was recently valued at £30,000, and a set of Sampson Low first editions fetched £1200 at auction (or £50 a book; they originally sold for 3/6, or 17½p).

Part of the success is rightly attributed to the brilliant illustrations of Harmsen van der Beek who, unfortunately, only lived to complete the first seven titles. It was certainly his illustrations that seemed to inspire Blyton initially, and together they produced some exceptional books for the period, with colour illustrations on every page. There were 24 books in the original Sampson Low series, though, in Blyton's lifetime, some

125 titles bore Noddy's name. It is the main series, however, that I analyse here, picking out what seem to me to be the significant discursive threads.

After a brief overview of the books' history and popularity, this chapter is organized around three themes. First, an exploration of the various discursive threads that led to the production of Noddy and to his subsequent development; this will involve examining Blyton's creative process, showing how closely her views accord with the modern notion of intertextuality, leading on to the recent rewriting of the texts. Second, a look at the order of things in the Toyland world, and last, a consideration of this world's overt consumerism.

Noddy: a brief history

1949 Purnell, with one of the largest printing presses in Europe (at Paulton, Somerset), were seeking a Disney-style figure to 'fuel' it. J.C. Gibbs of Purnell sent the work of Dutch artist Harmsen van der Beek to Sampson Low (owned by Purnell). David White showed Beek's work to Blyton and arranged a productive meeting. Later that year, *Noddy Goes to Toyland* appeared.

1951 The controversial *Here Comes Noddy Again!* was published, although nothing much was said about Noddy's 'mugging' by golliwogs until the sixties.

1953 Beek died, after completing the seventh book, *Noddy at the Seaside*. Robert Tyndall eventually took over, though for a reduced fee, and was not allowed to sign his work.

1954 The play *Noddy in Toyland* began its first Christmas run in London.

1955 A puppet series, *The Adventures of Noddy*, appeared on the new commercial TV, first shown on Sunday 25 September.

1958 The first substantial criticism of Noddy appeared in *Encounter*, written by Colin Welch (1958; 1998).

1960 The books had sold over 20 million copies.

1963 The last Noddy book, *Noddy and the Aeroplane*, appeared, although Blyton did have a title for a sequel: *Noddy Goes to the Moon*.

1968 Enid Blyton dies.

1975 There was a second ITV version of *Noddy*, by Cosgrove Hall, without golliwogs.

1986 A simplified second edition appeared.

1987	An unsuccessful attempt to launch Noddy in America.
1990	A third edition appeared, with remastered drawings by Mary Cooper and revised text by Stella Maidment.
1992	BBC Enterprises purchased the 24 Noddy book series for a reputed figure of £2–3 million, giving it control of world-wide distribution rights, although this was later disputed by Trocadero.
1992	Noddy books were reported to have sold over 100 million copies, with overseas sales of 46 million.
1992	New Cosgrove Hall puppet series launched by BBC.
1998	Noddy successfully launched in the USA, suitably American-ized, at a cost of £4.6 million, reaching audiences of 2.5 million.

My survey results showed the Noddy books to be fourth most popular with readers, with Noddy as a character coming second overall (just behind George). If we look at the different age groups, Noddy vies with Timmy for being the most popular of all with 6–14 year-olds. Interestingly, he is far more popular with boys than girls: second most popular with the former (voted so by 13.1 per cent), just behind Timmy, but fifth for girls (5.2 per cent). Unsurprisingly perhaps, the Noddy books were the most commonly 'first read' Blyton books (by 22 per cent), just ahead of the Five (20 per cent). They were also in competition with the Five for second place as the least favourite Blyton books (Noddy, 8.1 per cent; Five, 8.3 per cent). Reasons given for this were that the books were 'silly', 'babyish' and 'boring'. Clearly, it was important for more sophisticated readers to distance themselves from the little nodding man. As one pithily wrote about his least favourite character: 'Noddy – because it was.' Another respondent criticized his brother because he 'still reads Noddy books and he is 11½-years-old' (m, 13).

For many of the young, however, the Noddy books were 'magic'; unfortunately, few could articulate their appeal beyond such monosyllables as 'great', 'funny' and 'ace'. Older readers were more expressive, and for many Noddy still held a fascination: 'Now, I still just like the ideas in the Noddy books of living in toyland. The situations which the characters get into are quite surreal in parts. . . . I think it prepared me for Vonnegut (who I moved on to later)' (m). David Tibet, leader of the avant-garde group 'Current 93', lists Noddy as among his biggest influences, alongside Aleister Crowley and Tibetan Buddhism. He writes, 'We are the Final Church of the Noddy Apocalypse. He's a character in children's books who I find very, very surrealistic' (Tibet, 1987). No doubt this inspired the group to feature a crucified Noddy on the cover of their *Swastikas for Noddy* album.

Creativity: discursive threads and intertextuality

Blyton's creative process has often been the subject of critical attention, partly because of queries about whether she wrote all her stories herself, and partly because she personally was very interested in the process. My own interest in pursuing this matter (Rudd, 1996b, 1996c) is that it makes explicit the way that texts are weaves of discursive threads, supporting poststructuralist conceptions of authorship (Barthes, 1977b; Foucault, 1986). They argue that authors are far less in control of their material than previous ideas suggest; that any text is, in fact, a reworking of others, both literary and oral: snatches of conversation, idiomatic expressions, current news, personal experiences, and so forth.

It is curious how suspicious many have been about the way that Blyton said she wrote. She, though, was very interested and made a number of largely consistent comments about it over the years (Blyton, 1950a, 1952b, 1953a, 1959b; Sykes, 1962). She even interested a psychologist, Peter McKellar, in the matter, her correspondence with him (1953–57) being auctioned in 1994 for £5400. This provided McKellar with a useful case study of the creative process (McKellar, 1957; McKellar, 1989).[1]

In these letters Blyton admits that she recognizes 'many things that are thrown up from my under-mind, transmuted and changed – a castle seen long ago – a dog – a small child – woods long forgotten, in a new setting' (Stoney, 1992, p. 218). Later, she elaborates:

> I think my imagination contains all the things I have ever seen or heard, things my conscious mind has long forgotten – and they have all been jumbled about till a light penetrates into the mass, and a happening here or an object there is taken out, transmuted, or formed into something that takes a natural and rightful place in the story – or I *may* recognise it – or I may not – I don't think that I use anything I have not seen or experienced – I don't think I could. I don't think one can take out of one's mind more than one puts in. . . . Our books are facets of ourselves.
>
> (ibid., p. 221)

Certainly, this would seem to be the case with the Noddy material. In examining this material, I shall begin by looking at its pre-texts, then discuss its con-text, picking up both on contemporary issues and more enduring themes. Lastly, the post-text – the rewrites – will be examined.

What first made me curious about the books was the way that Blyton linked Toyland to the world at large. This is drawn attention to in only two places: in the first book, where we learn that Noddy was created by Old Man Carver, from whom he ran away; and in *N11*, where we are introduced to Father Christmas, 'King of Toyland'. The link between Toyland and our own world is explicit here, with toys being provided by the various villages, then dispatched via Father Christmas to children. Thus we find him exercising quality control, exploring a complaint that some of the balls do not bounce properly – in reply to which the Chief Bouncer 'promised to see that every ball in the village should have proper bouncing lessons before being sent to the world of boys and girls' (*N11*, p. 40). This seemed quite an alarming thought – that some toys were chosen and taken away to be the playthings of children. However, an earlier series of linked stories by Blyton, 'Tales of Toyland', made the links more explicit, and were clearly the basis of the Noddy books.[2] It is this earlier story that I shall describe in some detail, before pointing out the links.

We begin by meeting a Sailor doll, at first nameless, who lives in a big nursery with other toys. He is unhappy because the others don't like his jolliness, nor the fact that he sings loud, 'yoho' songs. At Christmas, a fairy-doll – also anonymous at first – arrives from the top of the Christmas tree. She too is resented by the others. They think she does not belong in their toy-cupboard. The Sailor and the fairy-doll pair up – naming each other Jolly and Tiptoe respectively – and escape to Toyland.

They ask directions fruitlessly till a rabbit directs them to 'a brownie who lives in the wood . . . in an oak-tree. . . . He might be able to tell you where Toyland is' (*Tales*, pp. 20–1). The Brownie obliges, directing them to a station where they can get a train to Toyland. They enter a crowded carriage and are 'all aboard for Toyland' (to borrow a later phrase), only to be refused entry on arrival because of Tiptoe being a fairy. 'She can't go to Toyland. Only toys live there' (ibid., p. 24). However, with the help of a washer-woman, who helps disguise Tiptoe (shades of *The Wind in the Willows* and Toad's escape from gaol), they manage to get inside. Yet they still have nowhere to live, there being no empty houses. Eventually, a policeman advises them to 'Build one! . . . Go to the warehouse where toy bricks are stored and choose what you want' (ibid., p. 29).

For readers of *Noddy Goes to Toyland* (*N1*), many parallels are apparent; for example, there is the Brownie who, like Big-Ears, helps them on their way (in her initial letter to Sampson Low she speaks of 'Big Ears the pixie'[3]); there is the train journey motif; Tiptoe, like Noddy, is accused of not being a toy and, of course, Noddy too has problems finding accommodation, until advised to build his own, and he and Big-Ears collect a box of bricks.

The parallels by no means end there. We meet other characters that will later find their way into the more famous Toyland of Noddy. There is a Wobbly man; there are some soldiers who live next door – that is, until their fort is completed, whence they decamp, and who should move in but a teddy-bear called Bruiny, which is also the name of Noddy's neighbours' son in *N22* and *N23*. In fact, it is this that may have caused Enid some confusion for, in the earlier Noddy books the bears' son is always referred to as 'little Tubby Bear'. On the other side of Jolly and Tiptoe lives a Clockwork Clown. We are also introduced to the Skittle family, a pink cat, and a 'fat clockwork policeman', who is unnamed (though so was Mr. Plod until *N5*).

The Noddy books also feature a Sailor Doll, who sings 'very loud and rollicking songs' around a 'yo-ho' refrain (Noddy, like the toys in Jolly's nursery, also tells the Sailor Doll not to sing so loudly in *N12*). Of more interest is the fact that one of the only times that Noddy changes outfit is in *N18*, when he dons a sailor's costume and goes off to sea. Jolly the Sailor doll does the same in *Tales*, travelling in the *Saucy Sue*, to 'Roll-About Town', a place of bouncing balls. On their way there, they also pass other districts familiar to readers of Noddy: Rocking-Horse Village and Humming Top Town. The behaviour of the bouncing balls should also be familiar to those who know *N4*. In *Tales* the balls 'came rolling up to see the ship. . . . Some of them bounced themselves instead of rolling, and one of them bounced right on top of the *Saucy Sue*, nearly swinging it over' (*Tales*, p. 67) – just as in *N4* it is Noddy's car that is bounced into. It is also worth pointing out that, while at sea, Noddy spies someone sitting in his car (which is following the ship); he remarks, 'Who's that in my car? It looks like a fairy doll from the top of a Christmas tree' (*N18*, p. 41).

I have already mentioned the common element of Father Christmas. In *Tales*, we are told that he comes to stay in a castle in Toyland once a year, in order 'to get toys from Toyland to put into his sack to take to children' (*Tales*, p. 89). Again, as in *N11*, Father Christmas arrives in the street with his four reindeer, but Jolly and Tiptoe, unlike the little nodding man, are not pleased to see him, fearful of being returned to the nursery. The 'grand Choosing Time' is a strange scene, reminiscent of Judgement Day, conducted by Father Christmas in a eugenically sound way: 'Only balls that bounced well, only tops that hummed properly, toy animals that were quite perfect, and dolls that looked happy and smiley were chosen' (ibid., p. 92). Fortunately, Jolly and Tiptoe are spared because they have 'been out in the big world before' (ibid., p. 97).

These threads have been teased out in some detail to show the links, but I'd like to pursue Noddy's name still further, for there are earlier stories about Noddy, showing that the nodding head was not the sole impetus for naming the character. 'Tom Noddy' (1931a) is about a boy who is always bottom of the class, mainly because he is so forgetful, whereas another story features 'Noddy the gnome', who sells chestnuts round Fairyland from his barrow. He goes round trying to find people to help him, among whom there is a frog called 'Big-Eyes' (Blyton, 1931b).[4]

We can see, then, that the origins of both Noddy and Big-Ears have their roots much earlier, in juxtapositions of names and incidents of which Blyton herself was probably only vaguely aware. In fact, it seems that the influences go back even earlier. Some Blyton collectors have discovered some undated postcards with movable parts, thought to be pre-First World War. The one illustrated here (Figure 5.1)[5] shows Nickleby Noddy with his dog – Timmy! Though there is no known connection, it is fascinating that this character has a bell on his hat (itself rather like a certain policeman's helmet), and pointed ears – just as we might have expected 'Noddy the gnome' to have. Also, if the tag is pulled, the doll nods his head! The colours of his outfit increase the likelihood of a connection: the hat is blue with bell in yellow, as is the cowl, the jacket is red, together with the shoes, and the trousers are blue – Noddy's colours exactly, as described in the first book, and consequently visualized by Beek (who already had the shape of Noddy and Big-Ears' figures from his earlier work).

The origin of the word 'noddy', to designate something simplistic, is also of note. Many seem to regard this as deriving from Blyton's creation. In fact, Hunt (1996, p. 69) claims that Noddy 'has entered the English language as a dismissive phrase for idiotic simplicity', little realizing that this usage is far older, appearing, ironically, in Nickleby Noddy's predecessor, *Nicholas Nickleby* (1838): 'To think that I should be such a noddy!' (*OED*, 1989, x, p. 459). However, apocryphal though Hunt's derivation is, it has become an actuality. In a 1994 work on education, the following sentence appears: 'A "Noddy and Big Ears" account of a skill or a concept can provide a basic framework, on to

Figure 5.1 Nickleby Noddy with his dog Timmy: a postcard thought to date from before the First World War.

which can be grafted more sophisticated understanding' (Peelo, 1994, p. 97).

A similar history occurs with the slang term for a policeman, 'plod', thought to derive from this series. However, a social historian has recorded its use in the thirties, referring to 'the slow-witted Constable Plod of the comics [who] popped up in many a guise' (Valery, 1991, p. 148). Thus, Blyton actually took the term from common usage (like so many of her names), and used it for several policemen in her stories before Noddy was conceived.[6]

The Blyton fan would also find other familiar characters in the Noddy books (Mary Mouse, for example, and the Saucepan Man from the 'Faraway Tree' books). Besides her own texts, Blyton was also influenced by the work of other writers. I have already mentioned Grahame, and Collodi will be discussed later; but Carroll is certainly there too. For instance, in the first book, the climactic court scene is clearly reminiscent of *Alice's Adventures in Wonderland.* There is also much sub-Carrollian word play, as for instance in *N6*, where Noddy says, 'I can't add up. I can't add down either' (*N6*, p. 32); or, in *N3*, where Noddy has established that he should charge 'sixpence all the way there and back' (p. 11), but doesn't know what a single fare might be, 'going there and not back'. Mr. Tubby replies, somewhat confusingly, 'It's exactly the same as if you go back and not there'. As the toy cat says, 'But can you go back if you haven't been there?' (*N3*, pp. 16–17).

The cat also brings Carroll's felines to mind, and some of the exchanges certainly have the feel of the semiotic word play in *Alice*. Thus, the toy cat complains to Noddy, 'I wish you wouldn't say *no* and nod your head at the same time. . . . It's very muddling' (*N3*, p. 16),[7] which is clearly reminiscent of Alice's cat, Dinah:

> 'If they would only purr for "yes," and mew for "no," . . . so that one could keep up a conversation! But how *can* you talk with a person if they *always* say the same thing?'
>
> (Carroll, 1970, p. 341)

These are just a few of the mainly literary pre-texts that helped fashion Noddy. Before I move on to the context – the wider cultural reference points that inform the work – let me mention one other influence: the work of Froebel. It was he who stressed the importance of scaling an environment to a child's size, and of using bright colours. He also laid great stress on geometrical shapes that would foster development, such as the ball and building-block. In a sense, Toyland is exactly this, a child-sized land of bright colours, fashioned out of building-bricks. Froebel even talked of children building houses from these shapes, as a way of encouraging the child 'to reflect upon larger patterns of order in society' (Shapiro, 1983, p. 24). Lastly, Froebel emphasized singing and dancing games, also structured to encourage the child to see the unity of society, in that all the participants would come together at the end. Once again, this is how most of the Noddy books end, in celebration and song.

Now let us look more closely at the context of the books' production. The post-war period in which the books were conceived was a time of social upheaval, with the class system of the pre-war years shaken up; there was also a new sense of cosmopolitanism, after many English had encountered foreigners for the first time. Many had also seen their first black people, with the first wave of immigrants from the West Indies arriving in the late 1940s. Lastly, it was a time of homelessness, both in England and more widely across Europe.

In the series, we are introduced to Noddy as something of a refugee, literally, found naked in the woods having fled Old Man Carver's house, because he fears a lion that the carpenter is carving. Big-Ears takes him to Toyland, but there is doubt about whether he will be allowed to stay there, as voiced by the policeman: 'Only toys are allowed to stay in Toy Village' (*N1*, p. 27). There are certainly echoes of the plight of refugees and immigrants here. There is a general sense of people finding where they belong, of each having their separate patch, albeit all are thrown together in Toy Village. The next concern for Noddy is finding a house, when all are occupied:

> 'Could you just let Noddy live with you till he gets a house of his own?' asked Big-Ears. 'Or do you know anywhere he could stay? He wouldn't mind sleeping anywhere – even in a garage – would you Noddy?'
>
> (ibid., p. 30)

He is directed to a toy farm, 'but the dogs barked so loudly at them that they were afraid to open the gate' (ibid.). Noddy reflects on this:

> 'It's no good. I shan't be able to find anywhere to live here,' said Noddy, sadly. 'I'll have to take the train again and go back to Old Man Carver.'
>
> (ibid., p. 32)

Again, this could easily be the plight of any migrants seeking accommodation, to find nowhere available, to have dogs ward them off – and yet, it could just as readily be the plight of many of the dispossessed and homeless English; 'squatting' was rife at this time, particularly around London, with protests regularly being held to highlight their predicament.

Noddy then obtains some bricks to build his own house – a kit called 'House-for-One' – which seems very like the ubiquitous post-war prefabs: 'a back room for a bedroom and a front room for living in. No stairs. We can't manage those' (ibid., p. 33). After they've erected it they go next door to Mr and Mrs Tubby's, for tea. Their house does have an upstairs, with a 'nice little bathroom. Noddy didn't even know what that was!' – a point Big-Ears explicitly emphasizes, showing Noddy's naïvety (ibid., p. 41). This was certainly a common view of the ignorant, that the bath, that mark of civilized humanity, might only be used for keeping coal in.

I am not suggesting that Blyton has written a social allegory here, simply that the events of the time had an influence in shaping the narrative, calling forth certain elements of previous stories rather than others. Neither am I suggesting that young readers will pick up on this – it is merely the raw material that gives shape to her fantasy. However, I would suggest that children will relate to a parallel situation: the feeling of being thrust into a strange world, and of learning how to fit in, how to belong – part of which involves learning the order of things.

I shall enlarge on this shortly, but I'd like to finish this section by looking at the way the various discursive threads have been textually reworked since Blyton's time: what might be called the post-text. My aim here is to show how an author's works are not only open to different interpretations (through readers providing their own personal/cultural contexts), but are subject to more constraining pressures, through textual and pictorial revision. (Apart from physical revision, the reading of texts can also be constrained by more amorphous cultural discourses – as in the case of racism and sexism.)

One of the main accusations levelled at Blyton is the poor quality of her writing, with banal, deliberately monosyllabic vocabulary. Reading through this series, though, I was surprised at some less-than-expected words: for example, 'wrench', 'precious', 'dolefully', 'rapturously', 'extraordinary', 'unexpectedly', 'becalmed', 'horde, 'surge' 'mischievous', 'belching', 'gallivant', 'mournfully', 'overhauled', 'solemnly' and 'dreadful'. Interestingly, the second edition pandered far more to the stereotype of the Blytonesque, removing most of the above and generally simplifying her prose, resulting in stories about half the original length. Mary Tapissier, then director of children's publishing at Macdonald, justified this by saying that the original books 'seem very long and have language that they [the children] do not experience' (Bates, 1987).[8] In the third edition there has been more attention given to the original text, but even here, at times, the polysyllables have been removed; for instance, taking the above list, 'unexpectedly', 'becalmed' 'surge' and 'dreadful' have been replaced, respectively, with, 'just then', 'isn't moving' and 'come', while 'Oh, how DREADFUL!' becomes 'Oh dear'.[9] It is as if there was an acceptance that Blyton must conform to her stereotype.

Revisions are always contentious. Even classic authors have had their texts changed where it was felt that typographical errors had been made, or wrong words used, but, the more popular the author, the more the texts seem expendable. The third edition is certainly more sensitive than the abortive second, but it is still erratic. Thus there are attempts to standardize place and character names (for example, Toy Town[10]), and to correct some stylistic features, such as Blyton's sometimes ambiguous use of pronouns ('it knocked it over', *N2*, p. 30), her idiosyncratic use of prepositions ('built it of toy bricks', *N2*, p. 8) and use of the present tense instead of the past. But this is done in such an *ad hoc* manner that any policy is unclear: stylistic excrescences remain – for example, 'Fancy singing it all out without making a mistake', *N6**, p. 54 – together with difficult sentences like 'And I sold a bell to Mrs. Sailor Doll for the little donkey she has for Sammy Sailor Doll' (albeit Sammy has become 'Susie' – *N8**, p. 38). Even where Blyton has used the wrong word, this sometimes remains, as in 'parked nose to tail in a neat row!' (*N2**, p. 50), which should clearly be 'line', not 'row'. Though the words 'gay' and 'queer' have generally been removed, others, like 'jerked' and 'madly' have been replaced in some instances, but not others.

Certain changes have obviously been prompted by the illustrations. Since it is easier to change text than illustration, whenever there has been a conflict Blyton's words have proved the more expendable. For example, 'fluffy dress' becomes 'spotty dress', because this is what the illustration depicts (*N16**, p. 36). This said, in many instances it was felt essential to alter the illustrations, notably, of course, in replacing the golliwogs – although one observant child pointed out one that had escaped (*N11**, p. 23). But replacing them is itself problematic. It would obviously not do to insert black characters in their stead, although the series has also been criticized for the lack of black people. This problem is exemplified in *N10**, p. 49, where one could argue that a replacement black figure is dangerously close to being a minstrel stereotype. Avoiding stereotyping can be particularly difficult with toys, which are often stereotypically simplified objects anyway. However, the revisions have also attempted, in a token way, to increase ethnic diversity and redress the gender imbalance.

The children's views on the morality of changing a writer's text were enlightening. They were as varied as those of the adults, who were also asked, but, if one were to generalize, the majority thought it ethically unacceptable. As an 11-year-old girl put it: ''Cos if someone's rewritten them they shouldn't really be allowed to put Enid Blyton's name on it, really, should they? Because it's not Enid Blyton's work any more.' A 15-year-old boy is more legalistic: ''Cos like, if she had it in her will, or something, that they could change it, then they could have done but if they never, then she might not have wanted it changing.' Others simply saw it as historical fact: 'that's what it was like when she wrote about it', therefore it should stand. Many maintained this principle – even if, ideologically, they approved of the revision:

> Yes that's a good change . . . but it's still . . . they shouldn't change it because it's not, now, it's not actually Edin Blyton's real book and everything, 'cos they changed it. They should have left it how it is, or they should rewrote it and written it by whoever changed it. Instead of leaving it as Enid Blyton.

Here, a 14-year-old Asian boy is talking about smacking, the original Miss Rap having been replaced by Miss Prim.[11] As he argued, ideologically the change was 'right because them kind of books, only really young people read them. And if they get the idea of teachers hitting them they probably scared of going to school'. Many others took this view, but, like adults, they always spoke on behalf of younger, more vulnerable children – never themselves.

Others were also against modifying the text, but for different reasons: 'They'd have more discipline if they didn't change them' (f, 9). This view was endorsed by older children, too:

> I don't think they should be changed either because you've got to portray, I think you've got to portray like, sort of, discipline from an early age. . . . If you start showing them you should get away with it in books and things, they tend to get a general appearance of behaviour – just by reading . . . books that can . . . symbolize it. (m, 14)

Others, yet again, were simply amused at the concern over such a matter, given the prevalence of violence elsewhere:

> *Daisy*: Well they should read some of these modern books, I mean, there's worse than getting spanked. People get shot and things, in a lot of the books.
> *Dan*: Yeah, and strangled.
> *William*: Tubby Bear shot – shot Noddy! [laughter] (11-year-olds)

and

> I suppose, if you take it in – with the way that most cartoons, I mean little animals are getting anvils dropped on their heads, and being blown-up. I mean, a slap, compared to that! (f, 17)

As I said earlier, the variety of views is similar to that expressed by adults. It also needs to be emphasized that this was what the children thought *in the abstract*. In the context of the story, the smacking was thoroughly enjoyed, and, when they were asked about their favourite part, many would refer to it (one group talked animatedly about playing schools in their back garden, with smacks for naughtiness). Gillian Freeman (1969, p. 97), who also found that her children enjoyed this part, worries that it is titillation that is being gratified, which might lead to a 'need . . . to inflict or experience pain in later years'. One sixth-form boy ended his Five story on the same wavelength: 'They all went home to Aunt Fanny's for lashings and lashings.'

The children's explanations for the changes were also revealing. Most of them suspected some dubious reason, like jealousy: 'They thought, "if I change it people will think I wrote it"' (f, 10); even as young as 7 this was posited: 'Because, they wanted like, to get the same ideas, 'cos Enid Blyton had brilliant ideas, and they're just pinching the ideas' (m); commercial gain was another suggested motive, as this 9-year-old indicates: if it's 'the same old thing', 'They wouldn't enjoy it any more, and they'd say, "Oh, I've read that one before", but if they say it's a new word, they'll think that it's all a new book and it's new pages, new things and new words' (f). This 11-year-old is more direct: 'other authors are just rewriting the same thing with a few little changes and getting quite a lot of money out of it when it was like, all Enid Blyton's doing' (f, 11). As is apparent, the children are quite pragmatic, seeing the driving force for change as being commercial gain.

The above discussion has concentrated on the discursive constitution – and reconstitution – of the texts, but other factors should not be forgotten, particularly the technological and social factors that led to Noddy's existence: for example, the fact that the publishers were specifically seeking a Disney-style figure who could be extensively marketed; also, that the huge printing presses at Paulton were purpose-built to accommodate material with extensive print-runs. But let me now turn to see how the various discursive threads, mentioned above, are realized in two particular thematic concerns: the order of things and consumerism.

Noddy and the order of things

Many children's books are concerned with understanding 'the rules of the game', *Alice's Adventures in Wonderland* being the most celebrated. This is a concern of the Noddy books, too, both for the reader trying to understand Toyland society, and for the central character, Noddy, who, as said above, is trying to establish his place in the scheme of things. At certain times this becomes an almost existential quest, as at the very beginning when he is found in the woods by Big-Ears, naked and nameless. We learn that he was made out of wood by Old Man Carver. Remarkably, Noddy knows the order of his own creation:

> 'He made wooden feet, and then wooden legs, and then a round wooden body, and then wooden arms and hands, and then a wooden neck, and then a round wooden head,' said the little man.
>
> 'And did he stick them all together and make *you*?' asked Big-Ears. (*N1*, p. 10)

Like Pinocchio, there seems to have been some consciousness even in his wooden formlessness, though it is only collectively that these bits become a '*you*', as Big-Ears puts it – with the addition of blue bead eyes, and hair from a cat's fur. The illustration of his creator, Old Man Carver, with a cat by his side, seems to owe something to Gepetto in Disney's 1940 version of *Pinocchio*, which also added a cat, Figaro. However, whereas in Collodi's story the creation eventually becomes reunited with his creator, and learns to love him, in Blyton's Noddy, the creation never returns; in fact, Noddy never mentions Old Man Carver again. Noddy claims he left because he was lonely, but does not consider his creator's feelings. It is worth recalling Blyton's own inability, psychologically, to return to her mother (who died the year after Noddy's creation), and, physically, to her father.

I have called this concern 'existential' for several reasons, but mainly because of the distinction between being and non-being, which seems central to the series. In a way, this is the *raison d'être* of toys, to be invested with life of some sort, and Blyton seems to celebrate such animation throughout Toyland, whether it is in Bouncing Balls or Rocking Horses. Even more dependent things than these are given some form of volition – examples being teeth, raindrops and hats. Thus, in *N6* (p. 21), Big-Ears explains to Noddy that his hat keeps coming off 'because it's cross with you for getting a swollen head' (with possible echoes of Pinocchio's enlarging nose). A Piagetian might point to this as typical animistic thinking. However, though Piaget was a publishing contemporary of Blyton, it is more likely that she took her ideas from Froebel, who developed a stage theory much earlier:

> the child at this stage imparts to each thing the faculties of life, feeling, and speech. Of everything he imagines that it can hear.

> Because the child himself begins to represent his inner being outwardly, he imputes the same activity to all about him, to the pebble and chip of wood, to the plant, the flower, and the animal.
> (quoted in Lawrence, 1970, pp. 252–3)

It is of note that most of the stories begin with Noddy waking up – coming to life – for, having animated things, there is the responsibility of keeping them alive. Sleep, therefore, is a particularly tenuous state, which is why Noddy is so carefully lowered into unconsciousness:

> 'It's dark and it's quiet,
> I'm going to sleep;
> My eyes are tight shut,
> They can't even peep;
> I'll dream of old Big-Ears,
> And dear Tessie Bear;
> I'm going to Dreamland,
> And now –
> I –
> am –
> THERE!'
>
> And so he was, fast asleep, dreaming of having tea with Big Ears and little Tessie Bear. (*N17*, pp. 8–9)

This concern is found elsewhere in Blyton's writing, too, and I shall return to it later.

In general, Toy Town comes across as somewhere that everything has its place, even if some of the toys' sense of being is very different from our own:

> The road was full of skittles doing their shopping. Noddy didn't bother to hoot at them, because they never minded being knocked down.
>
> 'That's the best of skittles,' said Noddy, knocking over a small boy-skittle. (*N9*, p. 18; fortunately spared in the revisions)

It is only Noddy who, like any young child, has the problem of finding out where he fits. At the very beginning, when he and Big-Ears pass through various towns on the train, Noddy enquires, 'Is there a Nodding-Man Station?' (*N1*, p. 20). His search for identity and a place to belong is also a concern of others. Big-Ears tells him, 'You're not a brownie, so you can't live in my town', adding, 'You're not exactly a toy either – but you're very like one' (ibid., p. 11). The forces of law and order (sounding suspiciously like the House of Un-American Activities with their insistent questioning, 'Have you ever been a member of the Communist Party?') also want to know whether Noddy has a right to be in Toyland, for,

> 'Only toys are allowed to stay in Toy Village.'
> 'I *think* I'm a toy,' said Noddy, nodding his head in fright. '... Please let me stay here. I'm sure I'm a toy.'
> 'You might be an ornament,' said the policeman, sternly. 'Like a china pig. That's an ornament, unless it's a money-box pig, then it's a toy. You look rather like an ornament. Have you ever been stood on mantelpieces?'
> 'No, never,' said poor Noddy.
> 'Have you ever been played with by children?' asked the policeman.
> 'No, never,' said Noddy.
> 'Well, dear me – it seems as if you're not an ornament and not a toy either,' said the policeman. 'You'll have to come before the Court tonight, and we'll decide just *what* you are!'
>
> (ibid., pp. 27–8)

A concern with where one belongs, of course, is partly determined by issues of class and gender (and ethnicity). Obviously, by removing characters from the real world and making them animals or toys it is often possible to conceal these issues, though not to erase them. In Grahame's *The Wind in the Willows*, for example, the individualized animals are all of the leisured classes, whereas the amorphous rabble of stoats and weasels – the baddies – are distinctly working-class. The main characters are also generically male – 'Toad', 'Mole' and so on – with females marginalized. But Blyton, I would suggest, unlike Grahame, keeps these issues at least partly in view.

Taking the class issue first, there are a number of leisured individuals, while there are also those who simply serve, like the milkman and postman. The latter complain about their lot; the postman about delivering letters inviting people to parties, but never being invited himself (*N16*), and the milkman about others going on holiday when he cannot (*N15*). It might still be protested that these characters are hardly working-class. Certainly there is an absence of workers. One might wonder just what this economy is based on, given the amount of consumption: there are no miners, no road-menders or sweepers, nor factory workers. There is, however, one very interesting picture in the first book (dating from 1949), of Golly Town, which depicts it as significantly different from the usual rural settings. The characters here are in what looks like an urban townscape, with a background of belching factory chimneys. There is no textual justification for this depiction, though Blyton must obviously have approved it (certainly, the only other time Golly Town is depicted, it is shown as more picturesque, *N11*, p. 42).

One of the few explicit references to a social hierarchy occurs when Noddy is looking for work at a house where one of the servants goes to fetch the mistress, 'a very beautiful doll with curly golden hair and bright blue eyes' (*N2*, p. 14). Noddy, though, is clearly one of the servants, and is asked to sweep the chimney (again, amended in new editions). So, one could say that class is not particularly concealed in these books. More significant is the view we get of it, which is from fairly low in the hierarchy. Noddy certainly has to work for his living, and has a great deal of trouble being accepted (indeed, this never fully happens).[12]

Let us move on to consider gender. Toys are usually fashioned without genitalia and, therefore, provide the opportunity for a loosening of gender bonds. Certainly, there is the maternal Mrs. Tubby Bear, the deferential Tessie, and comments like Father Christmas's:

> 'I've just come to say that some of you dolls who go to live in doll's-houses in the playrooms of boys and girls are not very good at house-work,' said Father Christmas. 'You don't know how to dust or to scrub floors or clean windows. Well, you must learn, please.' (*N11*, p. 48)

But Noddy himself is more androgynous. In fact, this reputedly caused him problems in Australia (Knowles, 1988), where his long lashes were regarded as making him effeminate (a euphemistic way of saying he was 'queer'); not only that, but in many pictures, he often appears to have brightly painted lips – as a toy might.

However, it is not just the illustrations, for Blyton's text supports this feeling of androgyny. Thus in the first story Noddy puts on a blue doll's bonnet to wear (*N1*, p. 24), and in *N6* Mrs. Tubby lends Noddy a bonnet trimmed with flowers to wear in place of his hat. It is only when others laugh at him that he abandons it. Interestingly, some of the younger children I spoke to referred to Noddy as 'she', sometimes correcting themselves, or being corrected by others – but the slips were definitely there. This aspect of Noddy has often been criticized, but he could also be seen as refreshingly sensitive – a shining example of the New Man – bursting into tears without compunction. Though many snigger at his secure relationship with the avuncular Big-Ears, it is pleasantly unsullied:

> '. . . if you can squeeze into my tiny bed, you can sleep with me tonight.' . . . they squashed into Big-Ears' tiny, soft bed, put their arms round one another to stop themselves from rolling out, and fell fast asleep. (*N2*, pp. 33–4)

Unfortunately, the new edition has felt it necessary to curb such intimacy. Noddy has a similarly open friendship with Tessie Bear who, aside from Big-Ears, is his main confidante. Thus, when Noddy is upset and cries, Tessie Bear comes in and hugs him, and they hold hands, sitting on his bed (*N8*). In a later book, Tessie Bear has Noddy to stay – 'It *will* be nice to have you staying for the night' (*N17*, p. 32), she says. In a sense, being toys, this is all academic – what could possibly go on? And, as we know from *N11*, the toys are *made*, not *reproduced*, which might explain the lack of babies in Toyland. Yet it is unlikely that such close friendships could have been given expression if the characters were human – and, clearly, the revising of Noddy and Big-Ears' relationship suggests that even this was too much for the nineties!

Some commentators, though, have sought to give this open sensuality a more overtly sexual reading. Thus, the frequent references to tails being chopped off are oedipally instanced – 'What a nuisance tails are!' said Noddy, pushing the mouse's tail away. 'I'm glad *I* haven't one. I'd cut it off if I had.' (*N17*, p. 14) – and Noddy's relationship with the milkman has been seen as masturbatory: 'Well, the milkman just loves to nod my head as fast as he can . . . I have to pay him a lot more nods for cream, though – it's not so cheap as milk' (*N7*, p. 10). Short of a nudging snigger, though, such comments are rarely taken further – because, I suspect, commentators do not know what to make of them. I shall attempt to remedy this in Chapter 10.

Big-Ears is less often attended to so closely, though brownies are traditionally linked to the *pilosi*, or 'hairy ones' (Duffy, 1972) and he is the only regular hirsute character in the series. Brownies are also associated with sexual potency, which is reflected in their close ancestors, the gnomes, whom Big-Ears most closely resembles. Garden gnomes had been popular since the 1920s, originating in Germany. Significantly, they are male, and are seen as policing gardens, guarding that more female symbol, the garden pond; as Paul Oliver says, 'Their form and, in their pointed caps, their colour, was phallic; the postures of the standing figures priapic' (Oliver *et al.*, 1981, p. 170).

Although I find the idea of Big-Ears as a sexual being unconvincing, he is certainly a potent figure, 100-years-old and able to do almost anything from driving cars to flying planes – even challenging Mr. Plod at times (*N2* and *N24*). It is significant that when Mr. Plod is injured, it is Big-Ears who assumes his role. But Big-Ears also seems to be above the law, having magical powers (*N16*, p. 56). In many ways he is reminiscent of Badger in *The Wind in the Willows*, inhabiting an equally isolated habitat, outside the confines of Toyland, in the Dark Wood. His house, too, is the nearest to a natural habitat in the whole series. Toadstools, of course, are unusual plants, growing in darkness (a dark wood would therefore be ideal) and living off decaying matter; they are also renowned for being either edible or poisonous, though it takes expertise to know which is which. It certainly seems to suit Big-Ears' querulous character; also, like his abode, he is known for his sudden nocturnal appearances, being the nearest thing to a *deus ex machina* – established with his arrival at the beginning of the first book. It is no doubt this power that makes Big-Ears so popular with readers – eighth most popular overall in my survey – but fourth with younger readers, and more popular with boys (interestingly, he seemed particularly popular with Muslim children, for whom bearded elders would be more commonplace).

Overall then, the order of things that Noddy has to learn about is one that has markers of gender and class, although Toyland comes across as a relatively androgynous place, partly thanks to Beek's style of illustration. Noddy himself is certainly freer of these markers. He is a worker, but is quite lowly in the Toy Town hierarchy and, in many respects, appears surprisingly modern, confounding traditional sex-role stereotypes with his androgyny, his crying, his cross-dressing, his sensitivity and domesticity (both he and Big-Ears are regularly seen doing their washing). Ironically, it was for these very reasons that he was criticized for being wimpish (Welch's 'snivelling, sneaking doll') and banned in Australia! But again, these are adult discourses speaking. Welch's article is revealingly subtitled 'a parent's lament', for, as he admits, the character is immensely popular with young children, regardless of the social backdrop.

Consumerist Noddy and the work ethic

When I first re-read the 'Noddy' books, I was surprised at how much they celebrated certain values: of consumerism, of property, and working hard to attain this. However, on reflection, this made the books far more characteristic of their time: the post-war economy struggling to spend its way out of recession; the low unemployment until the sixties; and the general revolution in shopping and consumerism (television, car and house ownership all increased dramatically over this period, with buying on hire-purchase becoming acceptable). This ethos informs the Noddy books in quite a profound way. Rarely have I seen the economy of a 'toy' culture so dramatically laid out. In the first book, Big-Ears explains to Noddy about money:

> 'It's something you get when you work hard,' said Big-Ears. 'Then you put it into your pockets and wait till you see something you want. Then you give it in exchange. You will have to work soon, then you can get money to buy heaps of things.' (*N1*, p. 23)

However, there is never a sense of superfluity; one is always thrifty, as Big-Ears advises: 'But if I were you I'd go to the market. The shops are *so* dear' (*N1*, p. 22).

At the beginning, Big-Ears lends Noddy some money, so that he can establish himself – even to the extent of becoming a house-owner: 'I'm in my own little house! I'm so happy! I'll work hard and buy lots of things for my house' (*N1*, p. 60). It is not until the second book, however, that Noddy acquires a car and establishes himself properly as Toy Village's taxi service, receiving the narrator's blessing at the end: 'It *is* a good idea, little nodding man – and if ever we come to visit Toy Village, we'll ride in your taxi' (*N2*, p. 60). Before this he does other jobs, helping with spring-cleaning and working in Mr. Golly's garage. Noddy stresses the importance of this, since he must repay Big-Ears: 'People must always pay back what they borrow' (*N2*, p. 20).

Over the course of the books, Noddy's gradual accumulation of property can be seen. After acquiring clothes, house (*N1*) and a car (*N2*), he doubles his money in *N3*, builds a garage in *N4* (notably a great deal of property built after the war did not initially have garages – a lack soon found wanting). In *N5*, Noddy gets some new lamps for his car, besides saving for a new bike for Big-Ears; it is also in this book that he tries other means of making money: by planting sweets in his garden (Pinocchio was advised to plant money) and by composing and singing songs. This is an established practice with the milkman, from whom he also gets his goods 'on the nod':

> 'You can have this little pot of cream if you'll allow me to sing your song as I go on my rounds.'
>
> 'Oh yes, *of course*,' said Noddy, beaming at him. 'And you can tap my head three times if you like, and make it nod. . . .' (*N22*, p. 8)

Even when Noddy is prevented from taxiing, he is not idle. When his car has crashed (*N20*) he uses a barrow to deliver goods at sixpence a time. Big-Ears suggests that Noddy could go to market for fruit and flowers cheaply, and sell them in Toyland Village: 'You could charge an extra penny on everything you sell, to pay for your trouble' (*N20*, p. 18). Other characters are given similar advice. On a windy day at the fair, a bun-seller – obviously with a vested interest – suggests that Bumpy-Dog should retrieve people's hats at a penny a time; as he puts it, 'A penny a hat – a penny a bun!' (*N21*, p. 33). Later in the same book, Noddy, prompted by Tessie, suggests that the skittle children make money for themselves by lining up and being knocked down (ibid., p. 44). Even among friends, the importance of 'paying your way' is repeatedly stressed. In *N23*, when Noddy picks up Mrs. Tubby Bear, he comments, 'Mrs. Tubby, let me drive you home! I won't charge you even a penny because you made me such a lovely cake last week!' (*N23*, p. 18). It is this, rather than the recognition of her as a neighbour, that is his motivation.

However, it is in the Father Christmas story outlined above that the real twist to this consumerism comes. He and Noddy arrive at 'N. & B. Works' (*N11*, p. 50), where we find Noddy and Big-Ears dolls being made. These are new toys that the children have specifically asked for.

> 'N. & B. Works – of course, Noddy and Big-Ears Works!' said Father Christmas. 'I see that the children have asked for Noddy and Big-Ears toys, Noddy. I wonder why.'
>
> 'Well, there are lots of books about me,' said Noddy. 'Perhaps they have read them. Oh, Father Christmas – OH, Father Christmas – when I see all these little toys *just* like me I feel Very Very Important!'
>
> 'Now don't you be grand and important or you won't be the dear

> little Noddy that children love,' said Father Christmas. He looked closely at the tiny figures running excitedly round the car. 'Yes, I like them. Pity the Noddies haven't little cars like yours, Noddy. I'll have to make a note of that.' (*N11*, pp. 51–2)

He certainly does – and of eggcups, lamps, toothbrushes, and the rest! A bit later, just to consolidate this promotional line, Father Christmas comments, 'one of the nicest, kindest little toys I've ever met' (*N11*, pp. 58–9). Obviously, quite a *coup* to have your product officially endorsed by Father Christmas! This book, it should be noted, came out in September 1955, just in time for the Noddy series on ITV, and at a time of extensive merchandising with the play having been launched the year before (a 'Noddy Licensing Co' was formed specifically to cope with his merchandising, which, by the late 1950s, involved 52 separate companies supplying non-book goods – Anon, 1958, p. 98). But the careful packaging of this product seems to have been envisaged by its creator from the outset:

> I imagine we might have as a 'motif' a toy train rushing along . . . going all round the jacket top, sides and bottom . . . to give the books a 'series' look. The specific titles . . . will each contain the name 'Noddy'. In the end, if they are very successful, they'll probably be referred to and ordered as the 'Noddy' books.
>
> (Letter to Beek, quoted in Stoney, 1974, p. 158)

The whole thing stresses ownership and consumption, from the personalized bookplates at the beginning to the message at the end: 'Look for the Next Noddy Book'.

In sum, the books are very much part of the expanding economy of the 1950s – even if this was itself a fantasy in Britain's fairly bankrupt post-war years. The characters in the books are forever consuming, and Noddy aids them by ferrying them to the shops.

However, there is also the converse of this acquisitiveness: an overriding fear of theft. Coming back to the books as an adult, I was surprised at the level of concern over this in the fifties. But this is something that certainly gives the books a more contemporary feel. People who isolate the 'mugging' of Noddy by golliwogs in *N4* miss the fact that crime is rife in Toyland. The golliwogs aren't distinctive, despite their press. Car thefts occur in five more books – none of which involves golliwogs – besides other thefts in seven further titles.

Forgetting to lock your door even once is a clear invitation to burglars, as Noddy finds out in *N14*. The Wobbly-Man puts his faith in Mr. Plod – 'It's a very good thing we've a policeman to look after us all, and see that we aren't robbed at night' (*N22*, p. 16) – but Tubby Bear wisely borrows a dog for the single night he leaves his house empty (*N9*). Even in daytime this fear prevails, as Tessie exclaims after Bumpy Dog's barking, 'There must be someone outside – a burglar perhaps' (*N24*, p. 13). There seems to be more crime in Toyland than in the whole of the Famous Five!

What is even more disturbing is the lack of trust in the community. Noddy spends much of his time trying to clear his name. One might expect this at the beginning, when the toys are establishing who he is – but it seems that he never attains their complete trust. In *N2* he has to convince everyone that he is not a car thief. In *N4*, the jingling of a bell is enough to implicate Noddy in a crime. In *N5* he is accused of stealing from the Sailor Doll, and is arrested. In *N8*, Mr. Plod accuses him of breaking into the houses of Miss Fluffy Cat and Mr. Wobbly-Man and, as a consequence, no one in Toyland will use him as a taxi. In *N17*, Mr. Plod accuses Noddy of going to Big-Ears' and stealing his flowers as some sort of trick. Each time, Noddy has to prove himself afresh.

The books also seem surprisingly modern in the ambivalent attitude expressed towards the police. Mr. Plod's position is often undermined – Big-Ears, for instance, overrides it when he wants. However, it is in *N21* that it is most expressly challenged (interestingly this is at the fair, an area of Bakhtinian license, where authority is often stood on its head). When Noddy hears that Mr. Plod has taken the steering wheel of his car, he is incensed. 'How DARE he? I'll get his helmet and stamp on it! I'll pull off all his buttons! I'll . . .' (*N21*, p. 49). He is interrupted at this point by Big-Ears, but others also undermine Plod's authority: the coconut-shy man has a coconut wearing the policeman's helmet, with Plod's face drawn on it. He comments, 'It's funny how many people want to knock off that helmet. Anyone would think they didn't like Mr. Plod!' (*N21*, p. 47). And this whole book finishes unresolved, with Mr. Plod left at the fair while Noddy and Tessie quietly escape. Noddy then proceeds to sing a song, 'wasn't it FUN / To go to the Fair!' (*N21*, p. 60).[13]

Conclusion

In this chapter we have seen how texts are clearly weaves of earlier threads – personal, literary, and, more generally, social – and how Blyton held a quite modern conception of the creative process. She never spoke of individual creative genius (in the Romantic manner), emphasizing instead its mundane origins. We have also looked at what these threads constructed in terms of the two main themes that seem to emerge from the Noddy books: concerns with the order of things – with one's place in society, with existence and animism – and with the consumer ethic. I also indicated that these issues are double-edged. On the one hand the reader is gently comforted – very much a concern of the post-war society; on the other hand there is an underlying insecurity, a fear that the celebration of existence is in the face of nothingness; that if things are not animated, they become inanimate, inert; that consumerism is itself a conveyor-belt that has to keep turning, or its emptiness becomes apparent; moreover, that the acquisition of property also brings in its wake its opposite: a fear of its loss, of theft. Although it might be argued that children won't discern these themes, they will certainly pick up on their emotional resonance: the insecurity of existence, knowing where one fits into the scheme of things, being accused of misbehaving, and so on. Such undercurrents lurk even within the safe haven of Toyland and, however much their occurrence is dealt with and order restored, they recur – they return – as indeed I shall return to them in later chapters.

6
The Famous Five: from Discursive Threads to Cultural Readings

> 'This all sounds most interesting. Quite Famous Five-ish, in fact!'
>
> Julian, *FOST*, p. 74

Introduction

This series, alongside Noddy, typifies Blyton's work more than any other, hence the highly successful Comic Strip lampoons (1982; 1983). The Five is the most filmed series, with adaptations by the Children's Film Federation (1957; 1964), Southern TV (1978; 1979), and Zenith Films (1995; 1997). This popularity is endorsed by my respondents, for whom the Five was by far the most popular series, with almost one third rating it their favourite. Even before the latest TV series the books were selling a million copies a year. As for the individual characters, all of the Five appeared in the top 15, George being the most popular character of all (as voted by 21.5 per cent) with her dog, Timmy, in third place. Even Quentin crept in at nineteenth position. The sex differences are interesting here, in that not only was George pre-eminently popular among girls, but she was also the most popular Five (human) character with boys too, beating Julian into second place. Given the unwillingness of most boys to read fiction about girls (albeit girls will read fiction about boys) – let alone find them more popular than the boys – this is quite an achievement.

In this chapter, it is my intention to examine why this series is so popular. I shall look at the series from an 'adult' perspective, pulling out the major discursive threads that critics have put on the agenda: those of nationhood and class (sexism and race being dealt with separately). I shall then move on to consider what the children see in the books –

what might be termed the pleasure of the texts – much of which derives specifically from an oppositional stance to adults. Let me begin, however, with a brief overview of the series.

The first book appeared in September 1942, having been written, most probably, in late 1941. The books then appeared annually, apart from 1959, till the last, twenty-two years later, in 1963. This last, *FATA*, was one of the final full-length books written by Blyton, whose mind by then was clearly deteriorating. She had originally intended the Five to be a series of six, but their popularity made her continue, making it her longest running series. Contrary to some critics' views (for example, Druce, 1992, p. 120), not all of these books were first serialized in Blyton's magazines. Thus, the notion of her being so readable because of the climaxes, or cliffhangers, created at the end of the respective issues, is unfounded. Only eight of the Five books appeared in serial form, the first being the seventh, *FGOTC*, the only one to appear in *Sunny Stories*.[1]

The Five series is based around three siblings, Julian (12 years), Dick (11 years) and Anne (10 years), who have a cousin, Georgina – although she prefers to be called George – (also 11-years-old),[2] and her dog, Timmy. The relation is through their father's brother, Quentin, an irascible and absent-minded scientist. He is married to Fanny, who, we learn, has always lived at Kirrin Bay, the site of their initial adventures.

Englishness

On re-reading the Famous Five I was struck by the social context, which seems to have fed into the texts in a variety of ways, just as it was found to have done in Noddy. A discourse of Englishness is particularly powerful, especially in the early books.

In the first, *FOTI*, we have the story of George, with her friends, defending her island at a time when King George's people were also seeking to defend themselves from being overrun by 'wicked men'; and when St George's 'sceptred isle' was itself under attack. Indeed, it was a time when such imagery was rife. Wilson Knight's drama, *This Sceptred Isle: Shakespeare's Message for England at War* (1940) also had its first production in 1941. And Churchill, with whom Hugh Pollock had been closely involved, spoke of 'This wicked man . . . resolved to break our famous island race' (Warner, 1994, p. 81). One 1950s reader even suggested 'that a good signal [for Famous Five Club members] would be the Victory sign – two fingers held up in the shape of a V, which is the Roman numeral for five'. When Blyton later discusses a huge increase in club membership, she innocently remarks, 'I feel like giving you Virginia's V sign!'[3]

War, of course, was a time of secrecy, as Anne is continually reminded: 'Anne, the only way to stop you giving away secrets is to sew up your mouth, like Brer Rabbit wanted to do to Mister Dog!' (*FGAA*, p. 71). The merciless kicking and nudging she receives because of her loose tongue is particularly prevalent in the early books, bringing to mind the wartime slogan, 'Careless Talk Costs Lives'. Lest it be thought that I am making too much of this, it is worth noting that the wider context is often made explicit, as here by Julian: 'We're doing this for your father – and maybe for our country too' (*FGAA*, p. 162).

The idea of the country being under threat from traitors was a prevalent concern, increasing after 1945 with many Cold War spy cases. Julian finds such behaviour incomprehensible: 'That's a thing I don't understand – to be a traitor to one's own country. It leaves a nasty taste in my mouth to think of it', to which Dick adds, 'Beasts! There's too much of that sort of thing nowadays, it seems to me!' (*FHWT*, p. 28). This Five story is about scientists who turn traitor, who 'disappear to another country to sell our secrets!' (ibid., p. 15). Later, the rogue scientist makes the comment, 'They won't like life, where we're going!' (ibid., p. 135), obviously referring to the USSR. This book was written in 1951, the year in which the Rosenbergs were found guilty of passing atomic secrets to the Russians.

However, it is not only traitors that concern Blyton. There is also the growing influence and power of America over British destiny, arising out of post-World War II reparations, together with the more general cultural influence of America in these years. This is most clear-cut in *FOFF*, where the issue of 'Selling our birthright' (p. 92) is made explicit; the brash American, Mr Henning, retorts, 'You ought to be glad that a poor, run-down, back dated country like Britain has got anything to sell to a fine upstanding one like America!' (*FOFF*, p. 95). There is certainly a celebration of Britain here, and more specifically, of England:

> 'That was good,' said Julian, voicing the feelings of the others. 'Very good. I somehow feel more English for having seen those Dorset fields, set about by hedges, basking in the sun.'
>
> (*FOFF*, p. 77)

It is something that makes an impact on readers too, as we saw in Harwood's eulogy, above, and others made similar comments: 'I could see through her eyes, the brook, the villages, the surroundings of an old

English garden' (f); 'her books were everything "English" . . . the beautiful countryside and green of England' (f). Whether deliberately or not, some critics even become remarkably Churchillian when discussing Blyton:

> Never were so many fully armed blackguards so easily overcome by so few children; never were adults so incompetent or adolescents so invincible; never were boys so brave or girls so gaily indifferent to danger; never, alas, were parents so entirely non-existent or children so much encouraged to enter a world of fantastic wish-fulfilment.
>
> (Eyre, 1971, pp. 89–90)

From an adult point of view, then, the discourse of Englishness is plain. The very landscape in which the Five play, of hedgerows, village greens, rolling hills and woodlands, is iconically English (Howkins, 1987) – or, more specifically, the south (the nearest the Five get to the north is Wales). It is also the countryside, rather than the town, that is seen to epitomize the true England, with its cottages and large country houses (*Country Life*, which helped forge this myth, was itself founded in the year of Blyton's birth):

> 'Why is it that people on farms always have the most delicious food? I mean, surely people in towns can bottle raspberries and pickle onions and make cream cheese?'
>
> 'Well either they can't or they don't,' said George.
>
> (*FOHT*, pp. 89–90)

Even Quentin's science is presented as an individualistic cottage-industry. This belief in the 'beauty and moral worth of England', as Arthur Mee termed it, was one that was common at the end of the nineteenth century (Smith, 1987, p. 271). It celebrated the Elizabethan age, even down to its 'Tudorbethan' houses – of which 'Green Hedges', the name itself metonymic of this England, was a prime example. As a number of writers have commented, ideologically this celebration helped naturalize middle-class aspirations by linking them to older aristocratic values. The country and the soil were seen to capture the true character of the English, which was also being cultivated in the public school system, epitomized by such products as Julian: cool, manly, a born leader, and one who derides effeminacy.[4] Certainly the Five, in their journeys underground, are seen to reach down to the bedrock of English culture.

However, if we turn from text to reader, the discourse of Englishness is not so prevalent. Only a few respondents said they liked the books for this aspect – a comment confined exclusively to the adults. Moreover, overseas readers often found that they had been imagining a romanticized country: 'Many of us have been disappointed on visits to the UK because it is not Enid-Blyton'ish at all' (m). I would suggest that, though the discourse of Englishness is certainly a preferred reading for the student of popular culture, for others, it is far less important. Her minimalist descriptions can be linked to a great variety of actual landscapes, which is why so many readers seem to have personalized them. Even here, though, most admitted to being vague about location, seeing her landscapes as more imaginary than real: 'I don't actually remember where I saw the story happening, I don't really think that I related it to any country' (f). Certainly, where translations have attempted to capture more local colour, they seem to have been less successful. One respondent informed me that 'the Malay version was not popular at all – due to the fact that all the names and the places were converted to local names' (f). It will be interesting to see whether the latest attempts to localize the books will be successful in this regard, or end up losing that sense of a mythical landscape.

So, while the signifier 'Blyton' itself evokes a conception of Englishness, it is essentially a secure, cosy environment that is being constructed, one with minimal historical or geographical coordinates. And this homeland is set against all that is Other – 'We got fed up with French food,' said Dick. 'I came out in spots and Julian was sick . . .' (*FOST*, p. 70) – whether French, American, or whatever. The message is the same: the English (that is, the home team for readers in most cultures) are seen as the standard bearers.

Class

Not only is there a pride in being part of this team, but it is grounded in middle-class codes and manners. The middle-classes are paragons of deportment and behaviour, the Famous Five being their young ambassadors: 'We're on the side of the right, and it's worth while running into a bit of danger for that', as Julian puts it in *FOHT* (p. 168). Julian also believes in the liberal concept of 'one nation'. Following a comment from one of the circus people that, 'Us-folk and you-folk don't mix' (*FHWT*, p. 48), Julian responds, 'There's a lot of that kind of feeling about these days, and it's so silly. We're all the same under the skin' (ibid., p. 49). This, perhaps, reflects certain sensitivities of the time (it was written in 1951); for example, a concern with the breakdown of old class barriers following the war and the installation of a fairly radical programme of social reform with the post-war labour government.

So, does this mean that the books are 'class-ist'? Such a reading can certainly be sustained. We find a far more hierarchical society, with servants, cooks, gardeners, and a more deferential approach to authority; there are also travelling gypsies and circuses. The police, on the other hand, are the 'agents of middle class, keeping their established order and dignity in being and discriminating in their favour' (Jackson, 1991, p. 318), and are generally deferential to the Five. But it does not seem problematic that Blyton should feature these elements, given that they were part of the social landscape, just as they are in, for instance, Edgar Wallace, Aldous Huxley or Somerset Maugham. There is also a middle-class sensitivity to smell, about which some critics have expressed distaste – though, again, it is typical of the period, such that George Orwell once called it 'the real secret of class distinctions in the West . . . *The lower classes smell*' (1962, p. 112), continuing: 'Race-hatred, religious hatred, differences of education, of temperament, of intellect, even differences of moral code, can be got over; but physical repulsion cannot' (ibid., p. 160).[5]

Is there a concern, then, that children might see this world as reflecting contemporary society? It seems not. Even the youngest of my respondents were aware that the stories were part of a bygone age (though some, disconcertingly, had this age situated only as far back as the 1980s!). As evidence for this, they mentioned a number of the above elements, plus the stereotyping of sex roles, the clothes and the lack of television and computers. But most frequently they mentioned the freedom that the Five had to roam the country. One 12-year-old girl amused her group by joking about this:

Valerie: I said, 'Mum, can us, me and my cousins and Cindy (that's my dog) go – hire some caravans and go off like the Famous Five do?' [laughter] She says, 'No way!'
Daisy: [posh accent] 'Oh yes, dear, of course.' [more laughter]

Her friend's response shows an awareness of class that was common to many, adopting 'plummy' voices when imitating the Five. Past readers recalled doing the same: 'we tended to put on rather middle-class accents and say things like "I say, what's going on here, Ju?"' (f).

Some critics, though, seem to think that Blyton was not merely a product of her times; rather, that her books are more actively anti-working class. Dixon was probably the earliest to take this view, and it has been regularly rehearsed since. However, this type of reading is only sustainable from a very partial look at the texts. Most of the working-class characters, while they are usually background figures, are perfectly normal and acceptable – like Joan, the cook. In *FGOTC*, in fact, we find those involved in the black market, whom Julian calls 'the wrong kind of workers' (p. 59), contrasted with Will, who explicitly distances himself from these 'ninnies and idjits' (p. 58).

But, of course, it is those characters who are *not* acceptable upon which the debate tends to concentrate, some even seeing Blyton as making all the working-class characters criminals. This is not the case: eight of the 21 books have working-class villains while ten are middle class (there are two where the situation is more mixed, and one story – *FOFF* – has none). Nor is it true that the majority of crooks are foreigners – another common misconception – as only four of the series feature vaguely foreign-sounding villains.[6] It is also often said that the Five only deal with higher-ranking police, while 'ordinary policemen, who are working class . . . are often held in contempt' (Dixon, 1974b, p. 58). Again, this is false. In the Five there are more dealings with ordinary police, with whom the Five are mostly cordial.[7] I suspect that Dixon is here pinning too much on the character of Goon in the 'Find-Outers', who seems representative of a long line of comic policemen, from *Punch and Judy* through to specifically detective fiction police – as in Conan Doyle and Agatha Christie – placed in the story simply to be outwitted by the heroes.

Dixon and Druce also argue that the non-middle-class characters, such as Jo, are seen as more animal like, being compared with 'a squirrel, a monkey, a cat and a weasel'. They feel that this is about more than Jo's agility, being rather subhuman, or pet-like (Dixon 1974b, p. 52; Druce, 1992, p. 239). Unfortunately, other, acceptable characters are also described in these terms, such as Pierre Lenoir, mentioned earlier, or George herself, clambering 'up the side of the wreck like a monkey' (*FOTI*, p. 82). Druce (1992, pp. 224–5) even suggests that the names of the working-class characters are less than serious, with Nobby, Sniffer and the like. However, for each of these there is usually a middle-class equivalent, as, for example, Sooty or Tinker.

So, while middle-class values and behaviour are undoubtedly the unquestioned norm, there is no simple formula of middle-class equals good, working-class equals bad. As discussed above, Blyton plays with the stereotype. Thus there are quite a few middle-class children whose behaviour is also criticized – Cecil Dearlove (*FGOTC*), Toby Thomas (*FGTBH*), Junior Henning (*FOFF*), Henrietta (*FGTMM*) and Richard Thurlow Kent (*FGIT*), for instance. What these have in common is a lack of 'character' when put to the test – a common theme of folk tales. (A great number of Blyton's short stories deal with this – in terms of selfishness, cruelty and bullying – meting out exacting punishment to those who maltreat other children or animals.[8]) As Judith Rowbotham has argued – though speaking specifically about girls' school stories – 'character' is a neglected concept, often missed by those concentrating on such issues as gender:

> Character concerned itself with temperament rather than sexual nature; it was 'character' that marked people out as good, bad or indifferent. It encompassed the attributes that helped people either maintain their original station in life or where fitting, rise to a higher one. Equally, it was the factor that explained the downfall of people who were, in a superficial way, blessed by possession of natural talent. Both of these implied potential, but character summed up the merit, or lack of it, that accompanied them and ultimately, made them socially useful and worthwhile: one reason why middle-class society in this period accepted merit as an arbiter of fortune in life, and something that could overcome established class barriers.
>
> (Rowbotham, 1989, p. 101)

She goes on to indicate how character was fostered by good education, something that Blyton, especially given her Froebel training, was particularly concerned with. Blyton saw parents as bearing the brunt of responsibility. Thus, in *FRAT*, young Edgar's parents are described as 'no good to Edgar, and had taught him nothing but bad things. There might be a chance for the wretched boy if he were kept away from them, and set a good example instead of a bad one' (*FRAT*, p. 191). This is a key concern of the school stories, such that Miss Grayling, the headmistress of Malory Towers, reflects, 'Really, I think somebody should start a School for Parents too!' (*Sixth*, p. 120) – which is just what Froebel tried to do (for mothers in particular).[9]

Of course, the Five are the extramural barometers of appropriate behaviour, by which both the adults and children they encounter are measured. This said, the Five's norms are neither consistent, nor always middle-class (rather, they are child-oriented – 'Five-ish', in fact). For instance, Joan upbraids the Five for both greed and theft:

> 'last holidays I left a meat pie and half a tongue and a cherry tart and a trifle sitting on the shelves for the next day's meals – and when I came back from my half-day's outing there wasn't a thing to be seen.'
>
> (*FFIA*, p. 19)[10]

This is particularly revealing in view of the Five's subsequent encounter with Jo, 'a forlorn waif . . . going in fear of others, and often hungry and lonely', whom Dick upbraids for stealing food:

> 'Well, wouldn't you, if you were so hungry you couldn't even bear to look at a baker's cart?' said Jo.
>
> 'No – I don't think so. At least, I hope not,' said Dick, wondering what he really would feel like if he were starving.
>
> (*FFIA*, p. 63)

So, although Blyton had little insight into class, she could reflect such concerns effectively in terms of character, sometimes pointing up differences in value-systems. In this regard, those on the periphery of society – the gypsies, fair- and circus-folk (what we'd today call the 'underclass') – are allowed far more latitude, and clearly have a transgressive appeal. They tend to break the rules of patriarchy, their children are less sex stereotyped, and they are free of many of the social conventions. Jo is the prime example, so popular that she featured in more of the Five's stories than any other character. Notably, she is scarcely reprimanded for running away from her kindly foster-parents, whereas middle-class Richard Thurlow Kent (*FGIT*) is severely upbraided for a similar offence. Just as George can only escape the patriarchal yoke by running off and acting independently (see Chapter 7), so, it seems, the only way that others can escape the confines of society is by living in its interstices, between nature and culture.

This peripheral group is also more childlike, and their very fascination for the Five is bound up with their difference, the unsavoury smells and lack of manners; for instance, the circus children encountered by the Five in *FGOIC* are described as 'dirty and ragged, but most of them had beautiful eyes and thick curly hair, though it wanted brushing and washing' (*FGOIC*, p. 98). In this book, both Dick and Anne are seen to envy Nobby, learning how to do cart-wheels rather than fractions (*FGOIC*, pp. 86–7). The Five often enter this interstitial, forbidden world in their adventures, as in *FGDTS*, where the Five are particularly fascinated by the Barnies, a travelling group of players, whose pantomime horse, Clopper, the boys dress up in.

All in all, it is certainly the case that the Five are middle-class, and that differences between them and the working-class are marked, but most readers are already aware of this – some precisely because of Blyton, an example being this working-class reader, who claimed that 'reading Enid Blyton made me a socialist. It was through the Famous Five books [aged 8] that I first became aware of the class system' (f). However, this did not spoil her pleasure, any more than it did for others in her position: 'when I was 7 I certainly didn't want to read about the kind of life I was leading, and relished tales of scrounging chocolate cakes of [sic] the cook, etc.' (f) – the appeal for these being precisely their fantasy quality, 'completely different than my life on a council estate in Wigan' (f); with other readers, again, their awareness comes across in the accentuated 'plummy' voices they adopt, as quoted above.

However, moving towards a child's reading, one of the main pleasures of the books, as mentioned above, is the fact that the traditional framework of society is temporarily questioned: patriarchy can be challenged, and the Five can upset middle-class tenets by going below ground, both literally, with their tunnelling, and socially, in joining the circus and fair-folk. Thus Joan, the cook, describes all the Five as 'dirty little tatterdemalions. . . . You might all be sister and brothers to that ragamuffin Jo' (*FFIA*, p. 120), which they compound by eating like her. While Dixon and Druce make much of the fact that Jo is ritually washed by Joan, effectively baptizing her, they ignore the fact that the Five undergo their own initiation into Jo's world; for instance, spending a miserable night in the open. In a subsequent encounter, Julian has his hair 'whipped' by Jo's relatives before they become friends (*FFIA*). It is in this book that Jo also regains her strength by pointedly discarding middle-class trappings, her clothes and cleanliness.

So, despite the overall middle-class framing of the stories, as Sarland (1983, p. 171) says, 'it is the challenge to the cultural order that children find absorbing rather than the re-establishment of it at the end of the stories'. This aspect will now be examined in more depth.

Adults versus the Five

The challenge to cultural order is nowhere more evident than in the relation between adults and children. In fact, if Blyton is guilty of any *ism* it is age*ism* that is the real culprit. Adults are always suspect – and particularly so in the Five books. There may be good and bad ones, but all are tarred to some extent. Even George's parents are shown as untrustworthy, capable of doing exactly what they want by selling

George's island. Quentin's put-down is significant: 'You're only a child. Your mother didn't really mean what she said – it was only to please you' (*FOTI*, p. 108). Julian reinforces this view. 'It wasn't a bit of good fighting grown-ups. They could do exactly as they liked' (ibid.). The put-down, 'You're only a child' is, of course, also a key cry of their adversaries (ibid., p. 148), but to their cost, for 'what hope has a band of desperate men against four children?' And yet, what is asserted is not only superiority to the crooks, but to adults in general – a basic opposition that seems to unite readers, irrespective of differences in sex, ethnicity or class.

The adults shown to possess more sense are those who recognize that children should be given space. Thus George's mother deliberately absents herself in *FOTI*, as does Mr Luffy in *FGOTC*. This is in line with Blyton's Froebel philosophy that children should be left to their own devices as much as possible, and should be given a rich, natural environment; then they will grow 'straight'. Rural England is seen as the perfect nursery in which the Five can flex their moral and mental muscle. Of course, the absenting of adults is common in children's fiction. They are removed by illness, by work, or are simply dead. But Blyton seems to go beyond the convention. Not only does she have the children assert their freedom from adults, but she also emphasizes adults' right to be free of their progeny. (This might reflect Blyton's own concern to have time with her new husband. Baverstock (1989), in particular, records being suddenly dispatched to school for this reason.) For example, in the very first book it is suddenly put to the children that their parents want to go away on their own. In *FHPOF*, George's parents do the same. Fanny says, 'I'll go with you, Quentin . . . I could do with a quiet two days' (*FHPOF*, p. 77). They also, rather too frequently, remove themselves beyond reach: 'it's so like them not to give us an address!' (*FHPOF*, p. 117). They are not quite in the same league as Hansel and Gretel's parents, but they are far from exemplary.

Julian, with his expertise 'at getting porters and taxis' (*FOKIA*, p. 21), is an interesting creation in this regard, often being seen as 'very grown-up' (*FHMTS*, p. 138). He strives to live up to this image. In *FFIA*, when Joan, the cook, offers to lock up, Julian declines her offer. 'That's the man's job, you know, locking up the house. You can trust me all right' (*FFIA*, p. 25). Unfortunately for Julian, the house is burgled that very night, gently undermining his role.

This behaviour explains many readers' ambivalence towards Julian: he can be looked up to in the way that he aspires – like any child – to gain access to the freedom of the adult world; yet he can also, as a consequence, be no longer a fun-loving figure, but staid, boorish and overly rational. His bossiness is frequently in evidence. He even advises the other members on how to dress: '"I'm glad you girls took my advice and wore your thickest shoes"' (*FOHT*, p. 25); and, in *FGOIC*, we are told that, 'The children had all put on extra jerseys, by Julian's orders' (p. 157). This domineering nature does not escape attention. For example, when he rather over-zealously captains the raft in *FOHT*, George responds, 'All right, Teacher!' (p. 139). Earlier in the same book Dick also upbraids him, after the latter's remark:

> 'perhaps you feel able to tell us exactly why you ignored my instructions and didn't arrive where you were supposed to last night.'
> 'You sound like our headmaster at school!' said Dick.
>
> (*FOHT*, p. 71)

Even Anne considers him 'high-and-mighty and proud' at one point (*FHWT*, p. 91), though it is with George that most of the clashes occur:

> 'You know quite well that if ever you go against the orders of the chief – that's me, my girl, in case you didn't know it – you won't come out with us again.'
>
> (*FOHT*, p. 34)

Julian's rational approach to things can also distance him from readers, besides making him dismiss George's hunches. She is clearly the most intuitive – excepting Timmy, whose sixth sense is legendary (and who is always playful, never boorish; always sensual and exuberant) – and often shows Julian to be in error, which, to Julian's credit, he usually admits: 'You were right and we were wrong, George' (*FGAA*, p. 192).

Comments from respondents support this, many expressing the above ambivalence towards Julian. For some he was a paragon; in fact some females even admitted to having a 'hopeless crush' on him, and of being jealous of Anne. One juxtaposed him, rather amusingly, to Dick: 'I can imagine Julian being dead tall and nice looking, and Dick would just be small and spotty'. But this also made Julian suspect, as others said: he was 'like a father', 'the boring and sensible old one', 'too goody-goody', and 'really bossy' (a word commonly used). The following comment from a 12-year-old boy captures it neatly, contrasting the leadership styles of George and Julian. Whereas the former would 'just lead them into the wild', Julian 'sort of, gets the calculator out, if you know what I mean'.

George is generally seen as a more dangerous character, likely to go out on a limb over an issue: 'awesome', 'just the best', 'she's really the main person in the stories', everything sort of . . . goes round her'. I have already stressed the power struggle between her and Julian, but it is interesting to see respondents endorsing the view that Timmy is George's 'right-hand man', reinforcing her independence. The two are seen as a unit; and Timmy, of course, not Julian, was the second favourite Five character. George, in fact, annoyed some boys precisely because she did not seem to know her place:

> *Simon*: Yeah I don't like George because she was a girl but she was trying to be like a boy . . . Georgina. [. . .] She ought to be a proper girl.
> *Gillian*: That's sexist! (11-year-olds)

The other two Five members were certainly less popular, though each had adherents: 'When I was really young I always liked parts were [*sic*] Dick was given prominence' (m). 'He says interesting things and he's funny' (m, 14). Anne, too, though despised by many – described as 'really wet', 'a wimp', 'feeble', and 'namby-pamby' – was popular with others. For example, one immediately adduced evidence of Anne's brave deeds when the issue was raised: 'if you've read *The Famous Five Get into Trouble* [*sic*], well Anne climbs up a tree' (f, 10). Others were simply comfortable with Anne's dependence:

> I really like that yeah, 'cos . . . I always wanted . . . someone to look after me. I don't know. I'm just really different, aren't I? [. . .] I liked er, the boys looked after the girls, and it were just . . . I just liked it. [laughter from other girls] I like to get to do the chores at home.
> (Rebecca, 16)

What came across more strongly was that Anne, even if the butt of jokes, was an essential part of the Five. Thus a 10-year-old girl complained of one story (*FFIA*) that 'it wasn't really like the Famous Five adventure, 'cos Anne stayed at home all the time'.

As I have tried to show above, there is also a sense of power in Anne's role, and some readers certainly related to this. I would also suggest that Anne is important for another reason – not simply as a counterpoint to George, but as a signifier of the security of home, with her portable hearth. In fact, I think that many respondents were far more ambivalent about Anne than they made explicit: publicly they enjoyed despising her, but privately they found her presence comforting. This is borne out by the fact that she was the tenth most popular character with female respondents, whereas Dick was fifteenth.

But the main thing is the Five's unity. As George says in one story before the boys arrive, 'Why – we shan't be the Five – the Famous Five – if they don't come!' (*FOST*, p. 21). Many readers endorsed this, liking it when the Five were 'all together' (m, 15), 'all involved' (m, 15). As one adult put it, 'one relates to the camaraderie of the main characters' (m), and their friendship seems to be one of the main pleasures of the texts. Some explicitly commented on this: 'I liked the friendship between characters', the 'group feeling' (f), 'a happy collective' (m) – which added to the feeling of security in the books, especially as 'Everybody got on much better with each other than the children and adults I knew' (f). For others, the friendship went further, giving psychological comfort: 'I found the characters believable – and a lot more interesting than my friends in everyday life!' (f); 'The characters became my friends, I am an only child' (f).

There seems to be a recognition here that children's power lies in their solidarity – in being a unit, which we see being forged in the very first book. In the earlier volumes especially, the physical closeness of the Five, their bonding through touch, is quite explicit and unusual. For example, in *FGAA*, Dick and Julian hug the girls (pp. 17–18), and Dick repeats this gesture with George at the end of the story (p. 192). Dick calls Anne 'darling', and sends Julian to George with their love (p. 136). In one way, there should be nothing unusual about this, but given the stereotypical division of the sexes in many books, it is quite exceptional. This said, there is a suggestion that if anyone is left out of this emotional coterie, it is Julian, not George: 'George . . . linked her arms in Anne's and Dick's' (*FFIA*, p. 11). Timmy has already been mentioned in this connection, but the physical closeness that he can attain is a perfect metonym of their general unity, sometimes resulting in quite comical writing, as in *FGTDR*, when Fanny phones the cousins and asks for George; a neighbour replies, 'all the Five have already left, on their bicycles' (*FGTDR*, p. 13).[11]

Drawing on a poststructuralist notion of subjectivity, then, I would suggest that, for readers, the Five can be related to as a composite. Readers can enjoy a more 'grown-up' subject position in Julian, but also delight in George's obduracy and impetuosity, Timmy's intuition and physicality, Dick's appetite and cheeky humour, yet still have a place for Anne, as a more timid and homely self. As one male respondent put it, 'I came from a family of three boys and no sisters, and I suspect the brother–sister relationships portrayed in the books filled something I may have felt was lacking.' Though I shall deal with the issue of sexism in a later chapter, I am convinced that one of the main reasons that the books do not worry children in this regard is because of the Five's close affiliation, their bondedness, the close relationships, which some researchers have seen as a more female characteristic (Dinnerstein, 1977; Gilligan, 1982).

To sum up the three sections above, I have made the move from adult discursive threads about nationhood and class to the way that most children seem to read the texts. For them it is the empowerment of children against adults that appeals and, in this, 'St George' is the children's champion. She is the most outspoken against adults and their ways and, as we shall see in the next chapter, the one who most celebrates not growing-up, envisioning herself and Timmy on their island, forever. In this way we can begin to explain George's overall appeal across the sexes, while also recognizing her extra appeal for girls in standing up against patriarchy.

The Five and the 'F' word: pleasures of the text

Whereas adults might find some of the above discourses, on gender, nationhood and class, suitably serious, the young reader would probably code them as 'boring'. Children enjoy the companionship, as has just been argued, but this is just one of the pleasures of the texts. The word 'companion' is, literally, someone with whom you break bread, and it would be impossible to think of the Five without food – that is, 'Food with a capital F' (*FHMTS*, p. 11). But besides food, also involved are freedom, leisure and the experience of holidays in general. I shall also suggest that for many readers the pleasure of the text is not merely a mental enjoyment, but a sensual one.

The food scenes in the stories are certainly memorable. Barker confesses that he always thought 'condensed' meant sweet, after Blyton's evocative description of condensed milk as a 'creamy, sweet liquid' (Barker, 1982, p. 10), and Jan Leeming (1982) admits that she tried to make her own 'honey-pop' biscuits, inspired by the 'Faraway Tree' books. Other readers readily endorse this: 'Whenever I eat popping candy now I still feel like I'm in erm, Enid Blyton books' (f, 17); and:

> The one thing which remains most valid in my mind next to the tension of each mystery is the food scenes. In every book there was

> at least three mouthwatering descriptions of the feasts (always with ginger ale). It makes me hungry just thinking about it now. (f)

Older readers, who experienced rationing up until the early 1950s, confessed that the books were particularly attractive in this regard. This was even more potent for overseas readers, for whom some of the items were pure fantasy:

> she made mundane things like fresh bread and butter sound so mouth watering. For years i lusted for hot buttered scones, treacle tart, blackmange [*sic*] pudding (without having the slightest clue as to what they were). I got the chance to taste the stuff years later when i spent some time in england. I don't think i've ever been so disillusioned. (m)

For some, the cultural shock was even worse, as this Hindu reader related:

> I found her description of food items and activities centered around eating, most delightful. I remember becoming extremely curious & fantasising about food items that I wasn't very likely to come across in my pretty vegetarian environment. A hilarious incident comes to mind. After reading several books, where 'tongue sandwiches' were mentioned, I had this amazing mental idea of what it might be (a kind of culinary exotica that people-who-are-cool-must-eat -at-picnics!! :-)). When my mother finally explained to me what it really was, I remember being quite shocked. (f)[12]

Certainly the texts are full of references to food, such that some critics have sought a psychoanalytical explanation.[13] Woods, for example, describes the food as more reminiscent of an orgy in an Edwardian emporium than a modern child's idea of a good 'blow-out. . . . This is not food it is archetypal feasting, the author's longing for the palmy days of her own childhood' (Woods, 1969, p. 13; also Barker, 1982). This does not seem to be so in Blyton's case, for she herself had little interest in food (Smallwood, 1989) and it certainly doesn't feature in her autobiography. Also, some of the foods she mentions were not even around in her childhood, such as Spam, which only became popular during the Second World War. Other writers, like Katz, see food more explicitly as 'the sex of children's literature' (Katz, 1980, p. 192). The two are obviously closely related, but ultimately this seems a reductionist move, in that each has its own pleasures; it is also rather adult-centred – as true, perhaps, as a child saying that sex might be the food of adults' literature.

If one were to make any psychoanalytical connection, Klein's perspective would seem most apposite, in that she sees the provision of food as associated with the offer of the breast, and its withholding in similar terms. Defined in this way, there are certainly many examples of good and bad mothers in the Five stories. Mrs. Stick would be a good example of the latter, with Mrs. Andrews exemplifying the former;[14] significantly, the latter is only described in terms of her larder: 'Did you get a peep into that enormous larder of his mother's? It's like a great cave, goes right back into the wall, with dozens of stone shelves – and all filled with food' (Dick speaking, predictably, *FGOTC*, p. 81). When the Five are given the sustenance they need, they are emotional putty: 'I could hug you', says Julian, when offered food in *FOHT* (p. 67), a sentiment the others endorse. Feelings are frequently demonstrated in this way, as the following extract shows:

> 'Best sandwiches I've ever tasted,' he said. 'I do like those sardine ones. Does your mother make them for you? I wish I had a mother. Mine died ages ago.'
>
> There was a sympathetic silence. The four could not think of any worse thing to happen to a boy or girl. They offered Martin the nicest buns, and the biggest piece of cake immediately.
>
> (*FOKIA*, pp. 76–7)

This is a common compensation, which their cook, Joanna (the name changes from Joan), also uses: 'If she thought anyone was upset, she offered them her best and freshest food' (*FOKIA*, p. 105). Dick feels that cooks should be seen on a level with scientists and writers, putting a traditionally female activity on a par with more celebrated male ones: 'You know, I do think good cooks deserve some kind of decoration, just as much as good soldiers or scientists, or writers. I should give Joanna the O.B.C.B.E. [Order of the Best Cooks of the British Empire]' (*FOKIA*, p. 105).

Food, then, is about bonding and companionship. And, in reading the books, many readers like to join in, sharing the oral satisfaction. I have already confessed to my own indulgence with 'Twiglets', and other readers have made similar confessions: 'memories of eating picallilli butties' (f) or reading with 'a copious supply of digestive biscuits' (f).

Clearly, the security of eating contrasts poignantly with the danger of adventure. But eating is only one way this emulation of their heroes is achieved. Other readers hid themselves away, creating, like Anne, little hearths, or nest-like areas. These are a few of the places readers confessed to reading: 'secret place – in winter in built in wardrobe (den) over hot water pipes (warm!)', 'by the fireside', 'sit hunched up in the cupboard half of the airing cupboard (having removed the lego and meccano, etc) with a torch', 'secret place – in a corner of the living room behind the sofa', 'on a sofa sitting upside down'. I am reminded of Ernst Bloch's description of the ideal reading environment for detective stories: 'The setting . . . is just too cozy. In a comfortable chair, under the nocturnal floor lamp with tea, rum, and tobacco, personally secure and peacefully immersed in dangerous things, which are shallow' (Bloch, 1988, p. 245).

It is also reminiscent of the pleasures mentioned by soap fans (Hobson, 1982) and romance readers (Radway, 1984), part of which is precisely the space that these texts give them to resist their usual activities under patriarchy. For the following Blyton reader, this resistance is more explicit: 'In the class room while a class was going on had immense satisfaction doing that :-). Used to have a competition about who can complete reading a full book without getting caught' (m). However, the most popular place to read Blyton was bed, 'Under the bedcovers with a torch when my parents insisted on the light being switched off'. Some would engage in their own personal 'midnight feasts', too. Obviously this is another challenge to parental authority, but it is also a way of emulating the Five; in *FGOTC* (p. 25), for instance, the Five are depicted in their 'warm, soft sleeping-bags' eating chocolate and biscuits.

Sleep is quite prevalent in the books. Despite their Englishness, the Five seem to be firm believers in the siesta: after a picnic, on a sunny day, the Five are likely to sprawl on the grass and doze (for example, *FGIT*, p. 23). Again, it clearly marks out leisure time. But even their night-time sleeping activities are alluringly described, particularly the shift in consciousness from what Schutz (1962) terms one 'life-world' to another. The following passage, for instance, with Julian falling asleep, is typical:

> He didn't hear Timmy howling outside once more. He didn't hear the screech owl that made the night hideous on the hill. He didn't see the moon slide down the sky.
>
> (*FGIT*, p. 111).

We, the readers, are privy to the background noise of the Blyton universe, where nature diurnally proceeds. As with Noddy, there is no danger of non-existence. However, sleep also functions in another way, which is to shift us into the adventure realm. This is most clearly done in *FGOIC*, where the Five fall asleep in the afternoon, waking to observe a circus going by (pp. 10–11), which provides the venue for their adventure. In *FOKIA*, there is a passage quite reminiscent of Carroll's *Alice in Wonderland*, with Timmy rabbiting while the children sleep. George wakens to find that Timmy has gone down an extra deep rabbit hole, and then proceeds to follow him (*FOKIA*, p. 79). It should also be noted that their adventures are themselves often described as dream-like:

> 'This is a most peculiar adventure to have.'
> 'It's probably a dream,' said Julian, and laughed. 'No – not even a dream could be so mad.'
>
> (*FGTMM*, p. 130)

The reader is then shifted into the 'mythic' time of the story: a fantasy realm from which normal life is bracketed off; a time in which to indulge one's leisure, preferably while eating. Dick expresses this in a quite sybaritic way: 'I can't think of anything nicer than lying down on hot sand with the sun on every part of my body, eating an ice-cream, and knowing there are still three weeks' holiday in front of us' (*FHPOF*, p. 9). The mood of this echoes Gabriel Josipovici's description of his 'earliest memory of the pleasure of books':

> I lie in the sun at the poolside in the small town in Egypt where I grew up. It is midday. I am suddenly overwhelmed with pleasure at the thought of the long afternoon siesta when I will be able to carry on reading Enid Blyton's *The Castle of Adventure*.
>
> (Josipovici, 1997, p. 165)

Holidays, of course, are the key markers of this mythic time – a legitimate 'time-out' for children. Dick expressly draws attention to this word as 'the nicest . . . in the English language' (*FHMTS*, p. 11). Holidays are counterposed with school, which features only briefly in one book (*FOHT*). Generally, any mention of school is forbidden – and we have already seen how the word 'teacher' is used as an insult. For the holiday period the rules of ordinary existence are in abeyance, if not occasionally inverted in the manner of Bakhtin's carnival time. Rules belong to 'the Law of the Father', where the Symbolic realm of school holds sway, where they have to suffer the fact that, as George puts it, 'Grown-ups were so powerful, and could dole out all kinds of punishments' (*FGAA*, p. 102). In the stories, Quentin is their chief representative – an unpredictable God. Even when he is not seen, his presence is felt throughout the house, and further afield – given that he seems to be known worldwide. Quentin is someone who sends his daughter away to school then resents her presence in the holiday; he is someone who cannot understand a colleague putting his daughter's safety ahead of work (*FHPOF*). It is only natural then that one of the worst impositions on the Five is being given a holiday tutor. This happens only once (*FGAA*), but his invasion is clearly resented, and he effectively spoils their adventure. It is fitting therefore, that this school representative turns out to be a crook and gets his come-uppance.

The holiday realm is also a place where normal rules don't obtain, where things take on heightened significance. Thus, in *FHMTS*, Julian reflects on their going out in a boat called *Adventure*. 'We might have *known* something would happen!' (p. 93). All that is necessary is their coalescence; as Anne puts it, 'I do think it's funny the way we always plunge into something peculiar when we're together' (*FOHT*, p. 110). And, of course, they are together as and when any reader opens a book and joins them, or envisions them. The transition into this fantasy realm is expertly achieved, though going back to the books as an adult, I was surprised at how long it takes for the adventure to begin. In fact, for a few readers, it was too long: 'I think that the beginning of her books are really boring but as it goes along it gets more interesting'. (f, 12); 'Though it was a mystery book, half the book was taken up with them just eating and partying' (m).

For others, though, it is precisely this period of anticipation that is enjoyable. Readers wallow in the new-found freedom of the children from the normal restrictions of life, as the Five re-unite and simply enjoy each other's company. And, of course, part of the contract with the reader is the expectancy this generates, for once the Five are together, the elements are in place, and something must happen. Druce describes this pre-adventure period as one of 'ennui', drawing parallels with the Bond books (where it is more applicable), but to me it seems more like a time of delicious anticipation, as one of the books has it: 'Really, the start of a holiday was the happiest thing in the world!' (*FGTBH*, p. 26). It is similar to what Freud calls 'forepleasure', a notion that Brooks (1984) picks up in his discussion of plot, and, certainly, we find Blyton teasing readers as they journey through the text. Sometimes she even toys with the notion of withholding adventure, as in *FGOIC*, where the other members go along with Anne's wish to have 'an *ordinary* holiday . . . not *too* exciting'; adventurous incidents are continually declined (pp. 32, 82).

Conclusion

In this chapter, I have re-examined the Five books in terms of some of the main social criticisms made of them: that they are anglocentric and class*ist*. I have sought to argue that they are not so *in any simplistic way*. I then tried to move away from the critics' home-ground – basically an adult's perspective – to find out what pleasures children derive from the books. Drawing on the comments of respondents, I have argued that, of any *isms*, ageism is the most appropriate, with children being empowered in a world where adults usually rule. I then finished by looking at other areas where readers find pleasure in her books. These focus on adventure on the one side, and comfort and security on the other: food and drink, setting-up homes, sleeping, and enjoying holidays are all given space in the books. But more than this, the pleasures are not just textual; they are sensual, visceral even, with readers emulating the Five's activities. Hence they are both *physically* comforted, secure within themselves, and *imaginatively* satisfied too, in fantasy, in being taken out of themselves.

I shall return to these issues in later chapters, suggesting some deeper pleasures to be found in Blyton. Briefly, though, it is worth emphasizing how much the books feature interstitial realms – whether holidays, the margins of sleep, or the literally interstitial world of passages between walls – unknown ways that most never encounter, but pass across. The Five open up these secret ways to their readers as readily as their readers open up the Five's books; and however dark the passages might be, the passages of text – themselves probed by torchlight – are always light enough.

7

Sexism or Subversion? Querying Gender Relations in the Famous Five and Malory Towers

Social readings: an introduction

When adults (as opposed to children) talk about Blyton, two of the discourses most ready to hand are those of sexism and racism. For much of her writing career such accusations were simply undeveloped: the sexual division of labour, codes of behaviour, sexual differences in ability, were regarded by many as natural, thus not subjects about which 'difference' was much debated. It was only in the sixties that social criticism of Blyton's books began to be heard. But, as with other areas so far discussed, here too we find oppositional views: not only contradictory opinions, but also blatant misreadings, some of which have become part of popular mythology.

Blyton became a standard target in works on sexism, with Rosemary Stones even taking her book title – *Pour Out the Cocoa, Janet* (1983) – from Blyton's Secret Seven.[1] This said, there is little that goes much further than the fleeting comment, usually about Anne being 'a proper little housewife', beautifully captured by the Comic Strip (1982), where Anne can be observed sweeping the grass at their campsite. Dixon (1977a), though fiercely critical of most aspects of Blyton, is surprisingly silent on her sexism, as were contributors to the celebrated *New Statesman* (1980) debate. Even Cadogan and Craig (1976), who do take a more serious look at this issue, inexplicably omit some of Blyton's key works – her school stories. In this chapter I intend to look at the most popular of these, the Malory Towers books, together with the *bête noire* of critics in this area, the Famous Five. But first, a few words about 'sexism' seem in order.

In some of the criticism mentioned above it seems enough to alight on a signifier derogating females to shout 'Sexism!'. However, I would argue that sexism is not a *thing* but a *process*. Nothing is innately sexist; rather, sexism draws its energy from relations of power. Thus, even terms like 'bitch' and 'dyke' have been appropriated by feminists and given positive connotations; but, to know the connotation, one must look at the word in context, and at the audience's perception of that context. Of course, as society is patriarchal (that is, the institutional sites of power are mostly controlled by males), it will be the case that certain meanings predominate – just as the concept of sexism is itself normally concerned with the power of men over women, not vice versa. But the concern is still with how these relations are played out, both in the texts and by their readers. For adults simply to attach the label 'sexist' to this material effectively underwrites a particular state of affairs, making it seem a *fait accompli*.

Five have a gender-ful time?

The daughter of a friend was told at school that she should not be reading Blyton's books because they were 'sexy'. The parents eventually established that it was 'sexist' that the teacher had meant, and explained the concept to her. For the girl this immediately made sense; she replied that it was obvious the books would be sexist given when they were written. In other words, this girl had enjoyed the stories, but was in no way being sold into gender slavery by them. Many of the schoolchildren I talked to endorsed this view:

> I think they should have left them, 'cos that's how things were done. (f, 15)
>
> When they were written they were – I don't know – they were a different type of times [. . .] I think they should keep them as they are, and if you don't like them as they are, then don't read them. (f, 10)
>
> I think the old ones are better 'cos it portrayed the better, like, Enid Blyton wanted to show how it was like in that time, and that was a sexist age then, so, if you change it like the revised versions where some of the sexism's been taken out it just doesn't work as well. . . . They shouldn't be altered. (m, 15)

The critics' view

It is George who has been most criticized, called 'the ultimate stereotype' by Margery Fisher (1986, p. 233). Dixon endorses this view, of her being 'a very bad case of . . . penis-envy' (Dixon, 1974, p. 53). Cadogan and Craig too, describe George as being in a 'false position . . . like all tomboys, she can be "as good as", but this implies a basic deficiency. She never can be the genuine article'. They say that 'there is no suggestion that . . . [George's] fantasy of being a boy is just as "normal" as Anne's acceptance of a "housewifely" role'; rather, 'the author's view of girls who "pretend to be boys" [is] that they are pretentious and silly. They will "grow out" of it; the growing out is a process of adjustment' (Cadogan and Craig, 1976, pp. 338–43).

Before looking more closely at the texts, let me begin by questioning whether Blyton's views were as orthodox as these authors suggest. The tomboy character does seem to have had a particular appeal for Blyton. She herself cited Alcott's *Little Women* as one of her favourite books, with its famous tomboy, Jo. Blyton certainly has several outspoken females in her books: George, of course, Susie in the Secret Seven, and a number of girls in her school series – Bobby, Carlotta and Claudine in St. Clare's, Darrell, Alicia and Bill in Malory Towers. Notably, it is these characters that are given the more positive qualities, whereas the more conventionally 'feminine' ones are criticized for being concerned with superficial matters, like their appearance. In other words, in a world of girls, there is no notion of penis-envy: the girls can be strong in their own right.

Cadogan and Craig also mention the 'author's view', which, in Blyton's case, also questions normality. We have seen how she resented domestic chores as a child; we also know that, even in her twenties, she liked to be referred to as Richard, or 'cabin-boy', and that she supposedly modelled the character of George on herself (Stoney, 1974). Finally, as an adult, she certainly asserted herself effectively in the intensely male world of publishing. In view of this, it hardly seems likely that she would portray Anne as the paragon, George the 'queer' one. Blyton had too much invested in George for this – something of which most readers seem keenly aware (she was easily Blyton's all-time favourite character): 'I like George best . . . she sort of liked getting into adventures, more than all the others' (f, 10), 'she was bold!' (f), 'she was definitely a role model much to the dismay of my mother' (f). 'I really enjoyed the way George would stand up against authority' (f); one 8 year-old girl added on her questionnaire, 'P.S. I would like to be called George'. But it was not only girls; boys, too, were impressed, like this 9-year-old: 'George . . . she's like, she's probably the most adventurous of them all. She's clever.' Although, for girls, there was undoubtedly the added thrill of her gender: 'it was good to see a woman doing it', as one 16-year-old said, elevating George still further. Even antipathetic critics unwittingly do the same, like Dohm (1955, p. 360) commenting that George 'is the one allowed to find most clues or unmask the criminals'. She also says that George is 'in her teens', as does Druce (1992, p. 115), reflecting the character's impact.

However, though impressive, readers were not indiscriminate in their praise:

> I liked George . . . because she refused to be patronised because she was a girl or left out of the most exciting parts of the adventures. I also liked the way she often rebelled against adult authority. I didn't totally identify with her though, because I myself did not want to be, or look like, a boy. (f)

The texts

Following my earlier comments, I shall argue that the Five books are particularly effective in dramatizing power relationships between the sexes. The first book of the series, *FOTI* (1942), demonstrates this struggle well. George is introduced as a loner, but it is precisely by standing apart from society that she manages to be powerful. As she tells Anne:

> 'if they're going to be nasty to me I shan't take any notice of *them* . . . I didn't want any of you to come, anyway. Interfering with my life here! I'm quite happy on my own.'
>
> (*FOTI*, p. 20)

The more she becomes part of the Five, the more she is expected to conform. Bodily, she can still present an image of empowerment, but in relationships, she comes up against the 'almost grown-up' Julian, and patriarchy in general.

Over the course of the first six books – which was all Blyton initially intended to write – George's power can be seen to erode. It is only by stepping outside the circle of the Five that she can assert herself. Timmy is particularly useful here, for although he 'naturally' stands apart from this struggle, he implicitly increases George's prowess.

In *FOTI*, George's powers are clearly foregrounded (and this, of course, was written in the early years of the war, when women were being called upon to step outside traditional gender roles; children, too, were more independent as evacuees). George can handle a boat like a man, whereas it is doubted whether Dick could even row it ashore. She can swim better than the boys, too. Indeed, she is given the most physical action in the book, destroying the crooks' boat with an axe. Even Julian defers to her;

for example, when exploring the wreck, 'Julian did as he was told . . . George clambered up'; and later: 'Julian had a torch. He handed it to George . . . George switched on the torch and then swung herself down the ladder. The others followed' (ibid., p. 82). Despite not appearing till the second chapter, George is given more dialogue than any of the other children in the book.

At the end, then, we might say that George has joined the Symbolic order: they – the Famous Five – are henceforward an entity, with their name in the public domain; that is, both within the text, in the local newspapers, and outside it, among readers. But even if George has accepted that 'no man is an island' – despite owning one, and being 'no man'! – she has not forsaken her independence. First, she maintains her own version of her given name, and insists others use it, rather than the feminized, *-ina* form (her father, Quentin, tries to impose this more than most: 'Don't be silly, Georgina' (p. 106)). She thus manages to define her own identity rather than accepting that of others. Secondly, she has Timmy – a formidable ally, and one who stands alongside her as something not quite civilized (as one girl said in interview, 'George and Timmy is like, not as individuals – they weren't really individuals, they were like . . . George-and-Timmy'). These things George insists on preserving, even though she accepts the idea of boarding school.

In the second book (*FGAA*) George's acceptance of a more socialized existence is developed. Greater patriarchal forces are ranged against her: not only Quentin and Julian, but also the tutor, Mr Roland, a big, bearded man, who tries hard to make her respond to 'Georg*ina*'. Anne's willingness to accept Mr Roland's positioning of girls is nicely contrasted with George's rebellion. In fact, Mr Roland and Quentin seem to collude in this – as do the other children, especially Julian. However, George's (and Timothy's) intuitions about Roland turn out to be right, as she unearths the secrets of her, and her mother's home.

The third book (*FRAT*) shows the continuing development of the Five as a team, this time against the malevolent Sticks. But there is also the question of Julian's increasing assertiveness. However, being Kirrin-based, George still has the edge. In *FGTST* (no. 4), Julian is more domineering, arguing for the boys' rightful position at the centre of any adventure. Interestingly, this is the first story to be based away from Kirrin, at a place owned by a friend of the boys. The Five do start at Kirrin, however, and George's parents still feature, whereas in the fifth book neither Kirrin nor George's parents appear at all. Away from George's seat of power, Julian is a more assertive leader:

> 'I'm old enough to look after you all.'
>
> 'Pooh!' said George. 'I don't want any looking after, thank you. And anyway, if we want looking after, Timmy can do that.'
>
> (*FGOIC*, pp. 16–17)

Julian's authority is endorsed by his father:

> 'You will be in complete charge, you understand, Julian. . . . You are old enough now to be really responsible. The others must realize that you are in charge and they must do as you say.'
>
> (ibid., pp. 20–1)

But George adds, 'And Timmy will be in charge, too. . . . He's just as responsible as Julian' – a statement taken up first by Anne, Dick, then finally, their Mother: 'You certainly wouldn't be allowed to go without Timmy'.

The struggle between Julian and George continues on their holiday, ending only when Julian manages to use Anne as an excuse for having his way, 'Timmy or no Timmy' (p. 67). Even so, the reader is left in no doubt that George has not given in for herself. Julian is imperious in victory: 'You get the breakfast, Anne and George, and Dick and I will catch the horses' (p. 68).

The sixth and, at the time of its writing, supposedly the last Famous Five (*FOKIA*), is particularly interesting. Here George's power suffers further erosion. First there is Quentin's appropriation of Kirrin Island (it is emphasized in the first book that the island was passed to George through her mother, not her father).[2] On it Quentin erects 'a tall, thin tower, rather like a lighthouse. At the top was a glass-enclosed room, which glittered in the sun' (*FOKIA*, p. 23). In Lacanian terms, we have here the phallus, the Law of the Father (this 'erection' pulses with energy periodically, and the whole thing blazes with light!). Even James, the fisher-boy, seems to delight in George's loss: '"Your father's got the island, I see," he said to George with a grin. "Bad luck, Miss"' (ibid., p. 66). It is worth noting that James calls her 'miss' here, whereas he has previously called her 'master'. Prophetically, he asks George if she'd like to leave Timmy with him; for George's next sacrifice soon follows, as her father asks to borrow Timmy. After this we find her uncharacteristically described making the tea and washing-up, without protest.

We might suppose from the above that the tamed shrew now knows her place. Not so: she reasserts herself by going off to her island, alone, at night (the only other time she does this is, significantly, in the very last of the series). Quentin, prompted by a crook calling George his brave 'son', is forced to recognize her on her own terms, and the book ends, significantly, with his erection being destroyed: '"Can we . . . watch the tower being taken down tomorrow?" begged George. "Do say yes!"' (ibid., p. 191).

These gender struggles are reinvoked in the following books, but I think the point is made. What needs emphasizing, however, is a gradual downplaying of George's power. Thus, by the seventh adventure, the growing control of the boys is clearly evident. Julian actually says to George at one point, 'This is my adventure and Dick's – and perhaps Jock's. Not yours or Anne's' (*FGOTC*, p. 112). The narrator, too, endorses this marginalization. Thus, Mr Luffy is described as a good swimmer, 'faster even than Julian' (p. 85) – not, note, 'George', albeit in the first book she was the fastest.

The undermining of George's independence is increasingly characteristic of the Five books, read in chronological order, with Julian seeking to bring her into line – even in her own home:

> 'Mother, how *could* you take people in when you knew we were coming home today?'
>
> 'That's enough, George', said Julian. . . .
>
> (*FGTDR*, p. 23)

In the final adventure (*FATA*) George is neglected to the extent of being mislaid by Blyton. In Chapter 4 we are told that George and the boys set off from a professor's house to Kirrin on the bus; then, in the next chapter, while the boys are still away, George is found patiently sitting inside the house!

Once again though, the patriarchal order is confounded, despite Julian laying down the law: 'There's to be no back-chat from *you*, George' (*FATA*, p. 23). This is made more explicit later, when Julian forbids her to go to her island: 'You heard what I said, George. You are *not* to go!' He will go instead, he says, after all, 'If danger was about, he could deal with it better than George could. After all, she was only a *girl*!' (pp. 134–5). To his surprise, she complies. But, as in that earlier 'final' book of the series, George takes matters into her own hands. She returns to her personal island, alone, at night, and thereafter dispatches the crooks. (This return is not necessary, but it is obviously a place of symbolic power for George, and for Five readers generally, one of whom referred to it as 'George's house' (m, 9).) In this book George ends up with one of the longest solo performances of the series. Not only does she do all this single-handedly, but the entire series ends on her: 'What an exciting time we've had! I really did enjoy every minute of it! So did we, George. Hurry up and fall into another adventure' (p. 176). In fact, it ends on such a celebratory note that the initial plot mechanism – the quarantining of George's family – is completely forgotten.

A token boy?

Despite George's overall triumph, Cadogan and Craig's criticism that George is a token boy – as good as, but not the real thing – warrants investigation. First, it wants stressing that the term used – 'as good as' – is Blyton's own: it is Blyton who makes this an issue, having both boys accuse George of being a fake. The point is, such discussions of what constitutes gender-appropriate behaviour occur throughout the series. For example, here is Toby, explaining why George should not go to see an airfield:

> 'But you're a *girl*,' said Toby. 'Girls don't understand the first thing about aeroplanes or motor-cars or ships – or spiders either, come to that! I really don't think you'd be interested, Georgina dear.'
>
> 'My name is *not* Georgina,' said George furiously. 'And don't call me "dear".'
>
> (*FGTBH*, p. 67)

Not only interests, but looks are debated too, as with Dick:

> 'Jolly girlish-looking boy you are, that's all I can say.'
>
> George flared up at once. 'Don't be mean! I'm *not* girlish-looking. I've far more freckles than you have, for one thing, and better eyebrows. *And* I can make my voice go deep.'
>
> (*FOKIA*, p. 64)

The problem of what is appropriate behaviour for the sexes is something that concerns children a great deal. Blyton, I am suggesting, did not just make George another tomboy; rather, Blyton put the whole debate about sexism on the agenda in this series. Nevertheless, it might still be claimed that George is nothing more than a token boy. What makes her different, I would argue, is her emotional reaction to things – something that Dick tackles her about later in this same book: 'Just like a girl, can't help blabbing' (*FOKIA*, p. 86). George shows her emotions more than any other character in the series, much to her chagrin, whether it be tearfulness, her love for Timmy (for instance, '"Lie down here by the fire, darling" . . . He put his head on her knee. She stroked him and whispered to him. . . . George settled down with her head on his neck' – *FGAA*, p. 110), or simply her passionate anger. It is this that distances her from the boys. In the first book, George cries five times – once more than Anne, and two of the latter's tearful episodes are a result of being kicked under the table; George's passionate nature is clear; she 'sobbed with rage . . . drying her eyes . . . furious with herself for crying' (*FOTI*, p. 104). In *FRAT* she loses not only her appetite but also her spirit of adventure, the former returning with a vengeance only when her mother is better (*FRAT*, p. 65).

Of course, I am not seeking to argue that girls should be 'emotional', boys 'rational' – although some feminists have sailed close to this 'essence of femininity' shore.[3] However, it is what makes George more intriguing, and not simply a token boy. Henry, another tomboy in the series, is cited by Cadogan and Craig to clinch their argument that George is not the real thing, in contrast to Anne. Yet a close look at the text shows that Henry (Henrietta) is depicted more as a contrast to George. Early in the story we find Henry cleaning her clothes and mending her riding jacket in anticipation of Julian and Dick's arrival (*FGTMM*, p. 19) – something George would never do. In addition, Henry is later to discover that she does not have George's mettle, deferring, unlike George, to a boy. Strangely, Cadogan and Craig omit to mention Jo, who is the main alternative tomboy in the series, and clearly a favourite of Blyton's, given her record three appearances. She effortlessly surpasses the Five in daring and capability – rescuing them all, boys included, from various scrapes.

Let us now turn to Anne, who is an obvious target for those adopting a crude approach to sexism. With comments like, 'You'd never get your bunks made, or your meals cooked, or the caravans kept clean if it wasn't for me! . . . I love having two houses on wheels to look after' (*FGOIC*, p. 40), it is easy to see why. But this is a narrow view, neglecting the fact that many girls do enjoy this behaviour, and are empowered by it, given the confines of a patriarchal society (Anne was tenth most popular character with females). In other words, they use their control of the domestic sphere to enable them in others. As Anne proclaims, 'although Julian thinks he's in charge of us, *I* am really!' Here is Anne in action:

> 'I'll just see what we've got in the larder, Julian,' said Anne, getting up. She knew perfectly well what there was in the larder – but it made her feel grown-up and important to go and look. It was nice to feel

> like that when she so often felt small and young, and the others were big and knew so much.
>
> (ibid., pp. 61–2)

There are various examples of Anne engaging in what Foucault terms the 'microphysics of power' to good effect, one of which I quoted earlier. Here is a similar instance from *FHWT*:

> 'There are twelve [sausages],' said Anne, giving Dick the bag. 'Three each. None for Timmy! . . . Julian, will you get me some water, please? There's the pail, over there. I want to peel the potatoes. George, can you possibly open the peaches without cutting yourself like you did last time?'
>
> 'Yes, Captain!' said George . . . (p. 29)

It is clearly because of Anne's power in the domestic sphere that some of my respondents came to see her as having a key role, like Diana (9), who thought Anne was the leader, alongside Julian. I asked her why:

> *Diana*: Well, she's the oldest girl and you need a, like a girl because boys are a bit funny sometimes, silly, and get silly and leave it . . .
>
> *DR*: What does Anne tell them to do then?
>
> *Diana*: Well she tells them to wash and stay clean when they're on adventures.

It would be wrong therefore, to belittle Anne's behaviour, particularly as it still represents a reality for many women. Rather than ignoring it, Blyton's books seem to engage in a dialogue about it – addressing it as an issue. By pretending that the world is suddenly free of these power struggles, that four-fifths of the Five habitually engage in washing up (as some revisions have it), is to miss the tensions that Blyton explored. The latter might be a desirable state but, as most ethnography shows, it is not yet a reality. To pretend it is so 'for the sake of children' is, I would suggest, to demean them. In the Five books, this sort of equality is not a given: it is fought for. Sometimes George wins – as in the instance below – but by no means predictably:

> 'You three girls must wash up for me afterwards' . . .
>
> 'Why can't the boys help?' said George at once.
>
> '*I'll* do the washing-up,' said Anne with a sudden grin. 'You four *boys* can go out to the stables!'

> Dick gave her a good-natured shove. 'You know we'll help, even if we're not good at it.'
>
> (*FGTMM*, p. 86)

So, George not only queries washing-up as 'women's work', but in this instance involves the boys.

Those who simply pick out Anne's behaviour miss the intricacy of the sex war being waged. Without the contrast of Anne, George's behaviour would not appear half so subversive. Moreover, without Anne's representation of the traditional female role, the books would all too readily celebrate traditional male behaviour – something in which George is overly willing to collude. Thus, when Julian congratulates George for being 'more like a boy than ever', simply because she acts magnanimously, we not only have George's smugness presented, but also Anne's 'indignant' reaction: 'It isn't *only* boys that can learn to give in decently' (*FOKIA*, p. 25). Elsewhere, Anne more explicitly disparages both George and males generally, calling her as 'ham-handed as a boy' (*FHMTS*, p. 78).

So, rather than stick this essentialist label, 'sexist' on the books, I would prefer to say that they explore sexism in a way to which children can relate. To take away this dimension is to deny children some of the pleasure of the texts – particularly in the person of George. At a time when boys' and girls' books were more clearly demarcated, it was to Blyton's credit that she produced 'adventures for boys and girls' (as the early subtitles have it) – and created a female character that boys not only find acceptable, but positively rate (more so than Julian). This seems to be the case even today. In Millard's survey of reading, the favourite writers for 11–12-year-old boys were, 'apart from Enid Blyton . . . all men' (Millard, 1997, p. 54).

Trying to launder the books in terms of 'political correctness' is to undermine children's own capacities – particularly those of girls; girls, it is often reasoned, need to be protected from such material. But to do this is to perpetuate the very discourse that many are trying to circumvent (that is, perpetuating the notion that girls really do need wrapping in cotton-wool). As the anecdote on page 110 demonstrates, this attitude can frequently backfire.

Some modern books miss the tension of the Famous Five precisely because they inscribe a world of unlikely equality – whereas many children experience a world that is not like this. The Five, I would contend, allow children to take part in the struggle, to fight it themselves, rather than be protected from it. It is interesting here to note the research of

Davies (1989), who found that some 'feminist' versions of fairy-tales were often resisted by children, chiefly, she theorizes, because the children were caught, insecurely, in a double-bind. On the one hand their sense of personhood was mapped out in bi-polar gender terms, while on the other, these tales confounded such gender expectations. Perhaps books that start from a position that mirrors what is still the gender reality of many children, might have more success in questioning that identity.

Blyton's Famous Five engage in this struggle. However, I am not trying to promote Blyton as a feminist *avant le lettre*. She may have toyed with her own childhood resistance to the domestic role, but her vision is decidedly circumscribed. The majority of her adults are stereotypically presented. Moreover, though the children are liberated from this stereotyping for a period, their ambitions are in keeping with the patriarchal views of the time. Hence George comments at one point, 'I shall NEVER marry a scientist' (*FFIA*, p. 18) – never considering whether she might *become* one, or even decide against marrying. Such speculation is only for the boys; it is Julian who says, 'I wouldn't mind being a scientist myself' (*FOKIA*, p. 28).

Having said this, the point about the Five is that their adventures celebrate the fact of not being grown-up, of being apart from the adults; and this is especially true of George. It is interesting that many find that George matures least over the course of the series, for George is undoubtedly the Peter Pan of the group: 'There can't be anything nicer in the world than this – being with the others, having fun with them. No – I don't want to grow up!' (*FGTBH*, p. 46).

It is also worth noting that not all the adults fit into the boring, stereotypical mould. But those that escape, who are less gender stereotyped, are those on the periphery of society. Thus, in *FHWT*, we have Anita who makes her husband – Alfredo – do some of the chores, much to Anne's surprise. This is specifically drawn attention to; Dick comments, on first seeing her, 'What a tiny wife he has! I bet he makes her run around him, and wait on him hand and foot' (*FHWT*, p. 43), but then Anne points to Alfredo fetching water for his wife. He also cooks the breakfast, and is later seen pegging out washing: 'It seemed a most unsuitable thing for a fire-eater to do, but Alfredo didn't seem to mind' (ibid., pp. 78–9). Like George, the only way that they can manage to maintain this difference is by standing slightly aside from mainstream society, by being Other. This is emphasized at the end of the book, too, for, though the gypsy fair-folk are on the side of good, they are also outside the law; as Jo puts it, 'No gypsy ever asked the police for help' (ibid., p. 142) and, sure enough, when the police arrive, 'Immediately almost all the fair-folk melted away into the darkness' (ibid., p. 180).

Schooling the female

Blyton wrote three school series plus the often neglected *Mischief at St. Rollo's* (1947b).[4] The Naughtiest Girl series came first (1940–45), St. Clare's next (1941–45), followed by the six Malory Towers books (1946–51). The last has been the most popular with readers (it was her third most popular series in my survey) and I shall give it most space here. But first, some comments on the Naughtiest Girl, which some have declared to be progressive, being set in a co-educational boarding school, with sexism challenged by 'the fact that the school is run by two women' (Ray, 1982, p. 197). Mullan (1987a, pp. 95–6) has taken issue with this, asserting that Ray is 'easily pleased'. However, he does not make a case either, simply quoting, without comment, a fairly extensive and inconsequential scene in which Elizabeth – the naughtiest girl – argues with a boy, Julian, about stealing. Mullan, one would have to say, is himself easily satisfied. There is no attempt to look at this passage in the context of the whole story (for instance, that Elizabeth later comforts Julian when he breaks down in tears – *nota bene* – and, finally, makes both Julian and another weak boy see the error of their ways). Unfortunately, neither critic really analyses what sexism means, so the debate goes no further. Mullan makes no mention of Frith, either, who also looked at the school stories, drawing on the views of fans. She found that the Naughtiest Girl series was actually less popular than the others with readers. One girl, Rachel, describes the series as more realistic, but not as enjoyable. Revealingly, the Naughtiest Girl series was not much re-read, but the others were, repeatedly – 'about twenty times' each, for one girl (Frith, 1985, p. 117); a finding confirmed in my own study.

Moving on more specifically to Malory Towers, it has received a detailed treatment by Gertrud Lehnert, but in German translation (re-named 'Burg Möwenfels' – Gull Rock Castle). Here, 12 anonymous sequels have been added to Blyton's original six (which charted Darrell Rivers' progress into the sixth form, with adulthood still in the distance). In the sequels Dolly, as she's called, losing her gender-neutral name, returns, marries a teacher and becomes, not a teacher herself, but a 'housemother'.[5] Lehnert argues that this is part of the 'implicit feminine ideology' of the stories, that learning itself is not so important for girls as becoming women '"who have their hearts in the right place"; that is, women who will find their place in life by making others happy' (Lehnert, 1992, pp. 112–13):

> Individual talent is important only so far as it can guarantee the success of extracurricular activities, such as Christmas parties; that is, to the extent that it serves a benign function in the world of school. Real professional achievement or even vocational training . . . is, in fact, clearly disapproved of.
>
> (ibid.)

Lehnert discusses Mavis, who loses her voice in the third Malory, thus showing the futility of girls seeking professional success. Unfortunately for Lehnert, in the final Blyton book we are informed that Mavis *has* 'gone to train as a singer' (*Sixth*, p. 15), with several other pupils also going into artistic careers: Belinda specifically as an artist, Irene to study music, and Darrell, after university, hoping to be a writer. Lehnert thus seems misinformed: professional success is encouraged (though not seen as the ultimate goal); also, the teachers in the English Malory are not married; in fact, most are quite independent, like the strikingly resourceful Miss Peters. On the other hand, the few males are mostly quite weak. It is therefore ironic that Lehnert should criticize Blyton for these qualities – her article is called 'The taming of the shrew' – when most of the evidence for it is from books which Blyton did not herself write, books where the patriarchal elements have been allowed to constrict the very space Blyton opened up. (Even the six original texts are only referred to in translation.)

The appeal of the Blyton school series, then, is in precisely the element that the translations have foregone: its presentation of a female realm:

> In a world of girls, to be female is *normal*, and not a *problem*. To be assertive, physically active, daring, ambitious, is not a source of tension. In the absence of boys, girls 'break bounds', have adventures, transgress rules, catch spies. There is no taboo on public speech. . . .
>
> (Frith, 1985, p. 121)

Although third overall in popularity, with the female readership in the survey, Malory is second favourite. It is also of note that it is the older readers that particularly appreciate these books. Among the 6–14-year-olds, Darrell is only the tenth most popular character. But, among the more mature readers, she moves up into second place, just behind George.

In the rest of this section of the chapter I want to argue that in these books Blyton constructed a liminal space in which girls, out of the bounds of patriarchy, could explore an alternative path of development. First, though, the word 'liminal' probably needs some comment. It is used extensively by the anthropologist Victor Turner, who developed van Gennep's notion of 'rite of passage'. He discerned three phases to this: the first is *separation* from one's former status, and the last is *reincorporation* into a new status. Between these is the *liminal*, when the person is literally 'betwixt and between'; it is an ambiguous position, often involving a dissolution of traditional hierarchies, and is a time of licence. Those in the liminal phase are also described as being in a state of 'communitas', or oneness; as Turner puts it, it is a 'communion of equal individuals who submit together to the general authority of the ritual elders' (Turner, 1969, p. 96). So, broadly speaking, the liminal is a period when normal notions of space, time and structure are disrupted. I'd like now to explore each of these in relation to the Malory series.

First, there is the notion of a magical space, which Malory Towers certainly gives, as many readers have found. In fact, some famous readers, such as Polly Toynbee (1982), have recorded getting themselves dispatched to what they thought would be similarly magical institutions, to their subsequent regret. Clearly, Malory has romantic associations, the name itself associated with Thomas Malory, author of *Le Morte d'Arthur*, which had its own magic centre in Camelot. Malory Towers is also likened to a castle, set against the backdrop of the sea in North Cornwall – similar to the Arthurian Camelot at Tintagel:

> She saw a large castle-like building of grey stone rising high on a hill. Beyond was the deep blue Cornish sea, but that was now hidden by the cliff on which Malory Towers stood. Four towers stood at the corners of the building . . .
>
> (*Fourth*, p. 7).

Gwendoline, in particular, responds to this image:

> 'Yes . . . I shall feel like a fairy princess, going up those steps!' She tossed her loose golden hair back over her shoulders.
>
> 'You would!' said Alicia, scornfully. 'But you'll soon get ideas like that out of your head when Potty gets going on you.'
>
> (ibid.)

Alicia's response suggests that the fairy-tale image of the feminine – of ornamental beauty, of being gazed upon and admired – is not appropriate. Others are also disabused of this notion, like Maureen, Gwen's alter-ego, and Zerelda Brass – the 'brassy blond' American girl who wears make-up and emulates film-stars. Gwen, it should be noted, is also frowned upon for wanting to go to finishing school – a place where the traditionally decorative beauty receives her final polish.

So, contrary to the fairy-tale stereotype, this enchanted place depends on one being active rather than passive for its magic to work. Thus Darrell and Sally's ambition to continue their education at university is regarded more favourably. And the key to this magical space is that it is a male-free zone – the male being the one who, traditionally active, consigns the female to a passive role. Even when men – such as Darrell's father – do make an appearance, they have to bend to female ways.

This notion of a female space extends to the very landscape of Malory, its description reminiscent of medieval courtly symbolism:

> The enclosed garden, set in the hollow square in the middle of the four-towered building, was very popular. It was crammed with hundreds upon hundreds of rose-bushes, and the sight and scent of these filled the fathers and mothers with delight.
>
> (*Sixth*, p. 86)

Elsewhere this is described in more detail, as a 'great circle of green grass sunk a good way below the level of the Court' (*First*, p. 11), round which are stone seats and a garden, all sheltered. The swimming pool is another, key, female spot:

> This had been hollowed out of a stretch of rocks, so that it had a nice rocky, uneven bottom. Seaweed grew at the sides, and sometimes the rocky bed of the pool felt a little slimy. But the sea swept into the big natural pool each day, filled it, and made lovely waves all across it. It was a sheer delight to bathe there.
>
> (*First*, p. 33)

The 'delicious coolness of the water' is often emphasized, and contrasted with the rugged coast. The periodicity of its renewal is also stressed (being regularly flushed out and renewed by the sea) as is its generally sensual quality:

> The pool was always beautiful on blue sunny days. It shone a deeper blue than the sky, and after a few weeks of summer got really deliciously warm – till the tide came in, swamped the pool, and left cooler water there! Darrell loved the pool. Even when she was not bathing she used to take her books down beside it and dream there, looking over the brilliant blue water.
>
> (*Sixth*, p. 30)

The description of Amanda Chartelow, an Amazonian athlete who swims regularly in the early morning, captures its appeal: 'She had a dip in the pool first – lovely! Her strong arms thrashed through the water, and her strong body revelled in it' (*Sixth*, pp. 121–2). Notably, the critic Jan Montefiore (1993, p. 179) describes her own addiction to the school stories in similar terms, as 'a pleasure like that of sinking into a warm bath'.

The whole realm, then, has characteristics of a female landscape: the medieval symbolism (à la Malory) of male castle walls surrounding a female realm, the sunken garden with sloping sides and rose bushes; the sheltered pool, at times mired, refreshed by the sea.

Moving from space to time, there is an insistent rhythm of return and renewal running through the series, and of female continuity. This is most obviously conveyed by the school terms, the rituals of arrival and departure, which are regularly observed. These markers are obviously important, given the liminal status of the pupils once 'out of bounds'; hence the transition between realms is carefully staged. Besides this, there is the general marking of the years, reflected in the book titles, and, within the books, captured in the changing seasons and turnover of pupils. At the beginning Darrell is told by the then head-girl, Pamela, of the joys of Malory, from first glimpsing it to becoming part of its 'communitas':

> 'You're lucky, Darrell . . . You're just beginning at Malory Towers! You've got terms and terms before you. I'm just ending. Another term or two, and I shan't be coming to Malory Towers any more – except as an old girl. You make the most of it while you can.'
>
> (*First*, p. 9)

Later, Darrell makes a similar speech to her sister, Felicity, feeling 'an intense desire to make sure that there were others who would carry on' (*Sixth*, p. 33). And Darrell, of course, herself eventually a head girl, leads the new girls to receive the ritual welcoming speech from the head, Miss Grayling, just as she had once been led down by Pamela to hear it.

Miss Grayling is a key element in this female tradition, but the matron seems to be its matriarchal core, crossing the generations, commenting to the girls, like Alicia, about how she remembers their mothers attending the school; and Alicia, in turn, speaks of her future daughters becoming pupils.

Time, then, has its own cycles, from the turning years and terms down to the periodicity of the tide sluicing the Malory pool. But despite the series charting a linear progression, there is a general sense of female time being more cyclical, hence more relaxed, which is again part of the liminal experience. Males, too, are forced to conform to this female time. One of the set pieces of the series, for example, is of Mr Rivers being kept waiting in the car, while the females get ready. From the final book, here are the opening and closing comments:

> 'Darrell! Aren't you *ever* coming? Daddy says do you mean to leave today or tomorrow?' . . . Their father was just about to begin a fanfare on the horn. Why, oh why was he always kept waiting like this?
>
> (*Sixth*, p. 1)
>
> * * *
>
> There was more hooting in the drive. . . .
>
> 'Darrell! Felicity! . . . Here we are! Where on earth were you? We've been here for ages.'
>
> 'Oh, that was Daddy's horn we heard hooting,' said Felicity. 'I might have guessed.'
>
> (*Sixth*, pp. 149–50)[6]

Moving from the matter of time to structural issues, I have suggested that in Malory we find an alluring, predominantly female world, where the bounds of patriarchy are largely set aside. Certainly, some facets remain; for example, the curriculum is predominantly arts-centred, but then again, public school education in general was criticized for this, and, even here, we find exceptions, with Irene being a gifted mathematician, Bill 'brilliant at Latin' (*Third*, p. 61) and volunteering for carpentry classes (*Fourth*, p. 34). Strong, independent women also feature among the teachers (none are married), especially in the person of Miss Peters, described as 'tall, mannish, with very short hair and a deep voice':

> The girls like her, but sometimes wished she would not treat them as though they were boys. She had a hearty laugh, and a hearty manner. . . .
>
> 'I really wonder she doesn't come to class in riding-breeches,' Alicia had said often enough . . . 'I'm sure she hates wearing a skirt!'
>
> (*Third*, p. 26)

Though the teachers do not always get on, there is no feeling of hierarchy among them – more a sense of community, where matters are talked through, and this seems to be passed on to the pupils as well: that to be open and share one's concerns is prudent. Thus we find female friendship celebrated, not only between the girls, but with teachers, too – as, for example, between Miss Peters and Bill (*Third*, p. 122; *Fourth*, p. 135). However, this sort of friendship is clearly differentiated from silly crushes of the sort that Gwen gets involved in: 'Oh, Gwendoline will always be silly over *some*body. . . . She's that kind. I expect she'll pick on somebody this term too, to worship and follow round' (*Second*, p. 4).

Male characters are few: functionaries like 'a hefty gardener' (*Second*, pp. 127–8), Jack the fisher-boy (*Sixth*, p. 85) and 'old Tom the boatman' (*Sixth*, p. 124). There are also two male teachers, but only Mr. Young, the music master, is memorable, largely for being the butt – literally! – of a practical joke. He is described 'with his funny little moustache twisted up at the ends, his bald head with the three or four hairs plastered down the middle, his too-high collar, and his eyes large behind their glasses' (*Second*, p. 24). The girls arrange it so that he comes to have 'OY' chalked across his behind, which the French mistress attacks. Mr. Young, we hear, is 'horrified at being tapped so familiarly by Mam-zelle' (ibid., p. 43). Male parents, it should be added, with the exception of Darrell's father, also tend to be characters of little worth.

But though a female world, which men enter at their peril, it is not simply a sensual and easy-going realm. This is the passive model of the feminine to which Gwendoline aspires, and of which she is quickly disabused. Malory Towers aims to bring out the best in its pupils, and each is therefore tested in its crucible. Going back to L.T. Meade's work, this is characteristic of the genre, but it is also central to the Froebel philosophy. Moreover, it is very much part of the medieval world of

Thomas Malory, where the knights were also tested for their worth. Finally, it is a key part of the liminal status, of 'communitas', where the initiates submit to 'the general authority of the ritual elders' (Turner, 1969, p. 96).

In Blyton's Malory the swimming pool is central to this, a place where the girls can come together as equals and celebrate their unity. Thus it is the obvious site for midnight feasts, but it is also the place where a levelling occurs. The girls are stripped of uniform and other pretension, as is made explicit in the case of Jo Jones: 'However much she swaggered and boasted and blew her own trumpet out of the water, she was of less account than the youngest first-former when she was in the pool!' (*Sixth*, p. 36). The pool is a site of testing, of baptism. Some come through it, like Mary-Lou, who has to conquer her fear of water in order to save Darrell, whom, she thinks, is in danger of drowning. Others, like Gwen (inevitably), Maureen and Jo, fail. And there are others who reach beyond the pool – like Amanda Chartelow, who is tempted to leave its security in order to swim in the ocean – and suffer the consequences.

This proving ground of Malory is made overt at certain points:

> 'It's queer how the longer you stay here the decenter you get. That's what my aunt told me. She came here, too, and she told me all kinds of stories about awful girls who got all right!'
>
> (*First*, p. 150)

Miss Grayling makes this philosophy more explicit:

> 'We all have good and bad in us, and we have to strive all the time to make the good cancel out the bad. We can never be perfect – we all of us do mean or wrong things at times – but we can at least make amends by trying to cancel out the wrong by doing something worthy later on.'
>
> (*Second*, p. 137)

We get to see the 'bad' in most: Darrell's temper, Alicia's hard-heartedness, Sally's jealousy, Mary-Lou's timidity. All these weaknesses visibly lessen; as do aspects of some of the more transient characters, like Zerelda Brass, who 'suddenly found a bit of character and quite a lot of wisdom' (*Third*, p. 141). Others, however, are less tractable; Gwendoline in particular: she is self-centred, idle, conniving, deceitful, hypocritical and more besides. Throughout the series she is a target for criticism, yet fails to improve – '"You're not fit to be at Malory Towers", said Susan, in a cutting voice. "I can't think why you ever came. You're getting worse instead of better"' (*Sixth*, pp. 105–6) – until the very end, post-Malory.[7]

What is shown is that although Malory is a superb proving ground, it depends on parents pulling their weight too, hence Miss Grayling's notion of a 'School for Parents', quoted earlier. In Gwen's case, it is her old governess and mother who spoil her. With Jo, it is her brash father who is at fault. But, given the right parentage, all should be well. All this is made explicit in Miss Grayling's exhortation to new pupils, which we hear three times. This is its first occurrence:

> 'One day you will leave school and go out into the world as young women. You should take with you eager minds, kind hearts, and a will to help. You should take with you a good understanding of many things, and a willingness to accept responsibility and show yourselves as women to be loved and trusted. I do not count as our successes those who have won scholarships and passed exams., though these are good things to do. I count as our successes those who learn to be good-hearted and kind, sensible and trustable, good, sound women the world can lean on. Our failures are those who do not learn these things in the years they are here.'
>
> (*First*, p. 22)

As Gillian Avery has pointed out, character building was central to the schoolgirl ethic, providing Avery with the title of her study, *The Best Type of Girl*. The emphasis, though, is on the *girl*, for the schools provided an imaginative space for development of character precisely because the pupils were free of other pressures. Those that strove to grow up too quickly, to become women before their time, were the ones that came unstuck. Avery interestingly quotes a guide to childhood from the 1920s which strongly condemns 'the tendency to loll, stay in the house and act like a lady'.[8] Gwen, of course, epitomizes the lolling approach to life, and despises those who indulge in exercise:

> 'I don't like the look of them much,' thought Gwendoline. 'They'll probably go out for games and gym and walks. Why aren't there any nice *feminine* girls here – ones who like to talk and read quietly, and not always go pounding about the lacrosse field or splash in that horrible pool!'
>
> (*Fourth*, p. 32)

Again, this is partly a fault of her upbringing, 'for she came from an overheated home'. Characteristically, she is seen as un-English in this: 'I wish I had been born French. Then I shouldn't have had to swim if I didn't want to, or tire myself out trying to hit a silly ball over a net' (*Second*, p. 27). The French mistresses are certainly shown to share this view: 'Neither of them understood the craze for games and sports of all kinds that they found in English schools' (*Sixth*, p. 30). And Zerelda Brass, the rather advanced American girl, is likewise suspect: 'Was America really so slack in its teaching of children . . . ?' (*Third*, p. 47); later, we are simply informed that 'Life was easier in America' (*Third*, p. 48) – which, following the War, was clearly how America was viewed by Britain. It was also how American children, especially girls, were frequently depicted in literature: as far more independent and grown-up (Avery, 1992; Macleod, 1994).

So, although there is an obvious upper-middle-class feel to the series, class is not the main criterion of worth. Character, as already explored in Chapter 6, is the key. Gwendoline, who lacks nothing in terms of class, is found wanting elsewhere, whereas other characters, like poor Ellen, who comes to Malory on a scholarship, and whose parents have had to penny-pinch to buy her uniform, emerges successfully from the test:

> 'It is easy not to cheat if you don't need to. Is it easy not to cheat if you *do* need to? When that test comes, you will know your character for what it is, weak or strong, crooked or upright.'
>
> (*Second*, p. 90).

As with the Five, nationality is more marked than class, though we do see British girls also lacking the requisite moral fibre. But each of these is outweighed by the main appeal of the books, which lies precisely in the fact that it is a female world – right down to the landscape. To be out of bounds here is to be on the periphery of patriarchy; paradoxically it is within the grounds of Malory that one is 'out of bounds'. It can thus be a world of particularly *active* females, doing the sorts of things that in most children's literature are reserved 'for the boys'.

It may be, of course, that this is only a liminal state, in which case, van Gennep's third phase, 'reincorporation', is just around the corner. But because the books don't follow the girls beyond school (unlike the German versions), the liminal state endures.[9] And, for readers, it is certainly the pranks, the friendships, the midnight feasts and the pleasures of the pool that appeal most. Clearly, the head's speech, repeated three times in the series, emphasizes that the espoused purpose of Malory Towers is to create more biddable women, 'women the world can lean on'. But the persistent message to readers is that this state of freedom is more desirable than a return to the Patriarchal Fold. It is summed up at the end of the series when Sally comments, 'That's one thing that still makes me think we're not really very grown-up, even though we sometimes think we're getting on that way – we always feel so *hungry*', to which Alicia responds, 'Long live our appetites!' (*Sixth*, p. 17).

Having said this, for many readers it was the image of Darrell as writer (one of Blyton's very few) that particularly appealed, suggesting a liminal realm that could be prolonged indefinitely, as it had for Blyton herself: actively becoming a writer of passages.

Conclusion

In this chapter I have argued for a more dynamic interpretation of sexism in an attempt to account for the popularity of Blyton's heroines. The relation of text to reader must be central, I have suggested, even if it means that the reader is ignoring a book's more patriarchal framing. Though most readers were aware that the books were situated dimly in the past, in earlier gender struggles, many could still relate personally to the scenario. Unfortunately, critics who simply read off sexism from isolated signifiers miss this, delimiting a text according to whatever is currently 'pc'. Banton calls this 'presentism' (another 'ism' regrettably), the interpreting of 'other historical periods in terms of the concepts, values, and understanding of the present time' (Banton, 1980, p. 21). This said, it is still Blyton who bears the brunt of such attacks, whereas the classics – Grahame's *The Wind in the Willows* (1908), Barrie's *Peter and Wendy* (1911), Milne's Pooh books (1926–28) Tolkien's *The Hobbit* (1937) or *The Lord of the Rings* (1954–55) – far less female-friendly zones, slip by.[10]

8
Golliwogs, Racism and Blyton: from Preferred Readings to Cultural Effects

Introduction

According to Ray, Blyton was the only children's writer to be included in the *Sunday Times* 'The Thousand Makers of the Twentieth Century' series – a series that was concerned with 'every person who had coloured the imagination of the twentieth century' (quoted in Ray, 1982, p. 65). Ironically, in Blyton's case, this was just what many of her critics accused her of doing – as in Dixon's provocatively titled 'All things white and beautiful' (1974a). Nevertheless, this was not an explicit issue until the 1960s. Until this time there was no defence of Blyton along these lines because there was no attack: it was simply not part of mainstream discourse. Dixon's social criticism of Blyton's work is the most extensive, and I shall consider his position below, together with those of others who take a similar stance. However, on the other side are those such as Inglis (1983) and Cullingford who, while acknowledging the charges of racism, deny its effects. 'These are innocent gestures; children are unaffected by them. They are not conscious of the implications', says Cullingford (1979, p. 291), and certainly many adults proclaim that they personally were never harmed by her works. Dixon, however, offers a rejoinder to remarks such as this:

> It's what *all* racist books have done to *all* children over a long period of time that matters. Whether a particular child was affected by a particular book or not is irrelevant. People exposed to infectious diseases don't always catch them. Also, of course, we don't have to take their word for it when people say a book never did them any harm. (1977, p. 121)[1]

Of course, by Dixon's own logic, neither do we have to take the word of individuals who claim that certain books *do* do them harm. And what of those, like Dixon, who speak on behalf of the harm done to others? For instance, he praises Paula Fox's *The Slave Dancer* (1974) though others have found it reprehensible for its racism. I say this not to undermine Dixon, but because of genuine problems with such an approach. It is inveterately subjective, ignoring the views of certain readers while privileging others – Dixon's own, in this case. This said, Dixon's main point still needs addressing. It is no good saying, on the one hand, that children 'are not conscious of the implications' of texts, while admitting, on the other, that the implications are undoubtedly there. If the latter is indeed the case, one would want to know how children *do* become conscious of the implications; at what age does such consciousness start; and what of the unconscious part of the process?

Unfortunately, in the bickering of the respective camps, such questions are rarely addressed. I shall approach the issues using the theoretical insights of Foucault and Vološinov, showing how Blyton has been caught up in the construction of this discourse. In fact, 'hi-jacked' might be a better term, for some of this chapter might seem a diversion. But the fact that Blyton herself stands as an active signifier of racism, in a strong if knotty discursive thread, necessitates that the matter be given thorough analysis. To my cost, I have had many discussions about Blyton close round this one issue. So, in order to avoid a superficial response, I shall begin by looking at the terms used, then at the chequered history of the golliwog, before returning to Blyton to take another look at some of the contentious texts.

First, though, it is worth pointing out just how rife what we now term 'racism' was, pre-World War II (setting aside other *-isms* for the present). Blyton is frequently singled out for such accusations, but, as Colin Watson has pointed out, 'Foreign was synonymous with criminal in nine novels out of ten, and the conclusion is inescapable that most people found this perfectly natural' (Watson, 1971, p. 123). Many are anti-Semitic, Blacks are criticized as a matter of course, and the 'yellow peril' is exactly that in Sax Rohmer's *Dr. Fu Manchu*. But the more general point is that foreigners *in toto* are Other, whether 'stinking Italianos' (Sydney Horler's phrase, ibid., p. 134), the Soviets, the French, the Germans (as 'the Hun'), even the Scottish, the Welsh and Northerners. Though Watson deals predominantly with popular writing, such prejudices are endemic to more highbrow culture too – and are readily found, for example, in Barrie, Eliot, Greene, Huxley and Nesbit.

This is not in any way to condone such attitudes, but to point out that it was not particularly Blyton who was a racist writer. She was part of a society that was racist; that is, one that 'naturally' foregrounded this way of speaking. So, to write that Blyton is worse than neo-fascism (as does Jeger) would seem to devalue such terms and be guilty of the 'presentism' mentioned earlier.

Racism

A remark by Robert Miles provides an apposite place to begin; races, he says, 'are either "black" or "white" but never "big-eared" and "small-eared"' (Miles, 1989, p. 71). This comment is ironic given the recent controversies over Big-Ears' name, but some 13-year-old children made a remarkably similar comment:

> *Pam*: Now it's not racist [i.e. the revised Noddy]. [. . .]
> *Charles*: Unless you've got big ears and a big nose! [referring to Big-Ears and the goblins]

But Miles' point is a serious one, for by collapsing the notion of race into colour distinctions, one is abetting the very process of making colour the determinant factor. As Colette Guillaumin notes, 'yellow' did not designate a human group till this century, when people first found that they were this hue (Guillaumin, 1995, p. 45). She also points out that this labelling is somewhat arbitrary, noting that South Africa designated the Chinese non-white, but not the Japanese (ibid., p. 66).

Blyton, it should be noted, uses the term 'race' not in the restricted colour sense, but with an earlier inflection, to designate a nation, speaking of 'the German children [being] more taken with my books than any other foreign race' (Blyton, 1950a, p. 3). This is an important point, for collapsing race into a black/white dualism actually helps foster a particular 'racist' discourse. In other words, the terms used to discuss the phenomenon themselves help generate the framing of that phenomenon; and this process of typification then helps forge the stereotype. This is clear in Dixon's article, where he makes exactly this slide from racism to a black/white dualism in his opening paragraphs (1974a, p. 70).

Guillaumin also looks at the history of the term 'black', demonstrating that it was only used to designate a people when they had already been identified as a social group; that is, after they were enslaved, whence their skin colour suddenly took on significance: they then became *black* slaves. Today, these particular social and economic relations are glossed over, and colour is pre-eminent – but we should not thereby hypostatize it.

Before we look at this in more concrete terms, let us also be clear about the term 'stereotype'. It derives from printing, the process of setting things down in 'black and white'. 'Stereotype' originally referred to the metal plates which, when inked, could be used to produce endless copies of an original. This meaning was then extended to refer to the way people might be seen as all the same, because of some mental stereotype that 'fixed' people's perceptions.

To slip into the easiest way of saying something, with a ready-made depiction of character type can, on the one hand, be seen as a basic tool of the storyteller, helping him or her convey shared meanings instantly.[2] On the other hand, it is also a way of obscuring individual differences. Returning to the Miles quotation, we can see how things come to be expressed in black and white terms, with subtler shades of grey lost. Attempts to reverse this process are very difficult because of the institutional weight behind such a discourse (of enslavement, economic dependence, colonial rule, manual labour, and so on). E.M. Forster explores this in *A Passage to India*, where an Indian and an Englishman try to break the polarisation by speaking of 'coffee-colour versus pinko-grey' (Forster, 1961, p. 254). But even leaving aside the political connotations of 'pinko', the term 'pinko-grey' would not stand a chance, as it expresses a colour, whereas whiteness is supposedly neutral, transparent: it is the norm from which others deviate. Therefore, because of the relations of power, whatever term is used for 'non-whites' will develop negative associations over time.

This can be seen in another novel, *The Lonely Londoners*, by the West Indian writer Samuel Selvon, where the character Galahad addresses his own hand, bemoaning its blackness as the cause of all his problems: 'Why the hell you can't be blue, or red or green', he says (Selvon, 1979, p. 88). Two key points arise from this statement. On the one hand, one could say that colour has very little to do with things. Had he been blue, then we would simply have a different set of terms – negative, doubtless – for this hue. Obviously it is the whole colonial history of slavery, of economic oppression and discrimination that counts – as Guillaumin persuasively argues. To blame this on colour is therefore a subterfuge, a scapegoat. From this perspective, the obsession with colour in children's books can be seen to be a diversionary tactic; that is, in leaping on every occurrence of the word 'black' or 'dark' (for example, rewriting 'Baa Baa Black Sheep'), the very discourse that is abhorred, solidifies – albeit unintentionally. Each usage of the term then becomes suspect and taboo. The result is a term that has even more of a negative stamp (literally 'stereotypical'). Thus the writer Malorie Blackman experienced problems publishing her book *Elaine, You're a Brat!* (1991), because her heroine was not only black but naughty, and 'black children shouldn't be shown in a negative light' (Macaskill, 1991, p. 21). On the other hand, because people will kill because of skin colour, or almost kill themselves in trying to remove it, one could argue that blackness has everything to do with the issue. The power of discourse once again shows itself.

Here we come to one of Vološinov's key insights, about the struggle over the sign – a struggle which has been played out over favourite words of Blyton like 'queer' and 'gay', with the male homosexual community seeking to replace the former with the latter, giving 'queerness' a positive, 'gay' spin (since which time, 'queer' itself has developed a more positive connotation). Likewise, in the sixties, the potentially derogatory term 'black' was adopted by African-Americans in a positive way, captured in the slogan 'Black is beautiful' (though, as suggested above, this was somewhat undermined by the concurrent witch-hunt against all other usages of 'black', thus making the word itself problematic).

If we now turn to the golliwog, we see a similar struggle. Some anti-racists fastened on it as a key symbol of racism and sought to ban it, thereby immediately elevating its status, which had differing effects on two other groups: one, mounting such campaigns as 'Save the Golliwog', argued that it genuinely did not see the doll in these terms, while another found the association attractive, precisely because of its racist potential. Hence Harvey Proctor, a conservative MP who wanted to disband the Commission for Racial Equality and repatriate immigrants, was also a supporter (Anon, 1986).

The material effects of such discursive practices can be seen in this letter to *The Guardian*: 'There is not much doubt in my mind that the golliwog . . . with its goggle eyes, spiky hair, and banana lips is in fact a distorted representation of a black person' (Matthews, 1984). This description not only helps perpetuate the stereotype of what a golliwog should be, but also the qualities that constitute the stereotype of a black person (especially the banana lips). The trouble is, we are so caught up in this discursive thread that it can be hard to see things otherwise. However, compare this supposedly 'natural' description with that of some of my younger respondents, those not familiar with the stereotypical associations: 'it's like a . . . a sun shape, and it has, like, like cotton things sticking out of its head' (f, 6, white). Others described it as 'a raggy doll', 'a scarecrow', while others again were less sure how to describe it:

> *Barbar*: Are they clowns? [. . .]
> *Matilda*: Teddies? [. . .]
> *Craig*: Are they bears?
> [Asian and white 7-year-olds]

Thus there is no 'natural' description, any more than there is for seeing the Chinese as 'yellow', or African-Americans as 'black' (Guillaumin, above).[3] We are simply embedded in a discourse of racism that naturalizes certain ways of speaking and categorizing; and, however politically correct we think we might be, we may be perpetuating.

There can, consequently, be no innocent discussion about golliwogs: not only does the word drag a long chain of signification in its wake, but in following the threads of the debate one is also caught up in a discursive practice with marked material effects. It is for this reason that many, as above, want to exorcise both word and image. However, such an essentialist view needs setting alongside the ultimate arbitrariness of the sign, the relational nature of language and the struggle over meaning. In fact, this constructedness has already been exemplified in the different views of the golliwog given above. So, let us now look at the history of this powerful signifier.

The unnatural history of the golliwog(g)

Blyton once said that she had depicted bad teddies as well as gollies (Stoney, 1974, p. 166), and they certainly are of similar vintage, though the former have a far happier history, with presidential origins in 'Teddy' Roosevelt (1907) and illustrious examples like Winne-the-Pooh and Rupert.[4] The golliwog was different, right from the start, losing its creator substantial revenue because it was never patented. It was the product of the young American artist, Florence Upton, who was having problems with a story she was composing – until she recalled an old doll she had, which, she says, brought the story to life (Peet, 1950). The resultant tale – *The Adventures of Two Dutch Dolls and a "Golliwogg"* – had little success with publishers till an employee at Longman took it home and, as with so many children's books, his children showed their appreciation. Published in 1895, the book was an immediate success. There were 12 sequels, with the Golliwogg (as he was then known) always central.

What interests me here is the ambivalence of the figure, which Upton herself recorded, speaking of both its ugliness and endearing personality (Peet, 1950). This is repeated in the early reviews, which mirror Golliwogg's reception in the story. In this the Dutch dolls initially 'scream' at his 'horrid sight' (Upton and Upton, 1995, pp. 23–4), before coming to like and respect him with his 'kind face' (ibid., p. 53). Upton's story thus shows how appearances can be deceptive, besides illustrating our fascination with the grotesque. Children's subsequent encounters confirm this. Lady Clive speaks about a golliwog that threw her brother 'into paroxysms of terror' (Clive, 1964, p. 31) and one of my respondents noted: 'As a result of reading the Noddy books, many of my childhood nightmares involved golliwogs'; though she pointedly adds, 'However it never occurred to me that there might be any connection between golliwogs and black people' (f). On the other hand, both Eric Bligh (1946, pp. 164–74) and Kenneth Clark are fulsome in their praise: 'I identified myself with him [Golliwogg] completely, and have never quite ceased to do so' – Clark, 1974, pp. 6–7).

The golliwog certainly possesses effective grotesque qualities: stark, staring eyes, hair standing on end (as hair does with fright, or an animal's does to scare others) and engorged lips, giving perhaps an erotic or engulfing emphasis. His power seems to derive precisely from his straddling of cultural categories, possessing an inveterately transgressive nature: black and white, bright yet dowdy, colourful and monochrome, human and animal (he often has paws rather than hands and feet), cultural and natural, friendly yet frightening. Like other such figures, it is this ambivalence, this hybridity that makes him disturbing, but also fascinating. In fact, similar carnivalesque inversion had been exploited in earlier incarnations of this figure, used in much older British customs; as Pickering notes: 'Blacking-up was already an integral element in such popular festive activities as plough-witching, pace-egging, mumming, morris and May customs' (Pickering, 1986, p. 78).

As for his behaviour, Golliwogg is frequently mischievous, but never an evil character. He is an explorer, an adventurer – in fact, more like the colonizer than the colonized, discovering the North Pole, going to a desert island (where he plays the 'Robinson Crusoe' figure, having his own 'Friday', called 'Monday') and venturing to Africa, where he meets some cannibals (Bligh, 1946).

What then, of the golliwog's relation to black people? The unnamed doll from which Florence Upton conceived the 'golliwogg' is often seen to have links with the minstrel figure.[5] However, the Golliwogg confounds this, and there are other elements that run counter to the Negro stereotype. Thus the two Dutch dolls also encounter an African, depicted as a black doll (Upton and Upton, 1995, p. 42) and, more interestingly, 'Sambo', who 'sings a song' (ibid., p. 45). The latter is depicted as much closer to the traditional minstrel, with banjo, striped pants, tails, top-hat, and the more traditional burnt-cork face. Moreover, Golliwogg is not given the artificial dialect often used in minstrelsy – though in a later story, *The Golliwogg at the Sea-side*, a Negro waiter features, who does speak in this manner. Golliwogg also has a thin 'beaky' nose, besides lacking other stereotypical associations: for instance, being musical, lazy, savage or superstitious (Davis, 1992, p. 106; see also Walvin, 1983). Lastly, it is worth noting that the original Golliwogg is a singular figure – not a type.

If not originally a minstrel doll, though, is there any other possible origin? Van Nieuwkasteele has made a convincing case for Upton's doll being based on 'Zwarte Piet', who was Saint Nicolas' helper in Dutch lore. Of course, 'Sinter Klaas', as he was known there, became Santa Claus in America. His helper, Zwarte Piet, kept a record of children's deeds in a large book, and those children who had been good were given gifts that 'Black Peter' carried down the chimney – hence his appearance (Savage, 1996). Pieterse notes that this figure has a long ancestry, going back beyond the middle ages, when 'Black Peter appears to have little to do with Africa or black people' (Pieterse, 1992, p. 165).

This said, I would not want to deny that the golliwog signifier can all too easily be linked to black people – and has repeatedly been so linked. Thus the *OED* quotes from *A British G.I. in Vietnam* (1969), in which its author describes a Negro 'whose appearance reminded me of one of those golliwogs that decorate the labels of Robertson's marmalade jars' (*OED*, 1989, vol. vi, p. 662). Note, though, that the author of this piece reaches for this association; African-Americans in general are not automatically read as golliwogs. Hence I would not describe this usage as racist, unlike, say, the report of Pik Botha telling an ANC member to 'stop jumping up and down like a golliwog' (Walker, 1995), where a racial slur seems intended. There is no doubt that it is a term, given its powerfully transgressive nature, which lends itself to such abuse. Equally, there is no doubt that the features of the doll have been distorted for such effect, just as the Nazis created figures with exaggerated Semitic features in their propaganda literature.[6]

The crucial point, however, is that it is not the term *per se*, but the relations of power that exist between the respective parties – just as Guillaumin demonstrated with the term 'black', which became significant only after certain social relations had been previously established.

It is when the term is used *against* a people already seen as a socially distinctive group – usually because they are disadvantaged in some way – that the term becomes abusive.

Moving away from the golliwog as a doll, let us now look at the derivation of the word and its associated terms, 'golly' and 'wog'. Once again, we are immediately in the realm of folk etymology, though Florence Upton's views would seem a natural place to start. She maintains that the word just came to her when she picked up the doll. However, others have suggested that the word 'pollywog' might have influenced her, a name for a tadpole dating back to the fifteenth century. It crops up in E.M. Forster's *A Room with a View* (Forster, 1955, p. 138) and in Hilaire Belloc's poem 'Frog':

> Be kind and tender to the Frog,
> And do not call him names,
> As 'Slimy skin,' or 'polly-wog'
>
> Belloc, 1979

Others suggest 'scallywag', which certainly captures Golliwogg's character, and some of my young listeners, not familiar with the original term, spoke of 'scalliwogs'.[7]

Pieterse (1992, pp. 156–7), a key authority, finds the 'pollywog' etymology dubious, but supports the independent derivation of the abusive term 'wog' – which is erroneously thought to be a shortened form of golliwog. It was an acronym for 'Western Oriental Gentleman', or similar, he says. In a letter to *The Times* in 1945, it is said that 'the letters W.O.G.S. were worn on the armbands of the native workmen in Alexandria and Port Said' (quoted in Davis, 1992, p. 11). This derivation was then retrospectively tied to 'golliwog', in that, because these workers were so thin, wealthier Egyptians called them 'ghul' – an Arabic word for desert ghosts – which the British troops turned into 'golly' (ibid.) Note that this explanation reverses the usual chronology. It is not 'golliwog' that was shortened to the insulting 'wog'; rather, it is the independently derived 'wog' that was run into 'golliwog', in line with the existing word. The *OED* also notes that the term was originally applied to 'one of Arab extraction' (*OED*, 1989, vol. xx, p. 478), only later becoming more generalized.

Though it has been necessary to provide this detailed account of the word and the concept, I hope it has actually demonstrated the flaw of arguing from origins. Etymology, at its best, only shows what a word originally meant, in *langue*; not what it subsequently means, nor how it is actually used, in *parole*. This is the essence of Vološinov's (1973) argument, that language is always in the hands – or mouths – of its users, and that it is usually a site of struggle. Pointing to dictionary definitions unfortunately leaves this out, besides the network of relations a word has with other terms, linking it discursively into a web of expressions with, for example, a racist connotation. Such is particularly the case with terms that operate in the oral rather than the written realm, terms that develop connotations through interpersonal use, as do words connected with race and sexuality. This said, even if we could point to dictionary origins, what would this prove? If 'wog' does derive independently of 'golliwog', so what? or if 'golliwog' really does derive from 'pollywog'? It makes the term 'golliwog' neither more nor less offensive. What matters, of course, is its social connotation.

However, following Guillaumin once again, because it is the *material relationship* that is crucial, it is likely that any new term for a socially oppressed group is itself likely to develop negative connotations over time. Rumer Godden records her disappointment that her novel about travellers, *The Diddakoi* (1972) which she hoped would present gypsies in a more positive light, simply seemed to give children a better vocabulary with which to castigate them. Likewise, any neutral word can become racially tainted in particular contexts, 'Hindu' and 'Jew' being listed as abusive terms in Cohn (1988).

The confusion that arises unless this semiotic latitude is realized can be seen in a widely reported case of the withholding of a child-minder's licence because she had a golliwog in her antique-toy collection, coupled with the fact that she read Noddy to her charges. The visiting council inspector, a Rastafarian, insisted that the offending doll was a 'golliwog' – not a 'golly', as the minder called it – commenting that 'he didn't see himself as having big white eyes and a red mouth'; and, of course, there is no reason why he should (Nelson, 1993; Payne, 1993). We have here two people with very different notions of the term 'golliwog' each seeking to impose their meaning on the other; that is, giving 'differently oriented accents' to the sign (Vološinov, 1973, p. 23). One, commendably, was seeking to expunge racism in all its manifestations; the other, trying to preserve a long-cherished nursery doll.

So, where does this leave us? The golliwog, it seems, was not in origin a racist icon, whereas the offensive term 'wog' had a separate derivation. However, there is no doubt that the golly came to prominence in an age that was racist, and that he was all too easily implicated in racist discourses, both in name and image. The fact that gollies are frequently named 'Sambo' and 'Nigger' is incontrovertible evidence of this. What

I have tried to do here is to indicate the semantic latitude and potency of this signifier, without shutting it down round this one, racist meaning. Let us now, then, move on to look at Blyton's offending texts in the light of the above.[8]

Blyton in black-and-white

'The little black doll' produced the earliest written comment I have found on Blyton's racism (Jeger, 1966), though this was already too late for Blyton to respond meaningfully. Dixon, and later Druce, have subjected the story to a more detailed treatment. It concerns a doll, Sambo, who is disliked by the other toys because he is black. He therefore runs away and meets a pixie who is kind to him. Sambo, in turn, repays this kindness, going out during a thunderstorm to fetch some medicine when the pixie is ill. However, the rain washes the doll's blackness away, leaving him with 'the dearest, pinkest, kindest face'. Sambo thus returns to the nursery and, no longer different, is accepted: 'No wonder he's happy – little pink Sambo!' (Blyton, 1944, pp. 72–3).

The story is characteristic of its time and is, without doubt, unpalatable now. It was certainly insensitive that such a book should continue to be available into the 1970s. Yet it warrants careful consideration, for Dixon goes on to claim that in a 1976 edition of *A Story Party at Green Hedges*, 'a very confused attempt has been made to give this story a face-lift . . . the racism . . . has been toned down' (1977a, pp. 111–12); Druce, likewise, speaks of it being 'silently changed' (1992, p. 43). In this supposedly revised version, the pixie episode is omitted and it is the toys who see the error of their ways: they come to fetch Sambo and, when they find him no longer black, are sorry and re-ink him, commenting,

> 'We don't like you because you are black or because you are white,' said the golly. 'We like you because you are kind and friendly and good. You can be any colour you like. We don't really care.'
>
> (Blyton, 1949c, p. 19)

This story, it should be noted, is requested at the 'story party' by a girl who owns the doll in question:

> 'He's so sweet, and I like his black face, don't you?'
> 'Yes. He's a dear little doll,' I [EB] say.
>
> (ibid., p. 12)

As the date of the above quotations indicates, both Dixon and Druce are in error. The 1976 edition was not a confused attempt to rewrite the tale: the version in *Story Party* is simply a separate story with a different history, going back, unchanged, to the first edition of *Story Party* (1949c), though it was first published even earlier, in *Sunny Stories* in 1943. The other story with this title had originally appeared in that magazine six years earlier, in 1937, and was collected in *Enid Blyton's Jolly Story Book* (1944) before its later incarnations – including the ones noted by Jeger, Dixon and Druce.[9] Wrong as they are, though, this doesn't alter the likely reception of the book in a multicultural society. Yet neither does it warrant Druce's claim that '*The Little Black Doll* displays a deeper dislike of blackness, and so does her frequent casting of golliwogs, along with monkeys, as the wrongdoers in the Noddy stories' (1992, p. 230).[10]

The story is actually about the folly of judging by appearance, something which Blyton uses repeatedly. Thus there is another story where a golly is set to run away, thinking that others have forgotten him at Christmas, till he opens a suitcase and discovers some presents addressed to him. 'So the toys liked him after all! In fact they must like him very much. He was their "dear, dear Golly."'[11] Unfortunately, it is the stories featuring 'black' characters that have been highlighted, whereas the blackness is usually incidental. Thus, in another variant, it is a bird that laments, 'I am a queer, odd little bird. Nobody wants me' (p. 88).[12] Likewise, in that precursor of 'Noddy', 'Tales of Toyland', both the sailor and fairy dolls ('white') are rejected by the other toys. In many stories it is actually tails rather than colour that mark difference. So, in 'Michael's Tail', a party is held, but only those with tails are invited.[13] But most famously, this theme is used in the first Noddy book, when he cannot find a home. In fact, the similarities between Noddy and the little black doll go much further: Sambo, too, wears 'a red coat, and blue trousers'. He, too, runs away till he meets a pixie with 'big pointed ears' who has a toadstool house with a door cut in its stalk, and windows in the top part (the toadstool-living Big-Ears was a pixie in Blyton's original conception of Noddy).

So, as in many other Blyton creations, the main character is merely seeking acceptance, whether by acquiring a tail, changing colour or whatever. In one variant the doll becomes pink and acceptable; in another he becomes black again,[14] suggesting that blackness is being used far less pointedly than others have claimed. This seems to be supported by the golliwog character in the story being *persona grata*; in fact, the golly is actually party to the black doll's banishment; albeit, if we follow the social critics' argument that it is blackness itself that is unacceptable, this would be nonsensical. Dixon does have an answer, however, which is revealing. He argues that the golly's face is '(just) acceptable' – though there is no such equivocation in the story – because 'black people at the level of the golliwog . . . were assimilable to white racist sentiments', whereas 'Sambo has some pretensions to being a recognisable human being' (1977a, p. 111). This seems to make no sense, though, in that many of the other toy characters explicitly mentioned as rejecting Sambo are even less recognizably human: 'a clockwork mouse' and 'a humming top'! Once again, Dixon seems to be foregrounding colour – white versus black – at the expense of other features of the characters.

Moving on to Noddy, we find a figure so closely associated with racism that the mere mention of his name can prompt a ban, as occurred with a production of David Wood's play, *Noddy*. This ran into promotional problems when Hampshire County Council simply caught sight of the title, despite the fact that it was a socially reconstructed version. 'Golly!', the newspaper report predictably begins (Preston, 1993). It is, therefore, all too easy to accept a racist interpretation of the series without even examining the texts.

In the original series, golliwogs were an integral part of Toyland, being seen regularly around Toy Village. Aside from Beek's one strange 'industrial' picture (see Chapter 5), Robert Tyndall, the other main illustrator, produced a 'Wanted' image of a golliwog pinned up inside the police station (*N10*, p. 40), reproduced in two later books (*N19*, p. 50 and *N22*, p. 34). Though unsupported by the text, with hindsight it can be seen as an unfortunate depiction, but little more – unless, that is, the golliwogs were consistently found to be criminal types and were seen to represent more than dolls.

Looking at Blyton's actual words, what seems to be at issue is whether the critics are right in claiming that golliwogs are 'habitually presented by this author in evil and menacing roles' (Fryer, 1989, p. 81; also Dixon, 1974a, p. 71; Druce, 1992, p. 230), or whether, as Blyton herself claimed, she wrote about more good golliwogs than bad. Thus it would be easy to combat the negative 'Wanted' image with such positive instances as Father Christmas singling out the golliwogs for praise: 'I've had very good reports from boys and girls about their golliwogs – they love them very much. I want to give some praise there' (*N11*,

p. 40). But, lest this be seen as tokenism, we need to consider all the golliwogs.

Some basic content analysis easily refutes the above. The golliwogs are menacing characters in only one story (*N4*), with other characters fulfilling this role elsewhere; for example, it is bears that steal Noddy's car in another tale. Overall, though, goblins and monkeys are the persistent villains, featuring in three stories each. If we look at characters that are naughty, cheeky or mischievous, rather than actually bad, the picture is similar, with golliwogs receiving four mentions (three supplied by Gilbert Golly), and still lagging behind the bears, with seven. If we look at the issue from the other side, with mentions of characters being 'good' in some way, golliwogs still score better than bears, even though, overall, bears feature more than golliwogs. Excluding mentions where characters fall into any of the above categories (villainous, naughty, or good), bears receive 24 mentions while golliwogs get only 12. It should be said that the golliwogs also get two collective mentions in Golliwog Town, whereas bears tend to be seen more individually, although a Teddy-Bear Town does exist (*N22*, p. 57). But if we look at named characters, as opposed to mentions as part of a collective (a criticism that might easily be seen as detrimental to the golliwogs), then the gollies and teddies are more or less even with nine each. Lastly, if one were to look at the class representation of each, there seems to be a fairly even spread also: there is a bear doctor, but bears that are barrow boys; likewise with golliwogs. Clearly, such content analysis is fraught with problems: if something is mentioned more than something else it might indicate prominence, but prominent characters can be either good or bad, stereotyped or individualized. However, because such negative accusations as the above are so readily voiced, it has seemed necessary to offer a more precise analysis.

Let us now give closer attention to *Here Comes Noddy Again* (*N4*), which, unusually, flags up its theme on the cover: the standard train motif is changed here, with gollies and police replacing the regular carriage occupants. The gollies are clearly under police control, too, subtly indicating their containment. The action starts in Chapter 5, 'The Golliwog comes', with a golliwog entering Noddy's house without knocking. He asks Noddy to take him 'to a party in the Dark Wood at midnight' (*N4, p.* 34) for a bag of sixpences. This offer of money is sufficient to allay Noddy's fears about 'bad goblins' being there (ibid.).

Noddy collects the golliwog and drives him to the 'the Dark Dark Wood', only to be told that there isn't a party: 'This is a trap, Noddy. We want your car for ourselves. Get out at once!' (ibid., pp. 39–40). Then

'Three black faces suddenly appeared'. They take his car and leave him naked – the only time he appears like this apart from when he is initially found by Big-Ears. Noddy then crawls aimlessly through the wood, eventually coming to Big-Ears' house where he is put to bed to recover. Eventually the gollies are captured and Noddy is reunited with his car and clothes.

The story is one of the few of Blyton's that exploits the golliwog's cultural ambivalence, and it is certainly menacing. I can still recall the impact it had on me when I was four (it is the only Noddy book that I *can* remember), although – I have to say it too – I never equated the golliwogs with black people. What we do seem to have, though, is an obvious pre-text: Collodi's *Pinocchio*. In this tale the wooden puppet is also lured out at night for monetary gain, to meet the Cat and Fox. They too organize a rendezvous and, disguised, try to mug Pinocchio: 'in the dark he saw two awful black figures, all enveloped in coal-sacks' (Collodi, 1996, p. 42). Pinocchio also runs through a wood and after many hours knocks at the door of a cottage, where he meets his eventual rescuer, and is similarly put to bed to recuperate. Collodi's is a far more brutal tale, though, his adversaries having tried to stab and hang the wooden doll. But even toned down, the power of the story is very real. Let me now turn to the revised editions, to see how they compare.

Although there was an abortive second edition, I shall concentrate on the third, which involved far more scrupulous attention to the style of Beek's original artwork; in fact, the first seven books still declare 'pictures by Beek' on the cover, despite the fact that over 70 of his illustrations have been doctored (but then Blyton's text has been doctored even more). The bad golliwogs have been replaced by goblins, Gilbert Golly has become Martha Monkey and Mr. Golly (owner of the garage) is now Mr. Sparks, 'a kindly-looking doll' (*N2*, p. 21).

It is certainly the case that corporations like the BBC would not have touched the books without such updating, thus bringing Noddy to many new generations of children. We find Japanese, Asian, Mexican, African-Caribbean and other multicultural images here, although none are main characters. (It would be easy to comment here that the main characters are still all white, but this would be facile, and show how constructions of colour are socially derived. To call Mr and Mrs Tubby Bear – *brown* bears – 'white' is making the concept rather too elastic! It should also be noted that in the Cosgrove Hall series there is a slightly more prominent black character, Dinah Doll.)

But the question still remains as to whether erasing the golliwog from history was appropriate. Indeed, it might bring to mind other examples of presentism, where 'the past was brought up to date' so that there was no 'expression of opinion, which conflicted with the needs of the moment, ever allowed to remain on record' (Orwell, 1954, p. 35). In this connection it is of note that the 'revised edition' declaration has now been dropped from the covers of the Noddy books. So, let me now turn to today's children, to see what they make of the whole issue.

Children reading the golliwog

Taking on board Dixon's point that what matters is what children in general – rather than the isolated child – have made of the golliwog, I asked children from four schools for their views.[15] Once again, it should be emphasized that I do not see children as providing some unsullied reading of the books' *real* meanings. It simply seemed appropriate that the main readers of Blyton's works should be given a chance to air their views without prejudging their opinions as too immature or, worse, seeing children as too impressionable even to be consulted. Obviously many children are now themselves aware of the p.c. discourse of 'racism' – although sometimes they see it in quite different terms. Consequently, they will draw on this when asked about the books. Accordingly some I spoke to were clearly aware of a discourse about the golliwog's involvement in racism; some would simply trot out that Blyton was racist, while others – a considerable number – seemed oblivious.

All I can say is that, of the children who were not previously aware of the equation 'golliwog equals ethnically black person', none made it. This was equally true of the older children, though they could only speak retrospectively:

Sandra: I never associated that at all.
Claire: I didn't.
Rebecca: No, not till now.
Sandra: I just thought of the golliwogs as like . . . the golliwogs.
Others: Yeah. [16–17 year-olds]

Indeed, they still seemed distressed at the association:

Claire: So I don't see why . . . ?
Rebecca: As long as it's not encouraged that you're – you're not saying golliwogs represent these?
Sandra: I mean, was there a purpose, is that why, was Enid Blyton racist, I mean, was that what she thought?

Predictably, a number expressed their affection for the character, having had their own golly dolls, though this too had sometimes led to confusion: 'I used to have a golliwog and I got it thrown away, I got it taken off me [. . .] My mum wouldn't let me have it' (f, 13). These negative associations had led to some parents banning Noddy (or Blyton) in general: 'I didn't really read them because my mum said they were racist, and so I wasn't prone to read them.'

When I showed children the 'goblin' replacements and asked them why they thought the texts had been changed, I had a variety of responses. Briefly, it was suggested that it was for one of the following reasons: datedness (the characters were simply old and out-of-date); plagiarism (they wanted Blyton's 'brilliant ideas'); economics ('they've been taken over by the jam-jar golliwogs' – f, 8); or for reader appeal, to make the books scarier, or 'more evil', as an 8-year-old put it. Thus the golliwog versions were seen as 'for the younger children' (the view of a group of 9-year-olds). Several groups elaborated on this:

Daisy: I don't like the idea of the goblins, really. It makes them more. . . . Those [goblins] look wicked. Those look wicked and evil. They [gollies] look mischievous.
Valerie: They [goblins] look evil and a bit mean and horrible.

'Mischievous' was a term often used: 'When I think of the golliwogs I think of mischief, but when you're thinking of goblins you're thinking of evil and magic' (f, 13). I then asked this group whether they thought that this changed the story at all:

Sadia: It does, it makes it more serious, it makes it more scary.
DR: Why Sadia?
Sadia: Before it was just like, mess about thing, like, you're just being naughty and that, but that makes it more scary. Children could have nightmares and things like that 'cos they don't understand what it is properly . . . when they're little.

What is interesting is that these views were all expressed by older children, who were more likely to have had experience of golliwogs. The younger ones were more ambivalent, often changing their views in the course of discussion. When I asked why they had shifted their opinion the infants (4–5-year-olds) would only indicate particular features (for example, the goblins have 'got big sharp noses' or 'big nails'). The junior children (9-year-olds) were more forthcoming, but what is of note is that their considered opinions only emerged over time:

> *Hassan*: Those [gollies] look a bit scarier.
> *Sufia*: Because they're black, and in the night.
> *Qasim*: And they've got spiky hair.
> *Hassan*: Spiky hair like, they think they're ghosts.
> *DR*: So these are more scary than the goblins in the new ones?
> *Hassan*: Sir, yeah, these [indicating goblins now] look a bit scarier.
> *DR*: You think *these* are a bit scarier?
> *Hassan*: Sir, ghosts have like big ears [. . .]
> *Sufia*: Yeah, and long nose, like witches.
> *Hassan*: Old witches, and they have big-ears, long nose.
> *DR*: So which ones do you think are scarier now?
> *All*: Them [goblins].
> *DR*: You actually think these? You did before these [gollies] but now thinking about it, you think the goblins?
> *Aksa*: 'Cos them [gollies] look a bit like clowns ['clowns' said by two children, simultaneously]. They look funny.
> *Hassan*: Sir, yeah, they've got clown clotheses on.
> *Qasim*: These [gollies] are not scary.

There are two points to be made here. Methodologically, we can see the dynamics of how topics are discursively constructed: they are not static, but frequently change over time, often prompted by the discourse itself (Billig, 1996). This, therefore, makes it problematic in making truth claims from particular statements; in fact, a questionnaire response would have missed this dynamic entirely. Substantively – my second point – it is clear that there is a general uneasiness about the golliwogs when first encountered, which seems to diminish over time. This may have been the case with other groups, too, but I simply failed to notice it. Only in one group (6-year-olds) did I note that it was the one child with previous knowledge of golliwogs who immediately found the goblins scarier. The other three, for whom the golliwog was new, found this character more scary initially. This, of course, is exactly the reaction that Florence Upton captures in her original book about the character: an initial fear, followed by affection, which is also what many owners of golliwogs have recorded, and what makes it such an effective grotesque.

The ambivalence of the golliwog as compared to the goblin also made a reading of the revised edition more problematic for some groups. As they pointed out, it is only because the golliwog is generally trustworthy that Noddy can be excused for going off at night with one. But to go off with goblins, who are always bad, makes Noddy far less discerning. These are the responses of three groups to the question, 'Does changing the characters make the story different?':

Naomi: Yes [. . .] 'Cos Noddy would sort of, know.
DR: What would he know, Naomi?
Naomi: Because it, er, that they were actually bad.
DR: He should know that the goblins are bad, you're saying?
Edward: Yes [endorsed by all . . .]. And he wouldn't know if the gob- if the golliwog was good or bad.
Maurice: Yeah, because there's one good golly and one there – a couple of bad gollies, so he doesn't know . . . (7-year-olds)

* * *

Diana: Yeah, it does actually, 'cos I think he'd trust a golliwog but I don't think he'd trust a goblin unless it was dressed up.
DR: Right, so does it make . . . Noddy . . . ?
Diana: Well, it makes no sense actually 'cos the goblins look the most scary but the golliwogs are the most likely to let him go off with. (9–10-year-olds)

* * *

Lucy: Yeah, because like, he doesn't know the goblins, but he knew golliwogs. [. . .]
Patrick: He's silly going off with a goblin 'cos . . .
Lucy: You can't trust them.
Patrick: Yeah, you can't trust them, never. (9-year-olds)

Patrick had earlier remarked that 'If they [golliwogs] behaved and were nice to Noddy, I'd really like them. . . . But . . . goblins, you can't have them nice, else they're not really a goblin'. So, with this change, Noddy effectively becomes a more stupid – in fact, a more 'noddy' – character. After all, in the original it is the very thought of goblins being in the wood that causes Noddy to hesitate in taking a golly there in the first place.

While the reactions to these changes were varied, just as they have been to other alterations, they could be broadly grouped around those who endorsed the revisions (to avoid racism) and those who took exception to them, either because they thought the golliwogs innocent in the first place, or because they thought the changes introduced other 'racist' issues (I should say that, after hearing their views, I explained the racist connection.) In relation to this last point, one of the strangest conversations I had was with two Asian boys (14-year-olds) who were incensed at the changes. I had just asked them why the books might be racist.

Waqas: Because they deliberately – deliberately removed the black character . . .
Shahid: They've got . . . What – what's the reason, what's their reason for moving that character?
DR: That's what I'm asking you [. . .]
Shahid: I think it's because, if they want to change a character, they could have changed a different one. Why they have to deliberately remove that golliwog, or whatever?
DR: Right. Now the one that, let me show you now the one that was actually . . .
Waqas: He's one of the main characters
DR: Let me . . . sorry, let's go through this slowly, 'cos, are you saying, that it's like a black character?
Shahid: Yeah.
DR: And that they shouldn't remove that one?
Shahid and Waqas: Yeah.

This 'reverse racism' was quite a common response. It came either from those who already knew that the golliwogs were said to represent black people, or from those so informed during the progress of the interview, leading them to object to their removal.[16] 'Who's changing these books? Who's got the rights to change these books?' Shahid said, with passion. This becomes explicit at another point in the interview:

DR: Does it make Noddy seem any different if he agrees to go with a goblin . . . ?
Waqas: Yeah!
DR: . . . as opposed to going with a golliwog. Why Waqas?
Waqas: It shows that he's racist. He's not going with a black character, he's going with a white character instead.
DR: Right. I wasn't actually thinking of that but, I mean that's a good point . . .
Waqas: But it makes it worser, changing it, makes it like, makes the controversy higher, 'cos, like, people start talking about it more,

> when they find out that it used to be like this, so if they keep it like that there'd be less of it, less people talking about it . . .

This shows how an awareness of the discourse of racism can develop its own volition, disrupting the very open-mindedness it is meant to foster.[17] For example, some children suggested a rigorously systematic revision: 'they should have half the black ones bad and half the white ones bad as well . . . and half the black ones good and half the white ones good . . . so it's just they're equal'. Others suggested a complete reversal: 'you make Noddy black and the . . . Noddies [*sic* – that is, gollies] white'. This is reminiscent of the logic in a Joe Orton play:

> *Mrs Prentice*: What's Miss Barclay doing downstairs?
> *Prentice*: She's making white golliwogs for sale in colour-prejudice trouble-spots. . . . I hoped it might promote racial harmony'.
> (Orton, 1976, p. 387)

Others again, seeing the problematic nature of falling into a black–white dichotomy, opted for more neutral colours: 'They could have done the colouring schemes like green or purple, then it wouldn't come across as being white or black', to which his colleague perceptively responded, 'Seeing it's Toyland they could have done it as anything' (14-year-olds).

Let me sum up here. I have discussed the golliwogs in depth, and shown that in Noddy they are not the villainous characters often claimed. They are only so in the one infamous story. I have also looked at a *corpus* of 323 other Blyton stories, randomly selected, to see how she treats golliwogs more generally. Nine per cent featured golliwogs, 25 of which (8 per cent) were 'good' and only four 'bad'.[18] There do actually seem to be more naughty teddy stories than gollies, often explicitly, as in 'The naughty teddy bear' (Blyton, 1950b, pp. 129–37) and 'Teddy Bear is naughty' (Blyton, 1970c, pp. 115–24) – bearing out Blyton's own claim. In fact, the golliwog is often a character that comes up with solutions to problems – again harping back to Upton's original – the one in the Amelia Jane stories being particularly popular (Blyton, 1939).

As regards the children, their views were mixed, as one might expect, partly dependent on their knowledge of the relevant discourses. They were certainly fascinated by the figure, with their views on its relevance to the racist issue confounding many adult preconceptions. I was surprised at how many approached it with a fresh perception, showing how much the golliwog has been written out of our culture recently. Interestingly, the most common referent for the word seemed to be as a hairstyle. It was a term, I was informed, to depict someone with longish hair. For example, here are Shahid and Waqas, telling me what they understand by the term:

Shahid: Yeah, on jam, on Robinson's [*sic*] jam. We take mickey out of people like that.
DR: They're still on jam-jars.
Shahid: Yeah, and we still call people golliwogs a lot, like, you know [Waqas and Shahid:] curly hair.
DR: Who? You call them that?
Shahid: Yeah, we call them. For a laugh. Everyone calls . . . that name, and everyone knows that name.
DR: Anyone with curly hair you call that?
Waqas: No, someone with long hair.

The term might still be used derogatively, however. One (white) girl complained that 'when I was at primary school, I had me hair permed, and I got called a golliwog. [. . .] 'Cos it was like permed.'[19]

Conclusion

Some parts of this chapter might have seemed a diversion, but the centrality of racism in general, and the golliwog in particular, to any discussion of Blyton has necessitated its inclusion. I have tried to show the complex history of the issues, where fake etymologies are rife. Undoubtedly, Blyton was a product of an age we now consider racist, in which white people (male and middle-class especially), saw themselves as naturally superior (and this is something that certainly should not be erased from history). I have also shown how easily Blyton's books can be shutdown round a racist discourse and, perhaps, why this reading of Blyton became a central concern of the sixties and seventies, a time when civil rights issues were highlighted.

But I have also suggested that there is much more to the golliwog than this: both he and earlier black/white inversions create an inherently ambivalent, transgressive figure, which is what gives him (and the golly is usually a he, taking us into other issues) both his fascination and his dangerousness. He is not coterminous with the African-American, although 'black' elements undoubtedly inform his appearance, particularly elements from minstrelsy. Those who deny such association are, at best, subconsciously deceiving themselves. Lastly, the insulting term 'wog' was also seen to have a separate history, though the etymologies have obviously been run together (just as we have seen with other terms in this history, like 'noddy' and 'plod').

I have also refuted the related notion in Blyton's books that the golliwog is always the bad character. More often than not, he plays an innovative role. The fact that the opposite has been thought to be the case, even among scholars, is itself of sociological concern. As I have shown, a variety of characters function in the role of villain in Blyton's work, depending, as Propp said, on the exigencies of plot; occasionally – but only occasionally – as in the notorious *N4*, the golliwog.

So, what about the practical implications? Clearly, the golliwog is a powerful character, one that intrigues children, and it is a shame that it has had to be banished. However, the prevalence of racism makes it untenable, especially given the golliwog's history (however distorted). This said, I think the situation might have been resolved in less draconian fashion. From evidence quoted earlier, the term 'golliwog' does seem to have been recuperated to some extent, its most common referent being a scruffy hairstyle.

Personally, I think an opportunity was missed in the 'Noddy' revisions: rather than try to erase the golliwog from history – which, as indicated, results in a reverse racism in many cases – it could have been re-worked slightly, and I would therefore take seriously the suggestion, above, which reiterates a view expressed in *Midnight's Children*: 'blue is a neutral sort of colour, avoids the usual colour problems, gets you away from black and white' (Rushdie, 1982, p. 103). Though such a change might not have worked for Selvon's hero, it certainly could for a doll, thus maintaining some of the potency of the figure while removing its 'black' signification.

9
The Mystery Explained (I): Writer of (and on) the Oral Stage

Introduction

Although any dénouement should be swiftly executed, this one is spread over three chapters, the first of which is largely a social explanation, the second, a more psychoanalytical one, the final one pulling the respective threads together. First, let me briefly review the evidence so far, before I reveal where exactly I think the 'secret mechanism' is located.

When discussing earlier approaches to Blyton, I pointed out how they could not but belittle her, because of the tools they employed. But we also saw how contradictory were the statements made about her: whether her writing, her plots, her characters, her vocabulary, or whatever. The only thing that none dispute is her ability to relate a story (even if there are arguments about how varied these stories are). What really seems to perplex the critics is that a writer they thought so ephemeral should persist for so long; for despite what the gatekeepers have said, her stories continue to be passed down the generations, across classrooms, playgrounds, and from friend to friend. This oral transmission of Blyton's reputation seems to give us an insight into her success and, conversely, to explain why the literary tradition has such a problem in dealing with this.

Blyton herself preferred the term 'storyteller' to writer to describe her work (Blyton, 1959b), which term seems to fit her far more appositely. She certainly always closed the feedback-loop with her audience by encouraging them to write to her – and she would always write back. She also listened to children's own stories, which she would refashion. Like Mother Goose of folktale tradition, Blyton seems to celebrate the female teller, associated with hearth and home, as in titles like *Chimney*

Corner Stories and *Fireside Tales*. In fact, I know of no author who so endorses her home. Some, like Hardy and Trollope, are known for a region, but Green Hedges is known worldwide as the epicentre of a storytelling phenomenon. In *A Story Party at Green Hedges* there is an invitation card to complete on the first page, in order to attend the party – which perfectly captures this notion of sitting round a hearth, feasting in the twilight, while tales are spun. It should also be remembered that Blyton began as a teacher who taught through story, then running together what it now seems should be taught separately: story, history and nature (as did many contemporary authors, especially one of her favourites, Arthur Mee).[1]

I have already drawn attention to some of these elements – the animism, the clumsy constructions, the authorial presence – many of which have been toned down in newer editions. But I'd like to return to them now in more detail, juxtaposing the characteristics of a literary style with the oral.[2]

The literary tradition versus the oral

Style is paramount. At one extreme we have Alan Garner (1996, p. 224) averaging 14 words a day, whereas, at the other, Blyton can manage up to 10,000. Clearly, the storyteller has the audience in front of him or her, and is forced to compose 'on the hoof' – something that Blyton had practised as a teacher. The storyteller cannot revise, except retrospectively. This, of course, accounts both for the rate at which she and similar writers managed to produce material, and for its lack of revision. Interestingly, as she herself confessed in her correspondence with McKellar, when it came to writing non-fiction, she found herself in the situation that most others experience: she had to 'think hard – deliberate – write a sentence or two – erase one – rewrite – think again, and so on' (McKellar, 1957, p. 138).

Composing in this way also gives an immediacy to the stories, of them unfolding before the audience's very eyes – which of course, they were – with Blyton learning about events at the same time as the reader. There are a number of telltale traces of this. For example, when Julian says, 'push that huge, high chest or wardrobe or whatever it is' (*FHMTS*, p. 164) – it is clear that Blyton herself was undecided. In *N18*, where Noddy goes to sea, the Captain tells him that they will 'land on an island somewhere'. Blyton does not name it until later in the story – clearly, when she needed to think of a name. But whereas many writers would go back and amend the earlier text, Blyton leaves it. It is only in the revised version that it is named 'Shell Island' from the beginning (*N18**, p. 30). On the other hand, the island in *FHMTS* gets three names ('Whispering', 'Keep-Away' and 'Wailing' Island, p. 63), presumably because Blyton had not yet decided which she liked best – 'Whispering Island' only emerges as the favourite later.

A novel, or story, is unique, existing in one polished form. This is according to the literary tradition, whereas, for many oral tellers, there are only versions of a story, all drawing on basic plots and characters. The latter would therefore tend to re-tell a story, changing its emphasis as necessary, depending on the audience and the time available. Blyton certainly did this, reworking material for different age groups, different markets, and different word-length requirements – as we have seen in earlier chapters. Her stories, therefore, were more pragmatically developed, often lacking the unity of more considered works. Again, this is reflected in the titles, such as *Five Minute Tales* (1933) and *Ten Minute Tales* (1934b).

Literary works tend to be more causally and thematically integrated than the oral. In technical terms, literary tales tend to be 'hypotactic', highlighting causality, nesting information, having character traits motivate action, and so on. Oral tales, on the other hand, like speech in general, tend to be more episodic and 'paratactic', with elements given equal status alongside each other, often linked with connectives like 'and' and 'also'. This is clearly so with many fairy and folk tales, which frequently have 'loose ends' and unexplained events. Many of Blyton's tales – such as the 'Magic Faraway Tree' series – also have a loose, episodic structure. This paratactic appeal is also apparent in individual sentences, as, for example, in the remark, 'How lovely to wake in a strange place at the beginning of a holiday – to think of bathing and biking and picnicking and eating and drinking – forgetting all about exams and rules and punishments!' (*FGDTS*, p. 37). Here all sense of subordination is removed: everything is levelled out with nothing taking priority over anything else. Notably, the revised editions of Blyton have tended to move away from the paratactic; for example, the following, 'He would sing it loudly, and . . .', has become, 'He thought he would sing it loudly, so . . .' (*N6/**, p. 17).

Literary tales are imaginative rather than sensory. This is a somewhat nebulous distinction, but one that has been upheld since Plato's negative attitude to sensory information (see below); the inference is that by being tied to the world of appearances, the material world, one thereby misses higher, imaginative realities. This is not simply about visualizing images, then, but something much more refined, as captured in the Leavisite criticism mentioned earlier. Visualizing, in fact, is particularly suspect, hence I.A. Richards and William Empson speak of its 'special danger'.[3] Even Nell in his influential *Lost in a Book* (1988) states that imagery is not generally used by readers. However, Esrock, who has reviewed this whole area, points to the contradictions in Nell, drawing on some of the latter's other work, which actually demonstrates the opposite: that vividness of imagery correlates with reading involvement, and, significantly, that imagery is 'an important contributor to reading pleasure' (Esrock, 1994, pp. 40–1). Blyton's use of the senses certainly puts her in the sensory camp, writing for an audience which is almost literally 'there' – as instanced in her frequent exhortations for us to 'Look' or 'Listen'. In this way we become complicit in witnessing a scene; 'when you're reading them, you feel like you're in the picture', as an 8-year-old boy put it. If there is a notice, Blyton is likely to say, 'Here it is' (*N13*, p. 33), 'Have a look at it' (*N9*, p. 28), rather than 'It said' – as each has been amended. When a crab seizes Noddy's toe, she writes, 'Look at it, holding on with its claws' (*N7*, p. 42; again, the visual imperative has been removed). And when Blyton describes a song being sung, she tells us all, 'I'll pop my head in at the window and hear it for you. Listen!' (which has been amended to 'I think it might sound a bit like this', *N8*/*, p. 60).

Not only does Blyton involve her readers' senses, but she uses other conventions of the oral teller, to suggest her presence – just as an oral teller uses body movement and voice to convey information. In fact, the last example above shows how she suggests her physical presence. Likewise, various typographical devices convey her voice. She uses uppercase and italics to stress a word, or to indicate its loudness (just as ethnographic transcription uses the 'uppercase = loud' convention). Generally these emphases have been kept in the revisions, but whereas Blyton would often accentuate only one syllable, this has been amended to whole words. Thus, whereas Blyton wrote '*any*thing', the revised has '*anything*' (*N12*/*, p. 21); similarly, 'EVERYbody' has become 'EVERYBODY' (*N8*/*, p. 31). She also, famously, uses exclamation marks for emphasis, runs words together to indicate haste (e.g. 'couldyoulookaftertheponyhereforme?' – Blyton, 1968, p. 94) and spells onomatopoeically (e.g. 'EEEE-ee-OOOOO-oo-EEEEEEEEAH-OOO!' – *FHMTS*, p. 140).

Character is central, action secondary, and deriving from the former. This, again, is in the literary tradition. However, the oral tends to reverse this, with action coming first. Thus, the behaviour of characters, rather than driving the plot, tends to be a function of it. This, as noted earlier, is Propp's model, where a variety of characters can perform any particular function. As the characters need to be swiftly drawn for the audience to visualize them, there is a tendency to rely on traditional figures, whether archetypal or stereotypical, rather than exact and subtly drawn Jamesian individuals.

Plagiarism is taboo. This is true in literary culture, whereas the oral tradition has a completely different outlook on the matter. In the latter it is *de rigueur* to draw on the culture's stock of legends, stories, and characters, and to rework them in new contexts. It is not surprising then, that Blyton uses nursery rhyme, fairy-tale, myth and legend as her wellspring, quite aside from a number of literary sources.[4] Moreover, she frequently draws attention to these links:

> 'It's like the Open Sesame trick in Ali Baba and the Forty Thieves,' thought George.
>
> (*FGOTC*, p. 152)

> 'Put that pig down, Anne, you must be tired of carrying it,' said Dick. 'You look like Alice in Wonderland. She carried a pig too!'
>
> (*FGTBH*, p. 179)

Neither should it be surprising that she reworked her own stories according to the occasion, despite some critics' dismay.[5] This was particularly noted in connection with Noddy. Once again, Blyton can be seen as surprisingly modern in treating everything as an intertext – something that sometimes got her into trouble, as when she was charged in 1953 with infringement of copyright, unsuccessfully in the event, for retelling Chandler Harris's story of Brer Rabbit.

The verbal icon. The notion of a work standing coherent and unified, on its own, is also part of the literary tradition, whereas the oral tradition emphasizes open-endedness. Blyton's work is inveterately open – 'to be continued' – either because it is part of a series, or because the story itself is likely to be reworked in a different medium or context. In this respect, of course, it is very like today's soaps. This notion causes some critics problems, in that it is the works of popular culture that they would like to define as 'closed', as these works are said to dictate interpretation and ideological stance, leaving little imaginative space for the reader. But, as many have argued, the opposite is frequently the case, with readers importing more of their own local culture and interests and, to some extent, co-authoring the texts. Figurative language is therefore deliberately avoided. It would only pin down an image too precisely, or confuse the reader with unwanted associations.[6] It is the reader who provides the metaphorical resonances from Blyton's baseline words, each importing his or her own local associations. As one woman put it, 'when I re-read the Faraway Tree this year I was extremely disappointed because half the scenes and people I'd remembered didn't exist – except in my imagination'.

A certain definable corpus *of texts is intrinsically valuable.* This is celebrated in the notion of the 'great tradition'. Conversely, the oral tradition tends to be forever modifying its texts to suit circumstances, so there are more likely to be celebrated performances (that is, meetings of text and audience) than texts *per se*. This is something that clearly comes across with readers, who tend to remember distinctive reading occasions, often associated with particular, favourite texts, even though the content of the text can itself be hazy. What they remember is having enjoyed it. This seems particularly apposite to Blyton's work, which is part of a larger territory, of fantasies, games and further storytelling; indeed, of a whole culture. (Over half the respondents discussed her work, about a third wrote similar stories, and an equal number engaged in fantasies about them; a quarter formed clubs, a fifth engaged in Blyton-related games, one in eight emulated her characters and an equal number re-enacted adventures.)[7]

Language is precise and logical. This is the case in literary works. They prize *le mot juste*, with economy and variety of diction, whereas the oral tradition flaunts this – frequently because of practical considerations: the teller needs a space in which to think of what is going to happen next. Thus repetition and use of vague filler words are common. Blyton uses many of these techniques, which are often the very things that revisers tone down. So, in the following, the revised edition has dropped the second sentence: 'He couldn't believe his eyes. He really couldn't' (*N2*, p. 56).

Blyton also uses a simple, straightforward, albeit functional lexis. Her language is deliberately transparent, one that is worn to familiarity with use, so that the story 'goes without saying' (which is why words like 'gay' and 'queer' now obtrude). Figurative language is therefore avoided, as noted above. Also, as in Homer, we find a variety of stock phrases used; for example, whereas for Homer the sea is always 'wine red', for Blyton it is 'cornflower blue'. I find it interesting that Blyton herself mentions Dickens and Homer as writers she not only admired but in whom she found similarities (McKellar correspondence, Stoney, 1974, p. 207), for both are also intensely visual. Dickens, like Blyton, was also a good mimic, and renowned for becoming totally involved when composing, seeing his characters enact scenes before his eyes. He too has a liking for present-tense narration. Moreover, he too was capable of producing a vast daily output – although he found this more difficult in his later years. Lastly, Dickens, like Homer, was someone who also relished contact with an audience.

The literary tradition tends to approve of authorial detachment, 'showing' rather than 'telling'. Conversely, in the oral tradition, the author is more closely involved – in fact, strictly speaking, he or she would have been physically present. There is a sense of immersion in the stories, with both narrator and narratee being close to the action, complicit in it, which gives the stories vitality. On the one hand the storyteller had to conjure up a vivid picture for all concerned, but on the other, the audience had to visualize it; the latter thus feeling part of its construction. In fact, the audience was literally 'at the pictures', which is exactly Blyton's image for what happened when she wrote, seated at her 'private cinema screen', watching events unfold. I have included several elements of Blyton's technique under this heading, because this seems to come close to its heart.

There is Blyton's use of deixis, that is, words which 'point' to particular locations in space and time ('here' and 'now'). Blyton uses both temporal and spatial *deixis* to sustain a sense of immediacy in her work. Her frequent leaps into the present-tense add to this, as, for instance, in *N6*, when Noddy puts on inappropriate headgear and the narrator says, 'But, oh dear, it isn't a hat, it's the little lamp-shade' (*N6*, p. 44; in the revised version, this is rendered in the past, distancing both action and narratorial voice).[8] Related to this is her extensive use of pronouns, creating potential ambiguities as to the referents (for example, 'We'll take him with us and say we'll set him on to them if they don't clear out' – *FRAT*, p. 130). Not only has she been criticized for this, but revisions have sought to disambiguate such sentences. However, if one is visually present there is, of course, less ambiguity. This, in turn, is related to Vygotsky's notion of 'inner speech', often described as 'disconnected and incomplete' because the material discussed is already known (Vygotsky, 1962, p. 139); and, as Vygotsky notes, such abbreviated language frequently occurs in intimate groupings (just as Bernstein talked about a 'restricted code' being used among more closely-knit groups – see Chapter 3). It may well be, then, that Blyton's pronominal usage is more confusing to adults than it is to children.

The closeness of the narrator is also shown in Blyton's metadiscursive commentary – that is, her narrative gloss on what's happening. Thus, the example of 'oh dear' above, where Blyton gives an evaluation of what's going on. Another key metadiscursive feature that Blyton uses is apostrophizing – turning aside to address a character; for instance:

> If danger was about, he [Julian] could deal with it better than George could. After all, she was only a *girl*!
>
> Yes, Julian, she is – but, as you've often said, she's just as brave as a boy. Don't be too sure about tonight!
>
> (*FATA*, p. 135)

Labov (1972), looking at urban storytelling, noted the presence of such evaluative devices, and at what he calls 'codas' at the end. Whereas during the story these metadiscursive elements help shape the tale and give a sense of currency, at the end they are used to signal a return to 'real time'. This, of course, is very like the oral situation, where the audience would obviously be aware of the storyteller's presence, often with the latter's interjections; and the teller would finish with something like, 'my tale's done'.

Here is a blatant example from the end of a Five story – which one is soon apparent:

> 'How did you find out all this?' said the sergeant.
>
> 'It's too long to tell you now!' said Dick. 'We'll write it all down in a book, and send you a copy. We'll call it – er – we'll call it – what shall we call it, you others?' . . .
>
> 'I know!' said George, at once. 'I know! Let's call it 'FIVE HAVE PLENTY OF FUN!'
>
> Well, they did – and they hope you like it!
>
> (*FHPOF*, pp. 181, 183)

Another technique that Blyton uses to create this notion of the story unfolding in one's head is 'free indirect discourse' (FID), which is where, as Wall puts it,

> The narrator briefly recounts an action and then slides imperceptibly into the thoughts of the character, so that it appears as though the narrator is commenting on the action in the voice of the child characters. This has the effect of causing the narrator to appear to be confiding in the narratee.
>
> (Wall, 1992, p. 191).

The following, also quoted earlier, demonstrates it well. Mr. Plod's helmet has just blown off:

> 'Come back helmet!' But the helmet took no notice. It was having a lovely time, bumping and bouncing and rolling along. Ha – this was better than sitting still on Mr. Plod's head! (*N6*, p. 44)

We can see here how the narrator slides from telling what's happening, to giving the thoughts of the thing spoken about. Often it is just the presence of an exclamation-mark that indicates FID, as in the line 'After all, she was only a girl!', above. However, it can be used in a more loaded manner, as in Blyton's depiction of Edgar's smile:

> Julian called out to Edgar. 'You shut up! You're not funny, only jolly silly!' 'Georgie-porgie,' began Edgar again, a silly smile on his wide red face.
>
> (*FRAT*, p. 17).

Examples like this caused Hildick to accuse Blyton of being 'as irrational and abandoned in her irrationality as a child' (Hildick, 1970, p. 139). Rose picks this up to illustrate her thesis that the categories of child and adult must be kept 'safely apart on the page' (Rose, 1984, p. 69) – something that Blyton is seen to confound. However, I think both miss what Blyton is about. Her slide between thought and speech is not just 'vicious childishness', as Hildick calls it (1970, p. 138), for Blyton has characters make the same slide:

> 'I wish I was like George,' she [Anne] thought. 'She wouldn't really mind that toad. I'm silly. I ought to try and like all creatures. Oh my goodness, look at that enormous spider in the corner of the sink! It's sitting there, looking at me out of its eight eyes! Wilfrid, Wilfrid – PLEASE come and get this spider out of the sink for me!'
>
> (*FHMTS*, p. 49)

Though it might indicate sloppy writing (or sloppy copy-editing), its presence is also indicative of the dreamlike feel of Blyton's narratives. They are truly like 'narrative monologues', to use Cohn's (1978) term for FID, a term that Wall also favours.[9] Here are two more examples, one from Noddy, where Big-Ears speaks on behalf of the car, the second from the Five, where we have Dick answering himself:

> 'Sorry to frighten you, rabbits,' called Big-Ears, 'but we're in a hurry. Parp-parp!' (*N3*, p. 40)

> 'I never liked Willis or Johnson much,' said Dick, as they walked out of the school grounds. 'Awful swotters they were – never had any time for games or fun. But I take my hat off to them today! Because of their swotting they've won medals and scholarships and goodness knows what – and we've got a week-end off in celebration! Good old Willis and Johnson!'
>
> 'Hear hear,' said Dick.
>
> (*FOHT*, p. 16)

This is an egocentric way of writing, one that conveys a sense of the dreamlike, or the fantastic, in which the dreamer would create and speak all the parts him- or herself. In reading this, as I suggested earlier, the audience feels part of the process. Certainly, this is how many saw her stories: '[I] Imagine myself there with the characters, but just invisible' (m, 17); 'I feel like I'm there with them'(m); 'When I read them I escaped into them and became one of the gang' (m).

It might be thought that first-person narratives would achieve this more readily but, because they funnel perceptions through one particular consciousness, this isn't so; in effect, one witnesses a far more partial view of events. First-person narrative also requires more empathy from the author, which, as I shall suggest in the next chapter, Blyton was not really capable of. Hence, after an early experimental period, she avoided this form.[10]

Let me now link the above to two other facets mentioned earlier. First, I have suggested that qualities of Blyton's writing make it more like a form of inner-speech – qualities such as its easy lexis and its belief in a shared, communally visualizable world. Given this, it may be that Blyton's work is particularly suited to facilitating the shift from outer to inner, from reality to fantasy – to what I have termed the 'time-out'. Secondly, one outstanding quality of the oral tradition is its present-centredness: it strives to create a sense of a story happening here and now, as does any daydream, of course, its *raison d'être* being immediacy. Several of the features mentioned above are particularly pertinent to this, like Blyton's flagging up of her presence, her proximal deictics (literally 'here' and 'now'), her leaps from preterite to present, and her exhortations to look at particular things. This seems to give an interesting twist to the notion of her being 'ephemeral'. She is this, certainly, but this does not mean that she'll go away. Paradoxically, it is her ephemerality that contributes to her longevity, in that the 'ephemeral' is about being 'for the day', and Blyton is exactly that: a story for the moment, indulging the pleasure principle.[11]

I have summarized the elements of the oral tradition, in contrast to the literary, in Table 9.1, but I'd now like to probe this link more closely. With Blyton, her audience was that huge tribe of children, sitting round listening, having their deeds celebrated, while the adults are seen as what Kenneth Grahame disparagingly calls 'the Olympians'. One is initiated into Blyton's stories by password – to the heroic deeds of characters like the Famous Five and Secret Seven – to a shared world, in fact, as the games and fantasizing suggest.

This analogy is worth pushing further, for storytelling not only celebrates its heroes, but it also unites its audience with them in fantasy. The audience is captivated, metaphorically spellbound. And while the stories are told round the light and warmth of the fire, the teller's task is to make sure that the minds of the listeners are equally warmed and enlightened (Benjamin, 1973 (p. 101) speaks of storytellers rekindling a 'shivering life'). Certainly, Blyton saw herself in this role, as moral guide, cultivating it assiduously by maintaining a proximity to her audience, soliciting feedback, writing columns, editorials and letters, setting up clubs, and by personal contact. In the clubs, of course, like the Famous Five, children could wear badges to show their sense of community.[12] But her stories were the main method of promoting it, making children the centre of things. From Blyton's central hearth, then, whether 'Old Thatch' or 'Green Hedges', her stories extended to that worldwide tribe gathered round this imaginary centre, touched by her sunny stories. Enid used this conceit repeatedly, building on the traditional link of feasting and listening, both inside the story and out.

Table 9.1 Literary versus oral qualities of texts

Literary qualities	Oral qualities
Style is paramount – polished	Style is secondary – 'first draft' stories
A novel/story is unique, a masterpiece for all time	Story changes to suit circumstances, time, audience
The work is thematically integrated: organic, hypotactic	The work is more linearly organized: open and paratactic
Imaginative	Sensory (visual, aural, tactile, and so on)
Character is central, rounded and motivated; emphasis on individual qualities; psychological, introspective	Character is secondary to action; schematically drawn; stock figures; archetypes, stereotypes; external perspective
Plagiarism is taboo, originality a premium	Draw on 'the tradition', derivative, intertextual
The 'Verbal Icon' is celebrated; text not context	Series oriented, open-ended, audience involvement, work as springboard for other activities (games, rituals, feasting, and so on.)
Definable *corpus* of texts is intrinsically valuable – the Great Tradition, the canon	Performance (that is, individual reading) is valuable in its own right
Language precise, logical, metaphorical	Language simple, repetitive, formulaic, clichéd; 'degree zero' writing
Authorial detachment – showing rather than telling	Authorial involvement – telling, evaluative comment, proximal deixis
Privatized activity, cerebral	Communal activity, affective, visceral

Homer versus Plato on storytelling

I would now like to draw on another line of research, which not only connects Blyton's oral style with the Homeric tradition, but also with its critics. The fact that our brains consist of two hemispheres, and that these work in different ways is now a relatively well-studied area. The left hemisphere, usually the dominant one, works in a logical, piece-by-piece fashion. It is analytical, the seat of language. In contrast, the right hemisphere is much more artistically inclined, tending to see 'wholes', to work with patterns. It is intuitive rather than logical, and far less likely to rely on hard evidence for its claims. It is not only artistic, but musical too, being the seat of song. Some researchers have suggested that this right hemisphere, which is far more in evidence in young children, becomes gradually overruled by the left as we age and as analytical skills are called upon to a greater extent. Researchers have also suggested that this right hemisphere might be the location of Freud's Unconscious, with the left constituting the more conscious self (Blakeslee, 1980).

Of special interest here is Julian Jaynes' work (1976) which, drawing on such evidence, makes some startling claims about our ancestors. In particular, Jaynes points out that in Homer's time poets claimed to visualize and hear material delivered to them, hence their belief in being inspired by Muses. What they were really 'hearing', argues Jaynes, was their own right hemispheres, which literally took them over, delivering powerful imagery and sounds. This certainly seems so with Blyton, who claimed, 'I am a visual writer, conveying what I *see* (*and* hear – for my private mind-television set has sound, too). While I write I live completely with my characters . . .' (Sykes, 1962, p. 21). Other senses are involved, too: 'My simile of a "private cinema screen" is the best I can think of. But it's a 3-dimensional screen, complete with sound, smell and taste – and feeling! This is why I can describe things so realistically in my stories, "as if I had been there". I *have* been there – but only in my imagination!' (McKellar correspondence, Stoney, 1974, p. 210).

These early writers, then, of whom Homer is the most famous, would compose 'off the cuff', frequently singing their material – something that Noddy and other characters are also prone to do. Blyton actually talks about hearing some 25 songs while writing her Noddy play, songs that 'burst out spontaneously from the characters . . . I saw them dancing to it, and heard them singing it' (McKellar, 1957, p. 139). Although most of us have lost this ability to access the right hemisphere so readily, many artists still seem able to do so. As Blyton put it, she found it easy to 'open the sluice gates of . . . imagination, reach down into . . . [the] "under-mind"' (Blyton, 1950a, p. 3); it was 'easily-tapped' (ibid., p. 4), and the fact that she had a photographic memory was probably very much connected with this.

So, to conclude this aspect, the oral tradition seems a more apposite way of talking about Blyton's writing, moving away from the supercilious sneering of earlier criticism, while giving some indication of why Blyton holds such attraction. It shows not only how she composed, but how her readers were likely to receive her compositions – 'Feeling that EB spoke directly to me'(f), 'I *was* there as I read' (f) – as many readers have recorded.

Having noted some similarities between Blyton and Homer, the corresponding criticisms should sound more familiar. In *The Republic*, Plato criticizes Homer's work for being, at best, frivolous, and, at worst, dangerous (Havelock, 1963, pp. 3–4); it is seen as a 'crippling of the mind', a disease, 'a species of mental poison, and is the enemy of truth' (one thinks here of Fisher's 'slow poison' comment). The Homeric bard is also troublesome because of his 'superior memory' and encyclopaedic knowledge. He encourages listeners to aspire beyond their station and gives them a personal code of values and attitudes. Such power is particularly worrying given Homer's influence over children: 'Shall we therefore allow our children to listen to any stories written by anyone . . . our first business is to supervise the production of stories, and choose only those we think suitable, and reject the rest' (Plato, 1955, pp. 114–15).

But behind these criticisms of Homer – all of which have been levelled at Blyton – there is an enduring concern with the poet's 'power to make his audience identify almost pathologically and certainly sympathetically with the content of what he is saying' (Havelock, 1963, p. 45), 'putting the whole community into a formulaic state of mind' and exercising 'cultural control' over them (ibid., p. 76). From the storyteller's side this required that:

> He sank his personality in his performance. His audience in turn would remember only as they entered effectively and sympathetically into what he was saying and this in turn meant that they became his servants and submitted to his spell.
>
> (ibid., p. 160)

They did this by re-enacting the story with 'lips, larynx, and limbs, and with the whole apparatus of their unconscious nervous system' (ibid.), and Plato saw such identification as most easily evoked when words themselves described actions. The language of the storyteller was thus deliberately visual, 'a piece of language so worded as to encourage the illusion that we are actually looking at an act being performed or at a person performing it' (ibid., p. 188). This was Plato's central worry, that we, the audience,

> are seduced into identifying with its doings, its joys and griefs, its nobilities and cruelties, its courage and its cowardice. As we pass from experience to experience, submitting our memories to the spell of the incantation, the whole experience becomes a kind of dream in which image succeeds image automatically without conscious control on our part, without a pause to reflect, to rearrange or to

> generalize, and without a chance to ask a question or raise a doubt, for this would at once interrupt and endanger the chain of association.
>
> (ibid., p. 190)

Ironically, Plato recommends arithmetic instead of story as the key subject, since it requires 'personal separation' rather than identification (ibid., p. 210). Mathematics was, of course, the one subject that Blyton herself found impossible.

Conclusion

I have argued that looking at Blyton in traditional literary terms is not only to miss her appeal but precisely to highlight her negative qualities. It is far more productive to see her in terms of the oral tradition, where her appeal stands out. This tradition has a number of notable features: first, it closely binds teller and audience; second, in terms of content, it extols the deeds of that audience, or its representatives ('it was thrilling to read about other children as heroes', as one reader put it); in other words, children's own fantasies of power and honour are addressed. Third, in terms of process, the audience feels very much a part of the action (thanks to the visual, sensual qualities of the tales, and their present-centredness). Lastly, it is not only participatory, but dreamlike and egocentric, too – terms that bring to mind Freud's notion of creative works being like daydreams, fulfilling the wishes of their creators. However, though Blyton is often conceived as a wish-fulfiller, I shall suggest, in the next chapter, that the truth is more complex.

There are two other points worth reiterating. It was suggested that it is this participatory quality which is at the heart of adult worries about Blyton, and I showed how concerns about the oral writer's powers of 'identification' go back to Plato. There is a fear of children being controlled, becoming mindless beings, slaves to the Blyton text, from which some are presumed never to escape. Blyton is thus a modern Pied Piper. Of course, the gatekeepers had their own agenda for children, which was another set of texts, but ones they felt moved the children on, stretched them towards adulthood in some way. There is no room for children to have their own pleasures in the text: celebrating having tales told about them, themselves at the centre. The other point, again to be picked up later, is that this celebration of the in-group – the children – must be at the expense of an out-group: the adults whom the piper leaves out in the cold.

10
The Mystery Explained (II): Writer of Passages

The plot so far: I began by trying to clear up some of the many misconceptions about Blyton's work, in order to view the field more clearly. I also sought to put Blyton's work into its social context, finishing with a description of its oral qualities, which suggest ways that its appeal might be more positively valorized. However, this still seems to leave some questions unanswered, and for these I shall turn inward, to a more psychoanalytically informed reading. These questions have been hinted at already; namely, the egocentric, dreamlike quality of her work; the way that what is happening *within* the text is frequently mirrored *without*, in the reader's local environment. Outside this cosy arena, we have also seen how outsiders can be despised and derogated. Let me now try to give some shape to these issues.

Entering the dark wood

In terms of previous studies, there have been a few hints at a psychoanalytic approach to Blyton's work, but usually at the level of innuendo, such as Tucker (1971, p. 100) quoting an irresistible line about George wishing she had a lighthouse. Likewise, Saunders (1995) bemoans Blyton's 'vast wardrobe of Freudian slips', and cites 'a Blyton series about an oversized elf named Mr Pinkwhistle [sic] (oh yes), who was given to suddenly materializing in children's playgrounds. You will not find the BBC hurrying to dust off that shocking old pervert', she concludes.[1] Druce, meanwhile, picking up on Noddy's spring-mounted head, which the milkman enjoys nodding, writes: 'the underlying phallic symbolism is made virtually transparent. It is difficult to understand how Blyton could have been unaware of what she was suggesting' (Druce, 1992, p. 257). Unfortunately, Druce cannot seem to articulate it either. His final statement is little clearer, where he speaks of Noddy as 'the disembodied penis of psychoanalytically oriented literary theory, the phallic trickster whose naughtiness motivates the plot' (ibid.). I have to admit that some children interviewed were on a similar wavelength, although it was only later that I realized why they were sniggering:

> *Daisy*: 'Here Comes Noddy Again'.
> *Dan*: I love that title. [12-year-olds]

This aside, we would do well to bear in mind Freud's own admonition, that sometimes a cigar is just a cigar. Elizabeth Schneider's witty comments on this sort of reading are also instructive, although she is here discussing romantic poets:

> If rounded mountains always in human experience must mean breasts and caverns always mean wombs, one might write an illuminating essay on infantilism and regression in romantic poets, provided one can prove that they describe more mountains and caverns than other poets do . . . [but] it is difficult to see how this kind of interpretation can throw light on any given poem unless it can show something special in the use of caverns and mountains that is not present in other cavern–mountain poems . . . [for example] the precise degree of the angle moving from obtuse to acute that might be found to transform a mountain from a breast to a phallic symbol, or the determination of a dome as breast or womb according as the poet is outdoors or in.
>
> (Schneider, 1953, p. 10)

This said, there is, no doubt, much to explain in Blyton that a social reading cannot account for. It must be said, for example, that there are an exceptional number of tails, often detached from their owners – far more than in other writers, responding to Schneider's point. I have already mentioned some in Noddy, but they crop up everywhere. In the short stories they are particularly prevalent, almost characters in their own right, with entire 'tales' revolving round them. For instance, in 'Amelia Jane and the plasticine' there is a teddy who complains 'that he had no tail' (Blyton, 1939, p. 78), so Amelia Jane sticks a plasticine one on him while he sleeps. 'He would think he had grown a tail, and what fun it would be to see him walking about proudly, showing off his beautiful tail! What would he say when it came off?' (ibid.). 'The clockwork-mouse loved it', we are told, 'and the yellow duck said it was the longest she had ever seen' (ibid., p. 81). Then, when teddy is not looking, 'with her clever fingers she made the end of it into a snake's head! Fancy that! It looked exactly like a snake now, with its mouth open and two little holes for eyes' (ibid., p. 82). 'Michael's tail' (1945) is similar, with a tail sewn on, which he doesn't 'want to part with . . . [so] He still wears it . . .'. (Blyton, 1972, p. 159). In 'Snicker the Brownie' (1937) tails become detached from some cats, and 'wriggled away like snakes, out of the garden gate, past Snicker, and slid off into the wood' (Blyton, 1985, p. 43); later 'those tails fastened themselves to the back of him as he ran – and there was Snicker with two long black tails! . . . He couldn't get them off! They were growing on him!' (ibid., p. 47). And so on![2]

What are we to make of them? Clearly, we need to go beyond Druce's knowing nod; they need to be related to other aspects of Blyton's work. And it seems to me that the key lies in the juxtaposition of Blyton's desperate sanguinity with her aversion to unhappy and unpleasant matters; ultimately, in fact, to death. All this led me to Freud's later ideas, where that disturbing area 'beyond the pleasure principle' is explored: the area of the death-instinct, where images of castration and dismemberment abound (Freud, 1961) and, in turn, to more recent accounts of this process, in Lacan and Kristeva. Let me begin with a brief outline of some psychoanalytical ideas to inform the discussion.

In Lacan's psychoanalytic account of development, the mirror phase marks the child's first coming to see itself as a whole, either in a mirror itself, or as reflected in the eyes of a significant Other – usually the mother. This person confers identity, a notion of one being a complete human. Freud calls this a narcissistic stage for a number of reasons, a key one being that this image of wholeness is precisely that: an image, not a reality. Hence it is a mis-identification. However, it does prove very attractive in that it offers the child a sense of being entire unto itself, lacking nothing; in other words, the child has an image of omnipotence, even though it may still lack bodily control, being, in effect, a fragmented being. It glorifies in its power, yet is dependent on others – on their defining look, their attentions – to have this power realized. It is during this stage that the ego is formed, which seeks to preserve this sense of narcissistic unity, of immortality, false though it is.

Unfortunately, this perception of wholeness is challenged both from within and without. From within, there is the simple fact that the Imaginary is only a partial snapshot of the subject, based on a false notion of wholeness – which can, therefore, be undone by all that has been excluded (what Kristeva (1982) calls the 'abject': that which has been expelled, although it is only in the process of abjection, or expulsion, that the subject comes to see itself as a separate being in the first place). From without there is the oedipal challenge. In this, the presence of the father disturbs the child's wish to maintain its satisfying sense of unity, which depends on the supporting regard of the mother. But the father is bigger, more powerful; in Lacan's terms, he is possessor of the 'phallus'.

Let me pause here to make plain Lacan's reworking of Freud. Most significantly, Lacan has moved away from a biological to a symbolic explanation of the oedipal castration. This is why he prefers the term 'phallus', which he uses to signify difference – without which language would be impossible. This was Saussure's insight, recognizing that language could not be based on unity, on separate words mapping on to distinct entities in the world (if this were the case, there would only ever have been one, unchanging language). In other words, and other words are always necessary, one can *mean* only by dividing, by indicating what is *not* in the very instant one indicates that something *is*. Lacan uses the trope of the oedipal struggle to show how the phallus breaks up the unity of the Imaginary. In Freudian terms one is either with (+) or without (–) the phallus, hence divided into male or female (an either/or dualism). One is forced to take up a position in language – in this case, a gendered positioning as 'he' or 'she' – henceforth excluding parts of oneself (the female parts of a male, and vice versa).

Moreover, as noted earlier, because language cannot fully map on to things, because it can only express them indirectly, in a relational manner, there is always a gap between what one wishes to say and its realization: a lack persists, a residue, albeit there exists the desire to fill it. So the speaker moves on, along a chain of signifiers, forever falling short of complete meaning – of that immediacy of being felt in the Imaginary stage – yet forever aspiring to it. The Symbolic order, then, is the realm of language, which is seen as residing with the Father – the key possessor of power; or, in Foucauldian terms, of those discourses that arbitrate 'reality'. What is important to note in the above is that the *presence* of the symbolic signifier entails the *absence* of the thing itself; at its very heart, then, language has an emptiness: the signifier never fully represents the signified (just as a mirror image never captures the full presence of the young infant).

Where does this plenitude exist, then, if not in the false but comforting image of the Imaginary, or in the divisive partiality of the Symbolic, in language? For Lacan it is in a third order – the Real – that which language cannot represent, although the gaps exposed through our use of language might hint at it. In slips-of-the-tongue, nonsense words, rhythmic sounds, repetitions, and so on, we get a glimpse of this disturbing unrepresented. The real is implied in various descriptions, like William James' memorable 'blooming buzzing confusion' – that which we filter out; for Lacan it is excess, surplus, *jouissance*. In its lack of signification it is also associated with death (remember that the third Fate, she who cuts the thread of life, is Atropos – literally 'no turning': for in death there is no metaphorical refuge).

Though Freud introduced the idea of a death-drive lying 'beyond the pleasure principle', he wrote about it in seemingly contradictory terms, as though life itself were striving towards non-existence. Lacan reworks this, seeing this drive as being aimed not at death *per se*, but at the death of the unitary ego: a driving of unvoiced, unfocused energies against the boundaries of a narcissistic Ideal-I; energies that wish to deconstruct it, and which the ego therefore wards off. (Of course, this was the fate of the original Narcissus, who was so captivated by his self-image that he ceased to exist apart from it.) Kristeva expresses this more bluntly: 'refuse and corpses *show me* what I permanently thrust aside in order to live. But what threatens to emerge from the real is ultimately a part of oneself, one's own refuse, one's own corpse' (Kristeva, 1982, p. 65).

Of course, individuals will seek to ward off such disturbing intimations. Lacan therefore speaks of the narcissistic ego turning in a 'fictional direction' during development. That is, it tries to shore up its Ideal-I by constructing fantasies (narratives) of its supremacy; in Freud's words, of 'His Majesty the Ego, the hero alike of every day-dream and of every story' (Freud, 1959, p. 150). In order to be effective though, such stories need to be retold continually, which is why Freud emphasized repetition as a way that the ego tries to secure – to bind – the energies that assail it.

The most famous story of repetition is the *Fort–Da* game, where Freud writes of his grandson rehearsing, symbolically, the absence of his mother. The child had a cotton reel to which some thread was tied. Each time he threw the reel away – which then disappeared from view over his curtained cot – the child said a sound like 'fort', or 'gone'; he would then pull the reel back into view, saying 'da', or 'there'. Freud was perplexed as to why the child should persist in an activity that was unpleasurable, that emphasized his mother's absence. Freud eventually saw it as paralleling the compulsively repetitive behaviour of war victims reliving traumatic events. He surmised that all were seeking mastery over their experiences, trying to integrate them in some way, whether fractured by war or simply by a mother's absence. Not only this: they were also making a move from being passive victims to active participants, seeking to repair a disturbance of ego-equilibrium by binding the energies of the disturbing elements.

In the *Fort–Da* case the child uses language to stand for the absence of his mother – present signifiers for absent signifieds – except that the signifiers never fully replace her. Hence, as said earlier, signification is constructed on, or conceals, a sense of absence. Peter Brooks (1984; 1994) has applied this notion to story, noting how a tale moves one from a quiescent state into the machinations of plot, with its repetitions, delays and stirrings of suspense; striving, across a pattern of signifiers, for some unifying signified (a plenitude of meaning) – striving, in fact, for mastery. Whereas the only coherence in life comes with death, when we have not only a beginning but an ending too, 'face to face with the granite end page', as Cixous puts it (quoted in Sellers, 1996, p. 103), story allows us a safe way of playing this out, one in which we can participate time and again, just as Scheherazade warded off death in her nightly stories (which Blyton (1930b) also retold).

Finally, let me say some words about the uncanny, the other main area where Freud probes the death-drive. In his essay Freud starts with a philological analysis of the German term for 'uncanny', *unheimlich*, which, as he notes, is closely associated with *heimlich*, a word for 'homely' or 'familiar'. But this latter term itself has another and opposing meaning – hidden, kept out of sight – a meaning which *unheimlich* echoes. As Freud puts it, the meaning of *heimlich* 'develops in the direction of ambivalence, until it finally coincides with its opposite' (Freud, 1985, p. 347). This in itself reinforces the term's uncanny nature, which Schelling's definition compounds: 'everything is *unheimlich* that ought to have remained secret and hidden but has come to light' (ibid., p. 345).

The uncanny is said to be evoked by a number of things: by doubles, by the inanimate becoming animate (and *vice versa*, in images of death, dismemberment and castration), by repetition, by effacing the division between the imaginary and reality, and by the psychic overwhelming physical reality (as in wish-fulfilments, the omnipotence of thought). However, Freud adds the *caveat* that these things do not evoke the uncanny in fairy-tales, for such happenings are simply too common-place in this genre (ibid., p. 369). (Obviously, for children, newer to story, this might not initially be the case.)

In the course of analysing the term, Freud uses Hoffman's 'The Sandman' to illustrate his point. However, Cixous and others have suggested that Freud's analysis represses much of the story's uncanniness, actually seeking to explain away the *unheimlich*. He does this, it is argued, because the story is largely about the 'death pulse' (Cixous, 1976, p. 539), which disturbed Freud, who himself seems to have had a phobia about death.[3] Yet death is at the heart of the *unheimlich*: 'the uncanny always entails anxieties about fragmentation, about the disruption or destruction of any narcissistically informed sense of personal stability, body integrity, immortal individuality' (Bronfen, 1992, p. 113).

Blyton, as we shall explore, also had a vivid fear of death, so let us now return to her – a compulsive storyteller if ever there was – to argue, broadly speaking, that she told stories as frantically as any Scheherazade, striving to keep intact an Imaginary, sunny *Gestalt* at all costs; and the costs were, ultimately, great. I shall discuss this in two sections, beginning with a return to her autobiographical writings before moving on to her 'fiction' – while recognizing that these terms are somewhat interchangeable.

Storying life

One story that Blyton liked to hear repeatedly when she was young was of how her father had refused to let her die when she had whooping-cough. He had cradled her all night, refusing to accept the doctor's negative prognosis (Stoney, 1974, p. 16). We have here an example of a story where the teller is also the hero, and where the narratee is closely involved and celebrated; clearly, an oral tale of great appeal. It is also one that, in the above terms, wards off death. Her father, as we saw earlier, seems to have had a profound influence on the young Blyton. He seems to have been the significant Other who helped her create a strong and early sense of self-worth. But, as we have also seen, this unity is dependent on the Other maintaining his or her presence, so it must have been a tremendous blow when Blyton heard that the person who had effectively 'storied' her existence, had had his own so suddenly terminated: a part of her was effectively cut off.

Death, then, held a special fear for Blyton – whether or not this particular event played any part in it. She certainly never attended the funeral of either parent, and was known to dislike illness, both in others and herself. However, in line with what I said above, this is no simple 'thanatophobia'. It is death in the Lacanian sense: a fear that the narcissistic ego might be attacked and overwhelmed; death as a catch-all waste-paper-basket signifier of loss, absence, castration, non-existence, fragmentation, eternity, *jouissance*, the abject – anything, in short, that threatens stability and unity:

> I don't like thinking about eternity. You think about time, and the end of time, and then you think what's beyond the end of time, and it gives you a sort of gasping-for-breath feeling. . . . I don't like it, it's too big and overwhelming. . . . I don't like hearing sad stories if I can't help to put things right. . . . The feeling of impotence that comes when a story of suffering is related, is one of the hardest things to bear, that I know. If you could go straight off and put things right, it wouldn't matter – but you can't in ninety-nine cases out of a hundred.
>
> (Blyton 1926; quoted in Stoney, 1974, p. 193)

Blyton confesses her aversion to matters outside her control. She enlarges on this in a letter to McKellar, where she shudders at his mescalin experiments: 'I dread the feeling of losing my identity, of not being able to control my own mind!' (quoted in Stoney, 1974, p. 215).

As a consequence, Blyton will only flag up such matters if she can point to a happy outcome. Thus she relates how, when she was small, she used to lie in bed and experience disturbing 'thoughts'. Some were about bears coming to eat her, which she found terrifying until she determined to take charge of her dream and actively confront the bears. This move, she says, dispelled what she terms her 'night-fears' and she vowed to 'do that with everything that frightens me' (Blyton, 1952b, p. 63). In other words, she took an active role, achieving mastery by warding off the unwanted – just as she does when relating the following incident with her beloved smooth-haired fox-terrier:

> 'If I said "Die for the King, Bobs!" he would at once roll over and pretend to be dead. And there he would lie, perfectly still, till I said "Come alive!" Then he would jump up'.
>
> (ibid., p. 30)

This exactly repeats the structure of the *Fort–Da* game, discussed above: 'Gone–There!' But Blyton carried it beyond Bobs' death, keeping him alive in story, refusing to have any reminders that it was a fabrication (such as a grave-marker – that granite end-page).

However, though a keen animal-lover, there was one animal she thought it right to 'thoroughly dislike': the rat. 'I make war on him relentlessly. He is a cruel, savage pest, bringing disease with him, and I don't want him anywhere near me' (ibid., 1952b, p. 40). The rat, of course, has always been a symbol of the hidden terror that gnaws at our existence: a destructive, undermining, pestilential thing (Zinsser, 1935). In fact, in an early work Blyton speaks of how the rat 'sometimes destroys man himself' by carrying disease, so that 'this is the one animal above all that we really cannot have'; if their predators disappeared, she says, 'The rats would multiply so rapidly that there would soon be a fight as to which was master of the world – rat, or man!' (Blyton, 1928a, p. 50).

For Blyton, as for many, the rat symbolizes the abject. Like smell, which as Stallybrass and White note, has 'a pervasive and invisible presence difficult to regulate' (1986, p. 139), the rat enters not by the proper channels but by tunnelling up through floors and walls – which is exactly what happened at Old Thatch when the family was invaded. And, as we have already noted, home for Blyton was far more than a place to live: it was the centre of her fantasy, whence she created the *persona* celebrated in her writings. Consequently, such an intrusion could not be borne, and her husband and the gardener had to dispose of the pest. She, meanwhile, as Stoney (1974, p. 98) notes, storied a more heroic, Imaginary version of events. Blyton the Pied Piper, then, not only captivated children, but magically rid the world of the noxious rat. Death is dispelled (or 'dis-spelled', to maintain the story metaphor).

For Blyton, the child was to be protected from such 'home-truths' (a significant phrase) in that childhood was a site of innocence: whole and unsullied. Any threats to it were therefore fiercely contested, as in Blyton's reaction to American horror comics (which she saw as satanic, speaking in a poem of their 'sulphurous smell'); or in her versified arguments in favour of keeping the death penalty for child murderers (Stoney, 1974, pp. 199–200). This is the aggressive obverse of the anxiety experienced by the Ideal-I: it not only fears attack, but will itself attack all would-be threats to its wholeness. So when Blyton says, 'I do not write as I know some authors are forced to do, to express some side of myself repressed in ordinary life' (Blyton, 1959b), I think she is right. She wrote for an opposing reason: to escape that side of herself *also* repressed in ordinary life; in other words, to maintain 'the armour of an alienating identity' as Lacan put it (Lacan, 1977, p. 4). Seen in this way Blyton's claim that 'Writing *is* my ordinary life' (Blyton, 1959b) made more sense than she realized, in that she had effectively storied herself into existence (as noted earlier).

Once we see her doing this, warding off disruption, other issues begin to make more sense. Her notion of home, so central, is in fact a very ambivalent signifier. For one thing it stresses safety. She was, as we've noted, a writer who extolled home, whose own homes were seen as islands of security, the central hearth around which succour could be found in story. However, by associating home with storytelling so openly, there is also the suggestion that home is a site of make-believe, of untruth: that the homely fabric is a fabrication. We know from Blyton's own history that home-truths were something to be hidden from public view by more acceptable stories: as when her father left home, or when her first husband departed – both events glossed over in her autobiography. In regard to the latter, we see pictures of Old Thatch but no Hugh Pollock (is he concealed within, perhaps?). His absence, along with the clandestine fate of Bobs, had to be re-storied. In short, home is a place of great familiarity, yet is also somewhere that can suddenly be defamiliarized (or defamily-ized), becoming strange. The notion of the *unheimlich* is readily apparent. But let us now pursue this more systematically in Blyton's fiction.

Mysterical symptoms

As we have just seen, story simultaneously reveals and conceals; in telling one version of events others become submerged, hidden. Although Blyton's prose is renowned for its baldness, it is always worth exploring, to see what signifieds slide unseen beneath those seemingly transparent signifiers, for they might not be quite so empty: 'Suddenly . . . the panel slid silently back. . . . The children stared at the space behind, thrilled' (*FGAA*, p. 149). I would suggest that the image of the storyteller in command of her audience, explored in the last chapter, is a useful metaphor for the psychic process: the ego sitting cosily at the hearth, telling both itself and its audience reassuring tales, while the cold and dark lie without. The ego thus seeks to secure itself against that which lies beyond, which it sees as a threat. In this scenario the storyteller literally 'binds' us with his or her spells and images, in the same way that Freud spoke of 'binding' energies. Mastery is achieved as we project our majestic egos onto our mental cinema screens. To make this more concrete, let me show how Noddy is informed by such a reading.

At the beginning of the first book, it will be recalled, the little nodding man is going through the woods when he bumps into Big-Ears. The former is described literally as a fragmented body, an assemblage of bits of wood, cat fur and blue bead. With his nodding head there is also a sense that, like a young child, he is not yet quite in control of this body. Big-Ears, I would suggest, becomes the nodding man's significant Other, mirroring for the wooden creature his initial sense of coherence (the Imaginary). Certainly, when Big-Ears meets him, the nodding man is naked and nameless. It is Big-Ears who gives him both identity and a place in society. He even genders Noddy, to the extent that he finds Noddy appropriate clothing. After this, of course, Noddy is forced to come to terms with the prohibitions of the Law in the person of Mr. Plod – his interdictions being repeated throughout the series. However, Noddy always manages to appease such forces without ever fully bowing to them (like most tricksters). So, at the end of each book there is a communal recognition of Noddy's character, often at a party, in a most egocentric way: 'Now they are having a wonderful tea-party, and Noddy and Big-Ears are as happy as can be. . . . No wonder everyone is clapping him and calling for more' (*N7*, p. 60). 'His majesty the ego' is duly celebrated, as it is in other ways: with Noddy's identifiable outfit and its self-proclaiming bell – 'It was the bell jingling that made us think it was you' (*N8*, p. 57); even his name – especially in the French version, 'Oui-Oui' – emphasizes his role as affirmative yea-sayer. The Noddy books, then, celebrate the narcissism of childhood, when the ego is first formed, when gender identity is relatively unfixed, and when the Symbolic, though a threatening presence, is not fully embraced.

Not only is Noddy an optimistic yea-sayer, but everything in the books is affirmative, the antithesis of negativity. Thus anything inert is liable to be animated (see Chapter 5). Likewise, the leaps into the present-tense add to this vivacity, giving a sense of immediacy to the action, of on-goingness. Other elements also fit this interpretation, like those puzzling passages where Blyton gently lowers a character into unconsciousness, all the while stressing their continuity of identity.[4] The fear of nothingness, of one's identity dissolving as one loses consciousness – 'What is happening to me when I am not conscious of myself? Where do I go? Where have I been? Who watches over me when I am gone to make sure I do get back?' as a Joseph Heller character puts it (Heller, 1990, p. 172) – is carefully countered. In her retellings of Bible stories, Blyton could even re-animate the dead. Significantly, she singles out 'the little girl of Capernaum' as one of her favourites (Blyton, 1952b, p. 104), which she reworked several times (1943a; 1948a), once notably entitled 'The little girl who slept' (1947a, pp. 59–60). Given that Blyton believed that her own father had all but resurrected her, such tales might have particularly appealed.

The only hint of anything untoward lies in the relatively frequent loss, as has been said, of tails, both in Toyland and elsewhere. Such images of dismemberment, as I noted, can be seen as threats to the wholeness of the Imaginary order; just as the stories where tails are added are attempts to foster a sense of completeness, of an 'image' that fits. The tail figures in a similar manner to the phallus as a signifier of difference. It is a sign of the disruptive third term – the castrating destroyer of Imaginary unity. But though disruptive, by the end of the story harmony is always restored, usually with a celebration of wholeness (in contrast to the Mouse's tail in Carroll's *Alice*, which ends in oblivion).

For Blyton, then, story provides a realm where the happy ending can always be sustained. She had no time for narratives that didn't conform to this, and thought that 'ordinary, normal children' agreed with her, calling Grimm's works 'cruel and frightening' (Blyton, 1952b, p. 49). When a child was disturbed by a copy of *Struwwelpeter*, she immediately removed it from her bookshelves (Sykes, 1962, p. 21). And yet the sunniness of Blyton's work is sustained only by removing or ignoring the shadows it must inevitably cast – as we shall now see from her mystery stories.

As stated above, Blyton's homes are symbols of security, magic islands where there lives a storyteller who will never let any child worry. And yet, as we also know, her islands are riddled with underground passages and are set amidst rocky waters that have to be carefully navigated. Within the *heimlich* the *unheimlich* always lurks, whether it be a childhood denied, an abandoned family, rats, or an alcoholic husband. The very hearth that should define safety – a *Dunroamin'* ideal – harbours disturbing elements.[5]

So it is no surprise that many of Blyton's well-known characters only really establish themselves *apart* from their families, as did Blyton herself. Noddy forsakes his maker to set up house and, of course, the school series are premised on the existence of a separate realm where girls can grow-up more rounded, which necessitates being away from home. As for the Five, they are always shown happiest as a unit away from parents: 'They just wanted to be off and away by themselves – just the Five and nobody else!' (*FGTMM*, p. 99). The Five are forever drawing attention to the holes in the homely fabric – holes in the wholeness – frequently leading to tunnels and passageways. The Five inhabit these interstices, as houses are shown to open out onto more primitive spaces: caves, tunnels and seashores.

The Five, it should be said, come from fairly happy homes, but the series still opens with a father's oedipal gesture, informing the three siblings that they will be holidaying apart from their parents:

> 'Mother and I won't be able to go with you this year. Has mother told you?'
>
> 'No!' said Anne. 'Oh, Mother – is it true? Can't you really come with us on our holidays? You always do.'
>
> 'Well, this time Daddy wants me to go to Scotland with him,' said Mother. 'All by ourselves!'
>
> (*FOTI*, p. 7)

In many other Blyton books the homes appear more dysfunctional. For instance, in *The Secret Island* (1938b), one of her first full-length mysteries, the three siblings are physically abused by guardians, their parents being feared dead. As a consequence the children run away, setting up home for themselves on an island. In the 'Adventure' series, Jack and Lucy-Ann are orphans looked after by an unsympathetic uncle and housekeeper who, as Jack puts it, 'hates us to go home for the holidays'. Dinah and Philip, the other two, have no father and their mother doesn't live with them: 'She's a very good business woman – but we don't see much of her', the latter says (Blyton, 1944c, pp. 17–18). The 'Barney' series also features two children without parents – Snubby, who 'gets kicked about from one aunt to another, poor kid' (Blyton, 1949a, p. 11), and Barney himself, who is a homeless traveller.

Home, then, is a slippery signifier, concealing as much as it reveals, presence masking absence, just as walls occlude the passages behind them. But it is the children who frequently uncover its secrets; children who show the flimsiness of the walls, the fact that the fabric conceals openings, has flaws. Adults, on the other hand, are the ones shown to be wanting – the ones frequently responsible for the secrets. Though I have so far talked specifically about parents and guardians, it is worth emphasizing that adults in general are suspect in Blyton mysteries. They try to shut children out, to exclude them from the grown-up world. The sole function of the village policeman in the Find-Outers – appositely known by his catch-phrase 'Clear-Orf' – is to prohibit the children from meddling in the adult world. But, of course, this is just what children must do. Only in this way can they discover their destiny.

Criminals are most interesting in this respect. Colwell's famous quotation, noted earlier, captures what for many adults is both the essence and the fatuity of Blyton's mysteries: 'But what hope has a band of desperate men against four children?' It is an unlikely reversal – as unlikely as the folk-hero, Jack, against the Giant – but this is surely the point: that adversaries are more powerful, but abusive of their power.[6] More importantly in Blyton, these criminals are also, frequently, parents or guardians themselves, shown to be abusive of children and animals. Thus there is the crook Uncle Dan, who physically abuses his charge, Nobby, the latter appearing with 'a tear-stained face, bruised and swollen', and told, 'we'll show you what a real beating is! And if you can walk down to the camp after it, I'll be surprised' (*FGOIC*, pp. 120–1). The villains, then, are frequently more than crooks, their crookedness metonymic of adult duplicity. They attempt to shut the children out of their grown-up world, doing things behind closed doors: 'You were warned not to go down to that yard. . . . And you've got to suffer for not taking heed of the warning!' (*FGOTC*, pp. 164, 166).

However, Blyton shows that though powerless in the order of things, children can accrue power. For it is not simply imposed from above in some repressive way; rather, it is part of the fabric of society, involving us all, regimenting our behaviour, our deportment. So a discourse that constructs children as knowing their place, as being marginalized, simultaneously gives them the latitude to exploit these margins, to 'run off and play', eavesdropping and peeking through keyholes; in short, to inhabit the interstices of the homely fabric. In this way, the discourse of the powerful overreaches itself: 'Discourse transmits and produces power; it reinforces it, but also undermines it and exposes it, renders it fragile and makes it possible to thwart it', and while 'silence and secrecy are a shelter for power, anchoring its prohibitions . . . they also loosen its holds' (Foucault, 1981, p. 101). In other words, adult secrets are their own undoing. In terms of Foucault's power-knowledge coupling, the children mobilize the discourses (knowledges) that have institutional support (of law and order, of morality) for their own purposes.

It is through gaining knowledge, then – clues and the like – that the protagonists in Blyton's books seek to make a space in which children can be heard. This said, generally the children share their knowledge with adults only when they have plumbed the mystery, knowing that otherwise it is likely to be reappropriated (Clear-Off, above) or dismissed, as by this anonymous functionary of the law: 'You go away, all of you . . . I shan't report you this time. But don't you go spreading silly stories like that or you'll get into trouble' (*FOHT*, p. 85).

The children know that they must be in a position of mastery, where the various clues cohere; that is, when they feel that they have uncovered the plot, that they are party to the adult secrets:

> 'Ought we to tell our parents?' asked Pam.
> 'Or the police?' said Jack.
> 'Well – not till we know a little bit more,' said Peter.
> (Blyton, 1949b, p. 74)

This is the Secret Seven talking, a group which, like other Blyton collectives, forms its own elect society not only in order to *explore secrets*, but to *be secret*. Their initiations, passwords, ritual meals and home-building activities therefore all mirror and mimic adult exclusiveness:

> Janet looked round the clean shed, pleased with their work. Boxes to sit on – mugs on the little shelf, ready for any drinks that were brought . . . and an old, rather raggedy rug on the earth floor. . . .
> 'Nice!' said Janet . . . 'I've put the S.S. on the door.'
> (Blyton, 1962, pp. 17–18)

Once again, we can see the instability of the *heimlich*, which semantically encodes not only homeliness, but also that which is 'hidden from the eyes of others'. So, though displaced from home in some way, it is very important for Blyton's protagonists to establish their own cosy nests, their own happy families. This, too, is why both boys and girls need to be involved, and span a range of ages, mirroring the idealized family unit. Certainly a male is usually the oldest (itself mimicking society, where a husband was and still is usually the senior partner) and there is often a division of labour. But most important is the stress on the family being a whole – a family free of sex, of course, like Peter and Wendy's – seeking to fulfil the family romance by fantasizing it for themselves. Pets are very useful here, functioning as the equivalent of unruly youngsters.

The stress on the wholeness of Blyton's groups is paramount: the Five wanting to be by themselves, being 'Famous Five-ish' (*FOST*, p. 74). They fret about each other when they are not together (earlier I quoted one 10-year-old who said that *FFIA* wasn't a proper adventure because Anne was not involved). Blyton heroes are never loners – she has no Nancy Drew figure (though, of course, even this heroine had her helpers – one, a tomboy, even called George). In the family unit, then, Anne's role is crucial as a mother figure who can reinvoke the *heimlich* wherever they go:

> 'This shall be our house, our home. We'll make four proper beds. And we'll each have our own place to sit in. And we'll arrange everything tidily on that big stone shelf there.'
>
> (*FRAT*, p. 110)

But for all that Anne is teased, homebuilding is generally a communal activity, with the others enjoying it too – just as in the Seven, above. In fact, George responds with, 'We'll leave Anne to play "houses" by herself . . . *We'll go and get some heather for beds*' (ibid. my emphasis). They revel in their communal meals, snuggling up in sleeping bags, wallowing in the sun, and so on. And, secure in their wholeness, the holes in the social fabric can be repaired. As I noted earlier, the Five have a strong bond, physically and emotionally, and many readers also responded to them as a unit, being 'all together'. In fact, adventure cannot generally occur without them first coming together.

There is then the 'fall into adventure', as one title has it, the phrase effectively evoking that sense of loss of control as they are caught up in mystery. In moving into this time the protagonists also move, in Freud's phrase, 'beyond the pleasure principle'; that is, beyond a time of instant gratification into a time of lack, when the hardships of tunnelling, being imprisoned and manhandled (as it usually is) have to be endured. Most dramatically, it is a period of fragmentation, when they are divided from their former state of unity (with an individual being attacked or kidnapped, perhaps).

And yet, all this happens only in a very tempered way. In Blyton any darkness is soon dispersed. If there are shadowy recesses, they are soon illuminated by the torchbeams of the heroes, so that, once again, we have a celebration of wholeness, with no troublesome openings. But the fact is, though these ruptures are healed in each story, they continue to open; there is an excess of openings: the adult fabric is inveterately flawed.

In all this there are hints of the uncanny – but only hints. Thus doubles often feature, as with the confusing Lawler twins in *FOST*, or the 'two Harries' in *FOFF*; on a different level there is the tomboyish doubling of George with Henry in *FGTMM*, or Susie's mirroring of the Secret Seven with her 'Tiresome Three' (Blyton, 1959a). Likewise, the inanimate and animate are often confused, as with Fatty and Goon pretending to be waxworks (Blyton, 1947d), or the Five mistaking statues for real people (*FHMTS*). The dead are seen to return, like the parents in *The Secret Island*, Jeff in *FGTBH*, or Nobby's dog, Barker (*FGOIC*). Signifiers produce their signifieds – as with the boat proleptically called

'Adventure' (*FHMTS*, p. 93); thoughts become omnipotent, with the psychical ruling over physical reality – as for example in *The Mystery that Never Was*, where the invented mystery becomes a reality (Blyton, 1961). Most convincing though, are those intimations of being buried alive, which occur in many of the claustral, underground episodes of the Five – more than once involving George's father, Quentin. (Though Blyton could never repay the life-saving act her father had performed on her, she could always retrieve the fictionalized father from the underworld.) Here, for instance, is George discovering Quentin in an underground passage:

> Sitting at a table, his head in his hands, perfectly still, was her father!
>
> 'Father!' said George. . . . He stared at George as if he really could not believe his eyes. Then he turned back again, and buried his face in his hands.
>
> '*Father!*' said George again, quite frightened because he did not say anything to her.
>
> (*FOKIA*, pp. 140–1)

All these things occur, but their uncanniness is enervated – just as in Freud's interpretation of 'The Sandman'. Moreover, just as Freud noted that the word *heimlich* has two meanings, one of which carries it into its opposite, the *unheimlich*, it is as though Blyton were trying to produce a similar semantic shift with the latter term, turning it once again into something safe and homely, something hidden that is, when brought to light, comfortingly familiar: a passage, yes, but one with steps; a secret opening, certainly, but one with a mechanical device – a 'hidden spring or lever' (*FGAA*, p. 149). They find treasure, yes, in plenty, but never the bones of the owners (unlike Stevenson's *Treasure Island*). The villains turn out to be after material goods only, not children's bodies or minds (unlike *Peter Pan* or *The Lion, the Witch and the Wardrobe*). There is never anything truly supernatural or numinous. As Kristeva says, speaking of the enchanted world in general, 'artifice neutralizes uncanniness and makes all returns of the repressed plausible, acceptable, and pleasurable' (Kristeva, 1991, p. 187).

This move by Blyton avoids digging deeper, unearthing, for instance, real skeletons in the cupboard. We are instead led on a detour that returns the child to the safe haven of childhood. The opposite of Atropos, Blyton continually turns away from the blackness at the end of the tunnel. Instead, materialistic treasure is seen to be the answer to most problems. Thus, at the end of the first Five adventure, Uncle Quentin assures George and the others that things will be different in future; speaking on behalf of them all in responding to a question about their wealth, he says he'll be

> 'Rich enough to give you and your mother all the things I've longed to give you for so many years and couldn't. I've worked hard enough for you – but it's not the kind of work that brings in a lot of money, and so I've become irritable and bad-tempered.'
>
> (*FOTI*, pp. 184–6)

He is described as 'quite different now. It seemed as if a great weight had been lifted off his shoulders' (ibid., p. 187). In the first 'Adventure' book, the results are even more dramatic, with Philip's comment on his friends' mother realized:

> 'She's a mother, and she ought to live like a mother, and have a nice home of her own and you and Dinah with her.'
>
> 'We're going to. . . . There's enough money now for Mother to make a home for us herself, and stop her hard work. . . . And what about you and Lucy-Ann coming to live with us, Freckles? You don't want to go back to your old uncle and horrid old housekeeper, do you?'
>
> (Blyton, 1944c, p. 324)

This notion of everything being righted is, of course, an illusion, but solving the mystery provides a sense of mastery, a feeling that all will now be well and, more importantly, that it is children, by modelling a more ideal unit, who have been the agents of this process. In Freudian terms there is a sense of plenitude, of coherence, and of fulfilling the 'family romance', as mentioned above. This romance, as Freud elaborates, involves children moving from a position where they see their parents as all-knowing paragons to seeing them as faulted, so 'that other parents are in some respects preferable' to their own (Freud, 1977, p. 221). Consequently, children entertain the wish that their own carers be replaced in some way. Versions of this, as in fairy-tale, are a common narrative outcome in Blyton.

Secrets, then, are safely contained: crooks are caught and treasure recovered, often with a reward attached (though it is recognition that is crucial). All is summarily dealt with, and – most importantly – logically explained; the point being that the mystery itself is less important than its effectivity: its ability to empower children and right some aspect of the adult world.

Let me now bring in comments from readers on these issues. Certainly, many framed her books in terms of being 'exciting' and 'adventurous' but equally, of being 'safe'. Indeed, some tried to explain how her books fulfilled both these functions, playing around the *heimlich/unheimlich* border, being both secure and audacious:

> I think people like them because they're safe . . . it sounds a bit funny, but they're not as . . . they're not scary, they're not boring, they're just in-between, they're nice and safe and just . . . how you want them. (f, 12)

> For me, EB's books filled a need for security and escape from the stresses and boredom of life as an intelligent, but emotionally insecure working class child growing up on a council estate (f).

'Security and escape', something that this 12-year-old girl also emphasizes: 'Interesting, and exciting, and you know it can't happen, and that makes you feel safe.' This is also apparent in many of the illustrations that the children produced, often showing both the adventure space and 'home'. The children's favourite illustrations from a selection of representations of the Five, too, were of note. The most popular was an Eileen Soper representation of the Five running through a tunnel, armed with torches, with Julian holding Anne's hand. But, in discussion, many were also taken with a Betty Maxey illustration, which was a close second. Both show the Five together, being mutually supportive, 'going together, working as a group' (f, 14), 'doing it all together' (m, 15), 'all involved' (m, 15), but in the former they are in the adventure space, while in the latter, they are shown more securely, examining a map.

Hugh Crago, in a very interesting paper, movingly recounts how he 'compulsively re-read' *FGTST*, long after he had grown out of Blyton's other books. The reason was that its landscape and images – with the warren of secret tunnels – echoed his own family situation (Crago, n.d., p. 16), which seems to me to capture the *unheimlich* exactly. Other readers, some with their own particular problems, have also found Blyton intensely comforting. One, for example, continually re-read a passage from *Mr. Galliano's Circus* to help her get to sleep at night. It is the passage where a caravan is fitted out as a 'home on wheels', with curtains and carpet. As she put it in interview, it is 'a community, everyone dead happy' round the campfire. Another 'abused' child read one Blyton (1945a) almost obsessively for the security it offered:

> As an emotionally disturbed child, coming from a socially deprived and violent background, Enid Blyton stories, where [*sic*], in many ways an escape route. Her stories took me totally out of a very grim reality; they offered me a safe retreat. The *Hollow Tree House* was personally very significant because the characters would often visit a hollow tree that was large enough to adapt into a temporary home. They furnished this hollow and it became a retreat for the characters when they needed to escape the adult world. I also lived in this hollow tree house, imaginarily – at times of violence.[7]

A third reader, with a degree in English, told me of a breakdown she had suffered at 18: 'to comfort me my sister brought all the F F O [Five Find-Outers] again and we had a superb time re-reading and enjoying them'. Other readers, including the famous, have also recorded their dependence on Blyton's texts at troublesome times – like Alice Thomas Ellis, or Liz Hurley, who, when the media eye was upon her after the débâcle with Hugh Grant, retreated to her Blyton collection. More generally, it has been observed that Blyton's books are the ones reached for when exams are on the horizon – not just in the case of schoolchildren but university students, too (Gilligan, 1995).

So, Blyton's life and fictions not only helped her personally to construct a realm of security (an Imaginary identity) but also provided her audience with an equally safe realm.

Conclusion

Again, some of the above will be drawn on in the next chapter, where I shall attempt to pull together the whole story. But here I have tried to account for those elements that a more social account cannot encompass: that trance-like absorption that many have experienced, abetted by such props as comfy corners and private foodstores.

I have suggested that Blyton is essentially involved in creating fantasies that protect and strengthen young egos, though this is seen to be on behalf of children as a group. This not only helps the process of consolidating the Ideal-I, but also the complementary process of warding off the not-I: the threatening, unbound energies that Freud spoke of. Blyton's work is about staging fantasies of mastery, whereby such energies are bound back in place – either within the social formation, or cast outside it. Just as Freud noted his grandson gaining mastery by casting his cotton reel, so Blyton provided similar fantasies of mastery, maintaining that her own stories unwound 'like cotton from a reel' (quoted in Stoney, p. 135). But in both there is no Atropos at the end to sever the thread; instead the reel is hauled back into the security of the cot with the deictic, existential cry of 'Here!'. Hopeless, trope-less Death is foiled in another cunning detour. For Blyton, writing about such matters was both a matter of control – 'I *work* with my unconscious, it doesn't run away with me! It used to, of course, now I would not let it – it is in harness' (quoted in Stoney, p. 211) – and of pleasure: 'When I am writing a book, in touch with my under-mind, I am very happy, excited, full of vitality' (ibid., p. 207).

However, there is another twist to this tale for, in that very process, Blyton's audience gave her back the very thing that made it all make sense. I have already linked the social and the psychic above, but here we can see how her audience, in effect, acted as the significant Other for Blyton herself: mirroring back to her, in exactly the Lacanian sense, her existence and worth. In other words, it seems that Blyton needed her audience as much as they needed her: 'I for one cannot imagine childhood without Enid Blyton'(m); 'I lived for EB as a child'(f); 'My childhood (from about 7-years-old to 15/16-years-old) are synonymous with Enid Blyton'(f).

Such audience approbation, first and foremost in book-sales, but also in letters, club membership, fund-raising and general support, all reflected back the very persona she sought so hard to maintain as a reality: the very persona that can be seen narcissistically reclining by her pond, mirrored for all to see and admire yet, like all such reflections, little more than an ephemeral surface. The approbation is also apparent in her magazines and stories, like *A Story Party at Green Hedges* where, after the story, the fictional child praises Blyton. Likewise, the inclusion of her name in so many of her titles, though a most useful marketing ploy, was also of personal importance.[8] Writing, for Blyton, seems to have been an existential act, whether in her fiction, her autobiographical storying, or even in comments which tied together these activities. George Greenfield, her literary agent, particularly likes to relate how she turned 'as if to embrace the bookcases on the wall', saying, 'These are my children' (Greenfield, 1995, p. 133).[9] And, in claiming never to listen to a critic over the age of 12, she strove to ensure that nothing too threatening would ever intrude.

11
Conclusion: Is Blyton Bad for You?

The relative obscurity of Blyton's work in 1992 when I began my study is now itself history, her centenary year having come and gone. Such rapid change is a factor that any writer on popular culture has to come to terms with.[1] My study represents but a particular intervention at one point in time (although it did try to capture a longitudinal perspective by involving past readers). In some ways I was fortunate to do the study when I did, before Blyton's works were catapulted into the limelight by Trocadero, with worldwide marketing and adaptations of many of her best known series. To do the study now one would not only find that the Five were far better known, but that much textual knowledge of the series derived from the TV adaptation; hence, no doubt, the sexism would be far less an issue (Anne, in particular, has been empowered in the TV series); further, the children could not have avoided seeing the series as 'old-fashioned', in that this is how the new version represented it (set in 1952, the year of Elizabeth II's accession). This said, as I noted in an earlier study (Rudd, 1992), children do not compartmentalize texts nearly as much as we do; they happily run-together books, comics, cartoons, films, videos and computer presentations – which is what defines multimedia, of course.

In this last chapter I want to do several things: to summarize the main points made, connecting them to larger debates in cultural studies, and to make some final pronouncements on three issues: Blyton's so-called harmfulness, the updating of her works and, finally, the question of Blyton's relation to children's literature.

Main findings

In this text I have explained Blyton in a way which, I hope, does justice to her immense appeal without reducing it to crude commercialism. The notion of 'discursive threads' certainly helped this process, allowing me to set aside older value judgements, to give children their say, and to tease out the intricacies of what constitutes the Blyton phenomenon. Accordingly I have enumerated personal factors (upbringing, the influence of her father, her teaching and storytelling, her fear of death and illness, her love of nature), cultural matters (other children's writers, the work of Mee, Dickens and Homer, her Froebel training, Englishness) and social issues (contemporary events, especially those involving damage to the nation or its children, such as invasion, spying, homelessness, horror comics). All these, I have suggested, give certain inflections to her work. What did not emerge as clearly as I thought it might, were differences in how different groups read her – apart from some gender preferences for different characters.

More generally, the following points have emerged. First, as I indicated earlier, the different constructions of Blyton over time are themselves significant, and I suggested that we may now be moving back towards a more appreciative attitude – reflected in the Oxford Union's motion that 'Enid Blyton is still a writer appropriate for today's child' being carried three to one (Brennan, 1997) – and away from the generally negative view of her held from the 1960s to the 1980s. As I have also shown, though – a second point – much of the earlier criticism is quite contradictory, suggesting that it is only their *anti*-ness that unites the critics. Third, it has become apparent just how much her critics are implicated in the very crimes of which they would accuse Blyton. Thus her outdated, élitist attitudes are criticized, but by those envisioning the future Blyton reader ending up as a shop-assistant, reading Mills and Boons – as opposed, for instance, to sitting the Cambridge English Tripos. Furthermore, I showed that this notion extended to readings of her texts, with working-class characters being stereotypically derogated in a far more blanket fashion than ever occurs in Blyton. Equally, racist readings of Blyton were shown often to have been constructed by mischievous extrapolation from isolated examples. Many commentators, then, are caught up in unusually similar discursive practices – practices that I have tried to unpick in the course of this work.

Fourth, approaches to Blyton, whether for or against, are remarkably untheorized. They are generally just asserted, even by critics well-versed in relevant areas (Mullan, 1987a, for example), and fifthly, are often based on glaring misreadings, sometimes not even drawing on Blyton's own, original texts. This said, I have also argued that to study the texts in abstraction is counterproductive: the whole context of reading needs to be considered.

Sixth, as a consequence I rejected earlier educational and literary approaches because their agendas seemed inappropriate to works of popular culture. Instead, two more productive ways of reading the Blyton *oeuvre* were explored. In the former, Blyton was located in the oral tradition, which made sense both of her storytelling style, and of its reception by a child audience keen to hear tales about the deeds of their tribe's heroes. In the latter, this was linked to a psychoanalytical perspective, which suggested that in fulfilling children's wishes to be significant beings, Blyton's stories were psychologically satisfying, akin to personal daydreams. But it was also noted that the stories only worked in this way because the world wasn't really like this: children are not powerful; they cannot resolve the world's problems. Thus the stories represent magical, or fantasy resolutions in which holes in the homely fabric – particularly the inadequacies of adults – are drawn attention to and made 'whole'; something that frequently occurred, to pursue this pun, during the 'hols', that magical time-out period. Seventh, it was suggested that Blyton's way of writing actually linked the social and psychic: that because her stories are essentially sensory (pictorial in particular) rather than literary, they prompt the projectionist in each reader's head to screen the ego in action.

Locating the secret mechanism

I'd now like to pursue the link between the social and psychic more thoroughly, because it is on this that a response to the question, 'Is Blyton bad for you?' must depend. Let me begin by saying that the way this question is usually framed is itself problematic. In its baldest form it suggests that Blyton deliberately encoded certain unsavoury discourses (racist, classist ideologies) into her texts, which readers then 'decode' and uncritically internalize. Such a view conceives ideology as a 'thing' that 'gets' its audience. Readers are envisaged as being blindly hit by it, such that the simple act of reading the texts is enough to constitute the effect, whether it be the sexism, racism, or whatever.[2] Children are seen to be particularly vulnerable, imbibing ideology before they are rational enough to realize what hit them.

This notion is unacceptable for several reasons. First, precisely because it sees being rational as the solution; talisman-like, reason is seen to ward off ideology – as in Plato commending mathematics – rather than itself being ideologically inflected ('reason' as a particularly male, unemotional and abstract pursuit of truth). Second, this model presumes, *a priori*, that certain texts are ideological, whereas others are not;

and generally, it is works of popular culture that fit the former bill, whereas 'artistic' works rise above it. However, as has again been argued, this itself is an élitist, ideological construct. Third, this approach sees children as particularly passive and prone to ideology (women less so, men least); in which case, children worldwide, over several generations, have clearly been cultural dopes, choosing to read and re-read texts that, if the official view is to be believed, undermine half of them for their gender, and insult many more for their ethnicity or class. Fourthly though, if children are really so passive and prone, then presumably the effects cannot be too serious, for another text can just as easily come along and send them on a different path. Only an unrelenting diet of Blytons, with no other input (no TV or comics, no education), might then be problematic.

The mechanism by which the ideologically loaded text 'gets' its subject is also dubious. Children are usually seen to identify with it unwittingly (as in Plato's model), or, as Althusser (1971) saw it, once 'hailed' one was thence ideologically 'nailed'. But as Harding (1962) argued long ago, though notions of 'identification' are regularly cited, they actually futher our understanding very little. Do we mean by it that we empathize with a particular character? Do we mean that we simply see likenesses between that character and ourselves, or is it that we wish there were likenesses? Alternatively, do we actually go further and seek to imitate a character's behaviour? These are all different, so should not be lost in a blanket term. More crucially, they all demand the active engagement of the subject – a point made deftly by Martin Barker in his rejection of the term: '"Identification" suggests that we are spoken for. "Dialogue" suggests we are spoken to' (1989, p. 260). With the latter, children are not seen to be drip-feeding themselves slow poison, but are actively engaged in a dialogue whereby they negotiate meaning.

In a similar way I have tried, through dialogue, to elicit some of these meanings (especially in relation to the discourses of sexism and racism) though without privileging children as the site of truth – any more than children see Blyton's fictions as such a site. From this it is evident that children do not consume Blyton as 'Instant Reddymix pap' (Alderson, 1997, p. 7). Obviously not all children like her anyway, while those that do tend to be selective, liking certain series and not others. Within a series they are also discerning, preferring particular titles. And, at an even more fine-grained level, they will discuss favourite episodes and characters within individual books: 'I like more books better than others, 'cos I like *Upper Fourth* better than the *Second Term* . . . I like the midnight feasts, and the tricks, and erm, I like [laughing] hearing about Gwendoline when she's being all silly over things and stuff' (f, 10).

Much children's reading, therefore, falls outside the way that many adults conceive it: neither slavish identification, passive consumption, nor ideological servitude. Basically, children are out to maximize their pleasure, by personalizing it, revisiting favourite moments. As Barthes puts it, 'reading in this way is no longer consumption but play'; it 'draws the text out of its internal chronology . . . and recaptures a mythic time' – what I have called a 'time-out' (Barthes, 1975, p. 16). This type of reading is also play in a more physical sense, with many carrying her books into other activities. To adapt Laurie Taylor's analogy of riding a big-dipper (quoted in Root, 1986, pp. 64–5), one can object to the ride on a number of grounds: its flimsy construction, its exploitation of the punter, its use of brash and sexist imagery. But in doing so one denies oneself its pleasures: its excess, its very forbiddenness. Barthes expresses a similar notion in his famous analysis of wrestling:

> The public is completely uninterested in knowing whether the contest is rigged or not, and rightly so; it abandons itself to the primary virtue of the spectacle, which is to abolish all motives and all consequences: what matters is not what it thinks but what it sees.
> (Barthes, 1973, p. 15).

So the trick is to go with the logic of the tale, to understand the way it establishes a scenario that readers can fruitfully invest in. Other elements are subordinated to this: characters, setting, even morality. So we will certainly find stock figures – little else, in fact – but the use made of them varies considerably. Even Blyton's well-known characters have conflicting incarnations. Big-Ears, for instance, besides being a wise brownie is also a car-driving pixie (Blyton, 1947c), a cowardly goblin (Blyton, 1937) and a thieving, unrepentant one ('Hi, Feather-Tail!', Blyton, 1951c[3]). But so long as the story establishes a basic opposition between heroic ego and Other, the latter can be anything, regardless of nationality, race, class, or age-grouping, whether human, toy (gollies, teddies, dolls) or fairy (goblins, pixies, elves) – whatever, in fact, suits the particular machinations of plot.[4]

We have also seen readers taking up a range of positions within texts, covering all Harding's categories and more. They related to a large number of characters – not simply the predictable heroes. The Malory Towers stories produced probably the widest range, with some readers even nominating Gwendoline as favourite; in other series, animals such as Kiki or Timmy stole the show. And, for many, it was not individual characters at all but the group as an entity that they liked: the solidarity of the Five, the friendships of Malory. Another surprise was that some boys enjoyed the girls' school stories without compunction, just as many rated George their favourite character.

All this lends credence to a view that the stories operate outside the confines of the Reality Principle. Readers seem to derive pleasure from the whole spectacle of the stories: the play of identity, affiliative behaviour, the demonized Other. These concerns, of course, are those of Freud's primary fantasies: a concern with origins, with castration (that is, with taking up a gendered role in the divided world of the Symbolic) and with identity. Where do I belong? What is gender appropriate behaviour? Who am I? Unlike socially grounded readings where, for instance, girls can identify only with girls (and girls, of course, of similar age, class and ethnicity), fantasy both precedes our social being (before we take up a position in the Symbolic) and continues to lie outside its reach, unruly and transgressive. This is its defining character: what we lack in social reality is what we desire. So fantasies are not necessarily restricted to such sociological categories as gender, ethnicity, or personhood even; in fact, they are not restricted to 'beings' at all, in that we can fantasize about events – the person being secondary. In other words we can be 'present . . . in a desubjectivized form . . . [caught up] in the very syntax of the sequence' (Laplanche and Pontalis, 1986, p. 26). Blyton, in her best work, is adept at fashioning such scenarios of mastery, of the powerless struggling for definition against the powerful; of the outsider trying to find a place to belong.

The point to emphasize about all such fantasies is that they are there to gratify His/Her Majesty the Ego. Their *raison d'être* can never be altruism, but always ego-ism. With this realization we come closer to understanding the illicit pleasures of being an insider in Blyton's works. Miles (1993), in a provocative essay redefining racism, argues that the insider does not simply distance the Other as an external, foreign threat, but that the 'in-group', the civilized, also distances itself from perceived threats closer to home, whether in the form of the poor, the peasantry or the working class (or, one might add, women and children). All such groups, as he says, are derogated as 'not civilised', as 'dirty'. This is a useful development in our understanding, but I think that this disparagement goes even further, operating not only socially, but psychically, too.

Others have sought to explore this treacherous area, and I have found the work of Stallybrass and White (1986), Kristeva (1991) and Bhabha

(1994) particularly useful. Kristeva (1991, p. 191) puts it thus: 'The foreigner is within us. And when we flee from or struggle against the foreigner, we are fighting our unconscious.' As noted earlier, there is a profound anxiety for Blyton about what lies beyond the ego: a void that her fiction continually strives to a-void; an apotropaic reflex. So, in constituting the narcissistic ego, all that is not ego, or not in praise of this ego, is abjected, frequently being seen as 'dirty'. However, as Bhabha makes plain, this is not a once and for all castigation, for the boundary between insider and outsider, between clean and polluted, is far less stable. For Bhabha, stereotypes are not so rigid, which is why they are so relentlessly reinvoked: both to bind them and, in the process, to secure our own sense of identity.

Blyton, I would contend, is forever policing this boundary between ego and Other, compulsively reinscribing it, both in her fiction and in her pronouncements about what 'normal' children are like. Seen in these terms, not only do the villains continually need to be banished, but they also need to be repeatedly invoked in order to define and secure the hero. What hope have the criminals against our young heroes, certainly. Yet without these criminals, the heroes would themselves be undefined and rudderless. Just so, as we noted at the end of the last chapter, Blyton without her child audience would herself have been empty.

This is a sensitive area of course, so I'd like to draw on two related studies before moving on to relate my approach to some wider issues. Significantly, given Blyton's penchant for linking writing to the cinema, it is primarily film studies work to which I shall refer.

The studies in question are ones that have also tried to come to terms with what, on the surface, might seem reactionary, 'fascist' (their term) films, but ones that are hugely popular. *Dirty Harry* is the first, which perplexed many commentators, as James Donald (1992) notes in his analysis. Why, he asks, should this white policeman have such vociferous appeal to marginalized ethnic groups? His answer, like mine, is to move beyond sociological categories to see the film working on the level of primary fantasy. Even more revealingly, Valerie Walkerdine details her move from being an outsider to a position of 'emotional realism' (Ang's term) while watching *Rocky II*. She begins by expressing her revulsion at the film, which was being watched on video at a working-class home where she was conducting research. Not only was it 'on', but the favourite moments were being replayed continually by the father. However, when Walkerdine later viewed the film for herself, she confesses: 'No longer did I stand outside the pleasures of engagement with the film. I too wanted Rocky to win. Indeed, I *was* Rocky' (Walkerdine, 1986, p. 169). Rather than the violence and sex-stereotyping, it was the escapism that prevailed, which, Walkerdine argues, is the only way to explain why many Blacks, too, call for Rocky's victory over his black adversary, Mr. Big. She concludes: 'Although it is easy to dismiss such films as macho, stupid and fascist, it is more revealing to see them as fantasies of omnipotence, heroism and salvation' (ibid., p. 172; see also Zipes, 1992, pp. 119–23).[5]

As noted earlier, it is of interest that Blyton so readily evoked images of a private cinema for her writing process, because several film theorists have also sought parallels between the cinematic apparatus and the staging of fantasies of mastery. Let me here rehearse these in connection with Blyton's fiction, drawing specifically on Christian Metz' (1982) work. First, there is the sense of presence and immediacy stressed in both, of the fantasy unfolding 'before your very eyes'. Second, Blyton's omniscient narrator adds a sense of control and authority to the telling, just like the *auteur* in cinema. Third, in flagging up the constructedness of her tale, Blyton foregrounds the paradox of presence and absence that Metz argues is central to the cinematic experience. In Blyton this is clearly seen in the way that the reader is immersed in the story, yet also made aware, through metafictional devices, that it is only a story. Fourth, and relatedly, the reader is made to feel central to the whole enterprise, with a resultant boost to the ego, in that the reader is the one who constructs the tale in her or his head (as Metz maintains the cinema viewer does), and without whom the whole fantasy would be meaningless.

Lastly, and more explicitly, Metz argues that spectators or viewers (both words privileging the sense of vision) experience a feeling of omniscience in their own knowing look, which is enhanced by the technology itself. Blyton, I would suggest, also indulges the pleasure and power of looking, though she achieves the effect more simply through print. This 'scopophilia' is especially effective when the gaze is fixed on adults, with a view to gaining knowledge of their activities – often by pursuing them relentlessly. The focus of this gaze is often enhanced, too, by the frequent use of technology: binoculars, for instance, are often used, as is the camera (it is central, for instance, to *The Castle of Adventure*, while both these pieces of equipment are used for surveillance in *The Adventurous Four*); but more than anything else, it is the torch that is metonymic of the children's power of vision: 'The beam was strong, and the boys could well imagine how the dark secret passage would be lighted up, once they turned on their torches' (Blyton, 1944c, p. 122).

This sense of mastery, in that it usually involves a particular social group, namely children, also gives a glimpse of a more utopian world (what Ernst Bloch termed *Heimat* – 'home' again) where children have space and are treated as equals.[6] However, as Richard Dyer qualifies it, this is not utopia in an intellectual sense, 'rather the utopianism is contained in the feelings it embodies' (1992, p. 18). Dyer usefully lists some of these 'utopian sensibilities' (ibid., pp. 20–1), all of which have relevance, but I shall just mention two: abundance and community. Blyton certainly celebrates these, both of which seem to give readers much pleasure. *Abundance* – that is, 'the enjoyment of sensuous material reality' – is most obviously witnessed in connection with food, with the midnight feasts; but it is also present in other simple pleasures, like sunbathing, swimming, and sleeping. As for *community*, Dyer defines this in terms of 'togetherness, sense of belonging', which again, is central to the texts, whether it is the Toyland collective celebrations, the friendship of Big-Ears and Noddy, the closeness of the Five, or schoolgirl comradeship. These all contribute to this sense of an ideal home, or *Heimat* – which in many respects is quite traditional, usually involving a mother figure, for example, supplying the abundance of food. But while it might be thought invidious to speak of utopian feelings in a world riddled with such divisions of gender, not to mention class and ethnicity, as Ang has expressed it, 'where cultural consumption is concerned, no fixed standard exists for gauging the "progressiveness" of a fantasy. The personal may be political, but the personal and the political do not always go hand in hand' (Ang, 1985, pp. 135–6). Moreover, in Blyton it is precisely the solidarity of children over the bullying and belittling restrictiveness of adults that unites them against other potentially divisive *-isms*.

Can reading Blyton damage your health?

We can now more fruitfully return to this question – which can only be answered as something of a paradox. For it would seem that those who read her in social realist terms (as do most adults) will find little to enjoy; such readers are therefore unlikely to persist. Those that read and enjoy the fantasy, however, are doing so in a way that is, by definition, not realistic: the enjoyment depends on readers engaging in the play of the text, thus making it their own. This is so because fantasy can only work by meeting *personal* desires; not someone else's, by proxy; in which case, the reactionary discourses in Blyton are not an issue *for the initiates* any more than is Ransome's communism, Lewis's Christianity or Carroll's predilection for young girls. (This is not to deny, of course, that child readers can derive 'undesirable' meanings from Blyton's work, but amongst my readership these tended to be more idiosyncratic issues – like her attitude to games, to wearing glasses, or being ill, to give three instances.) It is when other discourses start to obtrude that the fantasy ends (which, of course, the foregrounding of social realist readings can accelerate). This is frequently abrupt, as in my own case, but for others there is a period when readers oscillate, becoming increasingly aware of adult discourses while keeping hold of a childhood realm, suspending their disbelief for the duration of the story.

This means that Blyton will never lead children on from a world where the letters S.S. on a shed door signify anything but a group of children cosily replete with their sandwiches and badges of identification. In her woodshed there is no place for a more vicious and sinister S.S., complete with guttural accents – the sort of threat that she saw epitomized in American horror comics. Hence Blyton wrote for the whole span of childhood. 'I want to know you from the very beginning, and go with you all through your childhood till you are old enough to read adult books' (Blyton, 1952b, p. 96). Like Holden Caulfield's 'catcher in the rye', she wanted to protect any child that ran too near the cliff edge in the rye field (Salinger, 1951). She relentlessly patrols this boundary, most anxious to keep children safe from adult things. For were children to unearth the real secrets of adulthood, they would then become part of that world – and no longer be children. Then there could be only one story, a *rite of passage* from which there would be no return, rather than a secret passage that compulsively loops them back to childhood, locking them into its mythic time.

This is why Blyton is such an obvious marker of childhood, with many children measuring their growth by her serials. Readers progress through the characters, often violently rejecting earlier ones and, sometimes half-regretfully, finding themselves leaving Blyton behind. 'I almost didn't want to grow up because I didn't want to get too old to read Enid Blyton', as Pat McLoughlin of *Woman's Hour* put it (Kirby, 1992). Crago has also documented his experience of mastering Blyton's format, then 'a sense of being constricted by it' (Crago, 1990, p. 103), and earlier I recorded my own sudden and dramatic dismissal of Blyton. Other readers similarly marked the spot:

> I had a Blyton phase of my childhood and then it stopped, and . . . it was dramatic, in fact I can identify a pre and post Blyton era in my life, which surprises me because I don't remember that being true of other authors. (f)

> I have discovered that my own personal insight gained into my childhood and adolescent experiences and emotions are partly due to her books acting as a marker. (f)

> At the age of 12 my sister (who was 6) said that she had grown out of EB books and that they were 'childish'. I remember this because I was hurt at the time that she had said this about my fave author and made a promise that I would never grow out of these books. At the age of 13 going on to 14 I did grow out of the books, when I tried to read one I found it babyish. (f, 15).

It is also because Blyton is such a marker of childhood that she is often as vociferously rejected by children as by some adults – at least for a period; for she represents precisely those childish things that need to be put away. This explains a Welsh study that found Blyton not only the most popular children's author, but also the most disliked, with the Famous Five coming top in both categories (Thompson, 1987). Moreover, it is not only children who carry this ambivalence. Many adults I spoke to also expressed an initial disapproval of her books, later to become mixed nostalgically with a more childlike discourse of remembered pleasure, often conveyed through facial expression and tone of voice. Frequently the latter would emerge only after a tape-recorder had been switched off, or in informal conversation. Several times, after being grilled by the media, the interviewer would subsequently confide how he or she grew up loving Blyton.

However, let me finish this section with a *caveat* about Blyton's perceived harmfulness – for some adults have used her work less innocently (aside from her involvement in issues of racism, discussed earlier). I am referring to that discourse, promoted in the 1980s by the Conservatives, especially under Margaret Thatcher, which sought to allay anxieties about the ills of contemporary society by reappropriating the past, especially the period from the 1920s to the 1950s. This period – almost exactly Blyton's writing career – was repackaged by the heritage industry as an ideal time, a time that we are now seen to have lost (Hewison, 1987; Bromley, 1988). In this, the nation also has its Imaginary, of a Tudorbethan Merry Olde England, of heroic deeds and events, where islands (the Falklands) could be won back from wicked foreigners, and where shipwrecks from our glorious past (the *Mary Rose*) could, just like the Kirrin galleon, be resurrected to help change the fortunes of a society fallen on hard times. This is a less innocent construction, with Blyton's works being used to endorse that mythical middle-England of Major's Mansion House speech. Innocuous in itself, what it sought to divert attention from (homelessness, unemployment, poverty, crime, and so on) was less so. However, this was not the children's fantasy, but an adult one.[7]

Updating Blyton

There are two aspects to this: the updating of Blyton's own texts, and the attempt to appropriate the Blyton 'formula'. Regarding the first, we have seen that Blyton updated herself throughout her career, reworking stories and themes, and adapting to new media as she went. Though many find the updating heresy, I am sure that Blyton herself would have been far more pragmatic. The precious stance towards every word written is, in fact, far more characteristic of a literary culture. But Blyton, as a storyteller, was always refashioning her work. She would have been the first to retell her stories without golliwogs – in fact, I have indicated that she often told a very similar story using a number of different characters – just as, had she lived, she would have updated her language from those rather passé days of 'queer' and 'gay' abandon.[8] What is often forgotten is that this is a common practice amongst writers – even amongst the classics.

This said, had Blyton been responsible for new editions they would, in effect, have been new texts – not the fractured works we now have. I have already drawn attention to the superficial updating, which makes the anachronisms of a computer- and car-free rural environment ever more prominent. A number of readers commented on this, drawing particular attention to the less successful French 'Fives' (Voilier, 1981, 1987). But more significantly, there is the danger of weakening the power of Blyton's stories by taking away the very elements that give them their distinctive voice. This was most brutally done with the abortive second edition of Noddy, but I have also indicated its weakening in the more sensitive third edition, playing down precisely those oral elements in the interests of a more orthodox 'literary' style. Likewise in the Fives, George's fierce individualism has lost some of its edge, all having had their consciousnesses raised.

As for the appropriation of the Blyton formula. I have quoted critics on this earlier, who recognize Blyton's power but want it without the sexism, class-ism, and so on (Leeson, 1985, p. 163; Hincks-Edwards, 1982). I can see the appeal but, based on what I have argued, I would suggest that many works of popular culture which are successful in their embodiment of utopian solutions work precisely because they counterpose this with an existing state of things that is clearly dystopian. Well-intentioned attempts to write texts that install p.c. values often founder because they lose this tension between reality and fantasy, trying to make the reality utopian (no sex discrimination, no inter-group tension, no violence, and so on); whereas the more successful, but often more criticized texts not only recognize the need for contraries, but are themselves written by people with a personal investment in such issues, giving their tales a deeper edge.

Children's literature: the final mystery

Like the Five at the end of their tales, I return to my title, *Enid Blyton and the Mystery of Children's Literature*. The basic mystery, I would suggest, is that it is kept mysterious. Its particular qualities seem capable of being learned only after long apprenticeship, when one, in fact, already has a fully developed, adult sensibility. Thus anything that is not seen to move the reader directly towards this – in other words, anything that, contrarily, celebrates a child-centred culture, where wholeness is expressly conceived at the level of the child working against the fractured world of adults – must be belittled.

It was Blyton's refusal to endorse this that makes her work such an interesting case history. We, as adults, might only see bare words, outmoded and problematic discourses, but that is exactly our position as arch-Other. If, however, we do not try to understand her appeal, we are engaging in just the sort of arrogant colonialist discourse of which Blyton stands accused: of being dismissive, of disparaging what might seem to us quaint superstitions. And, in the very act of doing this we are solidifying the discourse that re-makes children's literature in our own image: one that celebrates the adult as the site of wholeness: rational, worldly-wise, experienced – Piaget's pinnacle of creation, in fact. At the other end of this binary see-saw sits the child; and, not surprisingly, the scales are heavily weighted against it, given that it must be that which the adult is not: incomplete, helpless, dependant – a site of becoming, in fact. In Foucauldian terms, I have sought to unmask this power-knowledge coupling by teasing out its constituent threads.

Adult protests, then, add to the child's pleasures. They underwrite the child's justification both for reading Blyton's texts, and for being secretive about them (they were supposedly banned in South Africa 'because of the impertinence her young characters were alleged to show towards their parents' – Tucker, 1970a). The more that adults seek to control and define what children should be doing, the more that groups such as the Five will appeal. From the other side, Blyton's books are frequently disliked by adults because the adults feel shut out of them. Unlike the classics, these are not texts they find they can share with their children, not only because of the content, but the plots, the characters, the writing – all effectively distance the adult reader precisely because he or she cannot see that world beyond the seemingly threadbare words. Blyton's books would thus seem to challenge Auden's famous comment that 'there are good books which are only for adults . . . there are no good books that are only for children' (Auden, 1972, p. 11).

This recognition, that there are some texts that might be good only for children, has been slow in coming. Whereas adults have long indulged themselves in their own pleasures – drinking, having sex, reading/eating/watching 'junk' – it is often considered that children, as apprentice grown-ups, should have a diet only of material that extends them cognitively. Indeed, though we have the *Bildungsroman*, the novel that charts a character's development, there is no equivalent term for its opposite: for a character that resolutely stays in the same place; if anything, this is seen as a pathology, as in the 'Peter Pan' syndrome; indeed, antonyms of 'developmental' all tend to carry a negative connotation: sluggish, torpid, stagnant, dormant, unmoving and idle. Blyton, of course, provides just such a point of retrenchment, of consolidation and emotional satisfaction.[9] The sorts of play that children spontaneously engage in – their daydreams of being victorious, all powerful, and honoured – Blyton makes into stories. This area seems to have been neglected in the past, essential though it is, for there can be no other development unless a child feels secure and is given space to take stock. Blyton offers precisely this, her books nourishing the ego, fostering a sense of identity. Carol Fox's comment, though related to children's own story-writing, seems apposite: 'The children can achieve mastery of their own existential problems, simultaneously mastering the story discourse, and taking on all the powerful roles they do not have in their real lives' (Fox, 1993, p. 34). Forever saying the same, Blyton's works thus celebrate *being* rather than *becoming*, the timelessness of *Round the Clock Stories* (Blyton, 1945b), rather than the regulated time of growth and development. For ultimately, as we saw in the last chapter, being/storying is life, whereas becoming can only end in death.

Coda

It is indeed ironic that a woman who was, in many ways, committed to circumscribing and controlling children should provide a landscape in which they could roam so freely, indulging themselves, celebrating their own world, while simultaneously turning the tables on the adults. It is also ironic that Blyton was the only real casualty of this. While the child audience moved on, replenishing itself, having been temporarily nourished by her fiction – 'a literary security blanket' (f) as one reader put it – Blyton herself was doomed, endlessly, to repeat her sunny stories. A few times she attempted to write something for adults, but unsuccessfully. This seems to be why critics try to explain Blyton's success in terms of herself being a child. But rather than childish, I have suggested that it was Blyton's psychological make-up that made her hold on to this site of innocence, warding off all that threatened it. For Blyton, then, the 'Enid Blyton' *persona* provided not only an early protective shell but also, ultimately, a restrictive carapace.

In true Blyton fashion, though, we need a happier ending, so I shall leave the last words with two key exponents of being, George and Alicia:

> 'I don't want to grow up . . . There can't be anything nicer in the world than this – being with the others, having fun with them. No – I don't want to grow up!'
>
> (*FGTBH*, p. 46)

So,

> 'Long live our appetites!'
>
> (*Sixth*, p. 17)

Appendix I: Questionnaires

On the following pages are copies of the Questionnaires sent out to potential respondents, predominantly in 1993. The first is the adult version, the second, the children's, which is slightly re-worded and simplified. This said, many children got hold of the adult version, and completed this. Also, some parents were so keen to participate that they filled out their children's questionnaires!

Note: the findings from the questionaires are fully reported in Rudd (1997d).

Adult questionnaire

ENID BLYTON QUESTIONNAIRE

I am undertaking some research into Enid Blyton's enduring popularity. I would be grateful if you would complete the following questionnaire. All responses will be treated with strict confidence and respondents remain anonymous. Please tick on the dotted lines to the right of the appropriate responses, or write in the spaces between questions. Feel free to add extra information on a separate sheet.

1. How old do you think you were when you first discovered Enid Blyton's books?

2. How did you discover them?
   by yourself ..... present from adult ..... other (please specify) .....
   through friend ..... adult reading to you .....

3. What was the first Blyton book you remember reading, or having read to you?

4. What was your favourite Blyton book, or series?
   (If your views have changed, please add your current favourite.)

5. Who was your favourite Blyton character?

6. Which book or series of hers did you like least (if any), and why?

7. Why do you think you liked Enid Blyton's books so much?

8. Did you re-read Enid Blyton's books?
   never ..... sometimes .....
   rarely ..... frequently .....

9. Where did you do most of your reading?
   in bed ..... in a 'secret place' (please specify) ..... other (please specify) .....
   in a chair ..... anywhere you got the chance .....

10. Which of the following words best describes the time you spent reading as a child?
    briefly (1–7 hrs a week) ..... abundantly (15–21 hrs a week) .....
    regularly (8–14 hrs a week) ..... persistently (21 hrs + a week) .....

11. Did you discuss Enid Blyton's books with others?
    never ..... sometimes .....
    rarely ..... frequently .....

12. Did you do anything more than read Enid Blyton's books?
    fantasise about them .....
    play games around them .....
    re-enact them .....
    have clubs, passwords, badges, etc .....
    emulate characters (speech, dress, etc) .....
    write similar stories .....
    other (please specify) ....

13. What were your other favourite authors/books as a child? (Please indicate if you preferred any of these to Enid Blyton.)

14. What adult authors/books do you like reading?

15. What is the formal level of your education?
    left school at 14/15/16 ..... have first degree .....
    left school at 18 ..... have higher degree .....
    went on to higher education .....

16. Please indicate your age group:
    6–14 yrs ..... 25–34 yrs ..... 45–54 yrs ..... 65–74 yrs .....
    15–24 yrs ..... 35–44 yrs ..... 55–64 yrs ..... 75– .....

17. Sex: Female ..... Male .....

18. How would you describe yourself (national/ethnic background)?

19. Your occupation (or, if retired, your former occupation):

20. Your father's/mother's occupation:

21. If you would not mind further enquiries, please add your name and address (otherwise leave blank):

    Please feel free to expand on any of the above questions. Also if you'd like to add anything else that I've not asked about, you are most welcome to do so. Please enclose on a separate sheet. Many thanks for your time and help.

Children's questionnaire

ENID BLYTON QUESTIONNAIRE

I am trying to find out what makes Enid Blyton's books so popular. I would be most grateful if you could answer the questions below. Some of them only need ticks, while others ask you to write more. But whatever you write will be kept secret, so please be honest. Even if you no longer read, or even like, Enid Blyton's books, I'd like you to try to think back to when you did enjoy them. (If you never enjoyed them, I'd still be interested in your views. Just tell me why you didn't like them.)

1. How old do you think you were when you first discovered Enid Blyton's books?

2. How did you discover them?

by yourself ..... present from adult ..... other reason (please give details) .....
through friend ..... adult reading to you .....

3. What was the first Blyton book you remember reading, or having read to you?

4. What was, or is, your favourite Blyton book or series?
(If your views have changed, please list your favourites at different times.)

5. Who was, or is, your favourite Blyton character?

6. Which book or series of hers do you like *least* (if any), and why?

7. Why do you like Enid Blyton's books so much?

8. Have you ever read Enid Blyton's books more than once?
never ..... sometimes .....
rarely ..... frequently .....

9. Where do you do most of your reading of her books?

in bed ..... in a 'secret place' (can you say where?) ..... other (please give details) .....
in a chair ..... anywhere you got the chance .....

10. How much reading do you think you do each week?

1–7 hours a week (i.e. 1 hr a day) ..... 15–21 hours a week (up to 3 hrs a day) .....
8–14 hours a week (up to 2 hrs a day) ..... over 21 hours a week (more than 3 hrs a day) .....

11. Have you discussed Enid Blyton's books with others?
never ..... sometimes .....
rarely ..... frequently .....

12. Have you done anything more than read Enid Blyton's books?
fantasised about them .....
played games around them .....
re-enacted them .....
had clubs, passwords, badges, etc .....
copied characters (their dress, talk, etc) .....
written your own stories .....
other (please give details) ....

13. Who are your other favourite authors/books? (Please underline any that you preferred to Enid Blyton.)

14. How old are you?

15. Are you male or female?

16. How would you describe yourself (your national/ethnic background)?

17. What do your father and mother do for a living?

18. Please add anything else about Enid Blyton's books that you think might be of interest:

MANY THANKS FOR YOUR HELP!

Appendix II: Interviews

Interviews

Four schools in all, two primary and two secondary, were involved in looking at contemporary attitudes to Blyton. The primary schools each had populations of approximately 200 pupils, though from very different catchment areas: Barney School is in a predominantly white, commuter-belt, middle-class district, whereas Amelia Primary is a predominantly working-class, urban school, with 50 per cent black English (predominantly Asian) pupils. The two secondary schools were similarly juxtaposed: Whyteleafe Secondary is a suburban church school, with predominantly white, middle-class children (1200 in number); St Rollo's Secondary is, again, a predominantly working-class urban school, with mixed ethnicity (about 1000 pupils, one-third Asian – mostly Muslims, but with some Hindus and a few African–Caribbeans). Questionnaires (Appendix I) were distributed to classes in each of these schools, with either teachers or parents helping the younger age groups complete them.

An interview schedule was then drawn up (see below) and submitted to the schools, to give them an indication of what I would be asking pupils. Interviews were conducted with 170 pupils, in groups of four (with two exceptions, of five), ranging in age from 4–17 year olds. There were mixed sex, single-sex girl, white, mixed ethnicity, and Asian groups involved. The interviews were taped then transcribed, while recognizing the theoretically-laden nature of transcription (Ochs, 1979). Clearly, from the very moment that the flow of speech is segmented into sentences, one is re-fashioning the source. I have by no means sought the complex 'Jefferson style' transcription, as used by Conversation Analysts (Atkinson and Heritage, 1984). Transcriptions are *verbatim*, however, except where a passage was unintelligible, in which case the 'drift' has been indicated. Prosodic features have been ignored, except where they are dramatic (shouting, for example), or pertinent to the matter in hand.

Transcription conventions

DR David Rudd
. . . speaker ceases speaking, despite the utterance being incomplete
[. . .] material omitted, for various reasons (e.g. irrelevant to point in my text, confused, incomprehensible).
[ ] other material in square brackets is for clarification – e.g. of tone, context, non-verbal elements.

The sex of the speaker, or writer, has been added in brackets – i.e. (m), (f) – and, for children, the age has been added (despite this being an ageist move!) – e.g. (f, 10).

Interview schedule

QUESTION SCHEDULE

1. Do you like reading? How many books have you read? What sort of books do you like?
2. Do you own a lot of books? Do you borrow them from the library?
3. Who are your favourite authors?
4. Which Enid Blytons do you like?
5. Which is your favourite book/series/character?
6. Why? What do you like about it/them?
7. What are your favourite bits?
8. Are there any bits you didn't like?
9. Follow ups (who's the hero/heroine? who made things work? who's the cleverest? who's the stupidist? who has ideas? How many characters can you name? Can you describe them? How many are boys/girls/men/women?
10. Have you read any with 'gollies', or 'golliwogs' in? (Do you know what a golly is? Could you describe one?)
11. Are anyone else's books like Enid Blyton's?
12. Do you know if she's still writing books? (Is she still alive?)
13. Do you know how long ago that this book/her books were written?
14. Are there any of her books you don't like?
15. Suppose someone said you shouldn't read books like this, what would you think?
    (follow ups: Have you heard anyone say this? Can you think why they might say such a thing? (Do you think her books might be bad for you in any way?)
16. Do you read her books yourself, or does anyone read them to you?
17. Do you talk about the books to other people? (Do you play any games after reading her books? Do you imagine yourself in stories like . . . ?)
18. Do you think the stories could be real? (Could that sort of thing happen in real life?)
19. Are her books more for girls or boys, do you think?
20. Which character would you most like to be? Do you ever imagine yourself as any of the characters?
21. Are there any things in the book that don't make sense to you?
22. What are your favourite TV programmes?
23. Have you seen any of Enid Blyton's works on TV? (follow ups: Which? What did you think of them? Were they like the books?)

Notes

1 Introduction

1 See the References section for a list of abbreviations used for main texts.
2 See Appendix II for transcription conventions.

2 Theory and Method: Literature, Discourse and the Constitution of the Child

1 Going through the many commentators on Blyton, very few have thought to consult children (even their own). Frith (1985) is an exception, with a substantial empirical study; Sarland (1983, 1991) and Fry (1985) also deserve mention, besides the general children's surveys, which were not centrally concerned with Blyton (*pace* Ingham, 1982). Woods (1974) is a curious case here, having addressed questionnaires about Blyton to 100 schools in Britain, but for the teachers, rather than the pupils, to complete.
2 The Public Lending Right Office continue to separate 'classics', such as Beatrix Potter, from the likes of Blyton and Dahl.
3 Inglis' work is more complex, in that he finds a space for popular writers like Blyton, drawing on his own childhood reading. He argues that all the writers he discusses offer 'the promise of happiness', though he does not square this theoretically with his more polemical statements. However, he has continued to champion Blyton's positive qualities (Inglis, 1997).
4 Though I am critical of Tucker's theoretical approach, his practical criticism is exemplary. He was one of the earliest writers to take children's interest in Blyton seriously.
5 However, as Culler (1981, pp. 119–31) has suggested, it could be that it is the text that is at the mercy of the reader; that is, the text is seen to have gaps which have really been created by readers, who have appropriated the text for their own purposes.
6 This, of course, has been taken up by the New Historicists, though I have not generally followed their example (Veeser, 1989).
7 Elizabeth Frazer uses a similar term, speaking of a 'discourse register', which she defines as 'an institutionalized, situationally specific, culturally familiar, public, way of talking' (Frazer, 1987, p. 420). In her empirical work she certainly found her subjects using a variety of these registers. Unfortunately, Frazer does not discuss the power base that clearly gives some discourses more 'clout' than others. It is this power element that is so important in Foucault's work.
8 See the References section for a list of abbreviations to main texts.
9 This follows Michael Holquist, Bakhtin's translator (Bakhtin, 1981), that these are one and the same person.

10 In some senses the quantitative/qualtitative distinction is artificial, the terms being closely interdependent. Briefly, to know anything, to call it important, means that one has some internal scale on which one is gauging it, however subjectively. In textual analysis, to talk about themes, or particular uses of imagery, means that certain words and phrases have occurred more frequently than others.
11 See Jordin and Brunt (1988) for a critique of Morley along these lines. Also Gemma Moss (1993) makes the useful point that standardizing class, age and ethnicity is insufficient; one needs a longitudinal view of readers and their reading histories.

3 Person and Persona: the Construction of Blyton as Cultural Icon

1 Much of this section draws on Stoney's ground-breaking work.
2 I was 'wined and dined' as a potential contributor, only later to be dropped. Clearly, my involvement was with the work, which was hardly mentioned, so was seen as having little to contribute alongside stories about nude tennis and cheating at cards!
3 There was some controversy over this in 1995, which hit the national press. A previously unknown work by her, entitled *Sports and Games* was bought by Mason Willey for £125. He argued that it was very early, possibly 1918–19 (Willey, 1995), and the ensuing debate caused a few rifts amongst Blyton collectors. However, it has since emerged that the book was published in October 1924 (Summerfield, 1998). Interestingly, it was a colleague of mine from Bolton Institute who discovered the volume, and asked me for names of Blyton collectors.
4 The 1986 edition is a poor imitation, with only four black-and-white photographs, compared with 87 in the original. It has also been carefully edited, omitting much information.
5 Freeman (1993, pp. 58–80) discusses Keller's autobiography in some detail.
6 Ironically, Mullan, who wrote *The Enid Blyton Story*, also wrote *Are Mothers Really Necessary?* in the same year (1987b), but makes no connection.
7 Blyton remains factually accurate, however: 'my husband . . . and my two girls' (Blyton, 1952b, p. 117), she states – not *our* two girls. Blyton was very fortunate in having the War distract attention from her private life. A brief report in *The Evening News* is similarly tactful, saying that Blyton is the wife of Mr Kenneth Darrell Waters and that, 'She has the patient, good temper of the natural mother – she has two daughters of her own', later adding that, 'up to the time of her marriage she ran a school of her own at Surbiton' (Carpenter, 1944). This is factually true, although it refers to her first marriage, 19 years earlier!
8 In using 'Imaginary' with a capital I am referring to Lacan's work, which is dealt with more extensively in Chapter 10. Here it is sufficient to note that Narcissus became locked into immobility, achieving immortality, but at a price. Blyton is very keen on doubles, whether in reality or fiction (there are many confusing twins, or even threesomes, as in *The Three Golliwogs*). Doubles were originally seen as duplicates who created immortality for their

owners; however, they later became uncanny augers of death (Freud, 1961; Freud, 1985).

9 According to Druce (1992, p. 31) her signature was first used in *Teachers World* (see note 12, below) September, 1927. It did not appear on a book till *Enid Blyton's Readers, Book 1* (1942b) – as Tony Summerfield discovered. Several of my respondents confessed that they had always read 'Enid' as 'Gnid'; others, especially overseas readers, hadn't known whether the author was male or female.

10 J.M. Barrie and Nesbit are thus explained (Lurie, 1990), as is Dahl (Powling, 1983, p. 53) , Carroll (Cohen, 1995, pp. 190–1, 530), and Mee (Hammerton, 1946, p. 35). Carpenter (1994) and Hulbert (1995) make this claim more generally about children's writers.

11 There is an obvious temptation to link problems of the uterus to 'hysteria', the term itself derived from the Greek word for womb. Breuer and Freud's *Studies in Hysteria* (1895) might then be turned to and, in particular, their patient Anna O with her fantasies of being in a 'private theatre': 'While everyone thought she was attending, she was living through fairy tales in her imagination' (Breuer and Freud, 1974, p. 74). Blyton, as we shall see, frequently spoke of living out her stories in her 'private cinema'.

12 *Teachers World* is written with the apostrophe after the 's' by Stoney (1974), Ray (1982) and Mullan (1987a) – viz. *Teachers' World* – and before the 's' by Smallwood (1989) and Druce (1992) – viz. *Teacher's World*. However, the journal itself has the title without apostrophe – a convention I have followed. Blyton, incidentally, wrote it with the apostrophe following the 's' (Blyton, 1952b).

13 Following a theme pursued elsewhere, this character was not invented specifically for this venture. 'Miss Mary Ann Mouse' appears in a very similar story in *Enid Blyton's Sunny Stories* in 1938 (15 April); collected in Blyton (1948b).

14 Ray (1982, p. 43) quotes a librarian who stated that at least one Mary Pollock was not very popular till reissued in 1950 under Blyton's own name (from the dates given, this must have been *Smuggler Ben*, the only one reissued in 1950). This seems untrue, for although no sales records survive, all six books were reissued under the name Pollock between 1945 and 1947, and two of the titles had already been reprinted earlier. Clearly, in wartime, this must have been based on healthy sales. (My thanks to Tony Summerfield, for his encyclopaedic knowledge of Blyton's publishing history.) Druce (1992, p. 39) distorts Ray at this point, in suggesting that none of the Pollock books was popular, and that this was based on Ray's own library experience.

15 My thanks to Barbara Stoney for pointing these out to me.

16 Eyre (1952, p. 53) quotes Colwell as saying 'but what chance has a gang of desperate criminals against three small children'; Grove (1993), 'What chance have a gang of desperate men against five small children?'

17 Personal communication. Ironically, School Librarians at Nottingham County Libraries asked me to speak on Blyton recently. I also appeared in a British Council sponsored film to promote Blyton as a British author, which was shot in Newark Library (Anon, 1997). Times have certainly changed.

18 Not all such bans are apocryphal though, nor are they all 'history'. In Dunfermline, in 1996, there was an outcry in the local press that the District

Libraries were not stocking any Blyton – a policy confirmed by the Director of Leisure Services, David Arnott, reaching back to the 1970s. It was argued that as there were so many titles, and they couldn't buy every one, they should not buy any. Selective buying, it was argued, was an 'impossible . . . half-measure', as they didn't know what criteria to use – a strange thing for librarians to admit! (Anon, 1996a). Particularly, as other respondents pointed out, the library managed such selection with other popular authors (Anon, 1996b). (My thanks to Sheila Ray for these cuttings.)

19 I am ignoring *Oz*'s 1973 cartoon, showing Noddy and Big-Ears engaged in masturbation.

20 My thanks to Mike Humphreys, for drawing this to my attention.

21 Perhaps 'Die Funf Freunde' were influenced by the news that 'the recorded stories of Enid Blyton outsell even supergroups . . . in Germany.' World Wide Audio Products received eight gold albums from sales of over 2 million in Germany (Manning, 1980).

22 This sounds like a reference to the *Oz* cartoon, mentioned earlier.

23 Lipman (1995) herself does not mention Thatcher as an influence, only Joyce Grenfell – whom she had portrayed in a one-woman show. Grenfell herself had expertly mocked Blyton's compositional style:

> I go upstairs to my Hidey Hole . . . I pin a notice on the door and it says 'Gone to Make-Believe Land'. This is just my way of saying 'Please don't come and bother me because a book is writing itself to me and we mustn't disturb it, must we?'
>
> No I never re-write and I never read what I have written. But you children do, millions and millions of you children do and that is my great joy.
>
> (quoted in Lipman, 1995, pp. 96–7)

24 Carol Thatcher (1996), in a biography with several parallels to Smallwood's, inadvertently shows other similarities between the two, as does Beatrix Campbell, in *The Iron Ladies*. Thatcher also made children central in theory – 'When children are young, however busy we may be with practical duties inside or outside the home, the most important thing of all is to devote enough time and care to their problems' (Thatcher, quoted in Campbell, 1987, p. 236) – while in practice, engaging in other activities. It is reported that when Thatcher was in hospital, having her twins, she decided then and there to put her name down for the Bar finals: the children were given a nanny and sent off to boarding school. Thatcher also left her mother out of her *Who's Who* entry, only giving her father credit for her existence.

25 The original books are *Adventure of the Strange Ruby, The Mystery that Never was, Hollow Tree House, The Treasure Hunters, The Boy Next Door* and *Holiday House*.

26 Another cultural icon of the twentieth century, Tintin, had met the same resistance. America being 'the one major market Hergé never cracked' (Thompson, 1991, p. 48).

27 Ironically Blyton has stories involving characters with each of these names: 'Silly little Goofy' (1941; in Blyton, 1970b, pp. 127–32), about a pixie, and 'Big-Foot is very clever' – Big-Foot being a brownie, like Big-Ears (in Blyton, 1971, p. 80).

28 David Lane was reported as follows: 'We have done market research in New York and a lot of American children and their parents could hardly understand a word he was saying' (Boshoff, 1997). This is sad news, and also surprising, given America's own multiculturalism; even more so given that the U.S. took so readily to the much broader, regional accents of 'Wallace and Gromit'.

4 The Pied Piper Among the Critics

1 The phrase is Colwell's but has been taken up by others; for example, Eyre (1952, p. 49), *Where* magazine (see Blishen, 1967), Moss (1970), but most notably by Ray, who uses it as the title of her book (see Ray, 1982, p. 3).
2 I have listed some polysyllables from the Noddy books below. Here are a few from the first Famous Five books: 'encrusted', 'forlorn', 'festooned', 'deputation', 'disclosed', 'traipse', 'surly', 'dismal', 'doleful', 'ferociously', 'captors', 'ransom', 'impassive', 'affable', 'obstinate', 'monotone', 'beseechingly', 'bewilderment', 'niches', 'sarcastic', 'biddable'. A personal favourite is 'stentorian', which I used to drop into compositions and conversations, having long forgotten that I had picked it up from Blyton; that is, till I went back to her books as an adult. Blyton herself presumably took it from Homer.
3 Recent editions have changed the colour from 'red' to 'green', which is presumably more scientifically correct, but this is a different issue. Fisher is elsewhere guilty of such misreading. In the review where she calls Blyton 'slow poison', she manages to misname two of the main characters, P.C. Goon being renamed 'Goad' (Fisher, 1973, p. 2230).
4 Such comparisons are not uncommon. McDowell (1972) sets up a similar contrast between Clive King's *Stig of the Dump* and Joyce's *Ulysses* in order to make a point. See Rudd (1995c) for a critique of this tactic.
5 This is a particularly disappointing comment from Moss, given her famous article 'The "Peppermint" lesson', where she explores why her daughter found a particularly cheap and 'totally expendable' text to be 'pure gold', reading it repeatedly over the years. Moss, realizing its personal relevance for her adopted daughter, makes the sensible comment that 'a book by itself is nothing', one can only assess its 'value by the light it brings to a child's eye' (Moss, 1977, pp. 141–2).
6 There certainly are flaws, though, and I shall detail some significant ones in due course.
7 One thinks of A.A. Milne's response to Dorothy Parker's criticism of his work:

> When, for instance, Dorothy Parker, as 'Constant Reader' in *The New Yorker*, delights the sophisticated by announcing that at page 5 of *The House of* [*sic*] *Pooh Corner* 'Tonstant Weader fwowed up' (sic, if I may), she leaves the book, oddly enough, much where it was. However greatly indebted to Mrs Parker, no Alderney, at the approach of the milkmaid, thinks 'I hope this lot will turn out to be gin', no writer of children's books says gaily to his publisher, 'Don't bother about the children, Mrs Parker will love it'.
>
> (quoted in Thwaite, 1990, p. 336)

8 This article has now been published, in slightly different form (Crago, 1996).
9 In a joint survey by the BBC's *Bookworm* and Waterstone's of favourite books, this was her only title to feature in the Top 20, and that for the over-16s.
10 I have given Leng's study close attention because it is indicative of the problems of purely quantitative work. It is also highly regarded, being the exemplar for the later Schools Council study (Whitehead *et al.*, 1977). But for all its quantitative credibility – Leng looked at the reading of 1055 children, aged 6–13, who attended certain local schools, and lived within one mile of Llanfair Public Library – the study falls down in not exploring the meaning of its data. Druce picks Leng up on a similar point:

> A ten-year-old girl brought back to the Library a book by Enid Blyton which she had taken out the previous day and had evidently much enjoyed. Finding no other Blyton on the shelves, and presumably failing to find any other book to suit her tastes, she took out again the very book she had just returned, and on three successive days the self-same thing occurred.
>
> (Leng, 1968, p. 187)

As Druce comments, 'It may have been . . . that she was merely maintaining her hold on a valuable bargaining counter' (Druce, 1992, p. 41). Remarks like Brian Blessed's 'we were very poor, so we swapped our Enid Blyton hardbacks for marbles' (Ewbank, 1990, p. 8) suggest this might be likely.

5 Noddy: Discursive Threads and Intertextuality

1 The nine letters have not been published, but Barbara Stoney reproduces extracts from four of them, which is more than is quoted in McKellar's own work.
2 Referred to as *Tales* hereafter (Blyton, 1963b). These were originally serialized in *Sunny Stories* in 1942 (Summerfield and Wright, 1995, p. 7), and appeared in book form in 1944.
3 This is not so surprising, for she had earlier written about 'Big-Ears, the Pixie' (Blyton, 1947c); he's pictured on p. 67, and seems, in this tale, to be the only one with a car.
4 My thanks to Stephanie Main for this information. The frog also features eponymously in 'Big-Eyes, the frog' in *Sunny Stories* (1943), collected in *The Yellow Story Book*. There is at least one other story that features a character called 'Noddy': 'Tom Noddy's Imp' in *Sunny Stories* (1937), later collected in *A Book of Naughty Children*.
5 It was Stephanie Main who found the first of these. Norman Wright also has one in his collection. The character possibly also featured in a book, but no one has yet turned up a copy. This illustration is from Geoff Phillips' collection – to whom, many thanks.
6 For example 'I was here first' (*Sunny Stories*, 1946) and 'It's just a dream' (*Sunny Stories*, 1948) each feature policemen called Mr. Plod. They can both be found in *Bedtime Stories* (1970a). Druce's explanation of the origin of Mr. Plod – suggesting a link with S.G. Hulme Beaman, who has Ernest the police-

man going 'plod, plod, in the dusty road' (Druce, 1992, p. 127) – seems less likely. But many words are overdetermined in this way. Barbara Baines was kind enough to send me newspaper cuttings about her father, P.C. Rone, of Studland, Dorset, whom Blyton used to watch pushing his bike up a steep hill (plod, plod). Blyton told him that he was the original Mr. Plod (Harrison, 1990).

Morrison (1984) quotes a police chief who resents the stereotyped image that Plod gives, though Cathy Currie, a criminologist, has suggested that Plod's image is precisely what the force should strive for, Plod being the ideal 'community policeman' (Anon, 1988). Unfortunately for children's literature, this image has been superceded: 'Most policemen are corrupt. . . . We have moved from the dull but safe world of Mr. Plod to the bleak and dangerous milieu of P.C. Pig and the short sharp shock' (Hoffman, 1984, p. 183).

7 Big-Ears asks the same of Noddy in the first book: 'Why do you nod your head when you say "No"?' (*N1*, p. 8). The problem is exacerbated for the Milkman: 'You nod for one bottle, and you nod for two! How am I to know which you want?' (*N2*, p. 8).

8 The books were emasculated far more than this. For instance, in *Here Comes Noddy Again!* (*N4*), the goblins only remove Noddy's shoes and hat; they also say they're sorry at the end and polish his car.

9 They are from the following: 'unexpectedly' (*N1*, p. 48), 'becalmed' (*N18*, p. 44), 'surge' (*N19*, p. 55), 'dreadful' (*N24*, p. 59). The amendments are on the same pages in the new editions.

10 It is called predominantly 'Toy Village', but also 'Toyland Village' (*N13*, p. 34) and, in *N5*, p. 55, 'Toy Town', with Blyton perhaps thinking of Hulme Beaman's eponymous radio series. In the third edition it has been changed to 'Toy Town' throughout – apart from one missed 'Toy Village (*N13**, p. 49).

11 Interestingly, the name 'Miss Rap' meant little to most of the junior children, though they had several ideas: first to do with music: 'Because she liked rap music' (m, 8), ''Cos shouts, like in the fast talking that people do' (m, 9), or, more directly, ''Cos she always sings raps' (f, 6); second, to do with 'wrapping': 'Because she's wrapped up in clothes' (m, 9), or more observantly, 'Because she wears wraps' (that is, a shawl; m, 6); thirdly, it was her speed: 'She's rapid – goes fast'; lastly, it was suggested that it was because of her littering: 'Because she throws wrappers around' (f, 6). This said, the name 'Prim' was, if anything, less known. One or two did suggest that it was short for 'Primrose', 'Because she's like a rose'.

12 We should bear in mind that this is Toyland, based on the sort of toys that supposedly exist; hence there tend to be toys in certain categories, not others (for example no miners or factory workers). The same explanation might account for the absence of any church, in that there are few toy clergy. Toys, as Kuznets (1994) suggests, are themselves pagan idols, animated by children, hence religion would be inappropriate.

13 In fact, I have wondered whether *N22*, in which the value of the police is expressly endorsed (see the Wobbly-Man's comment, quoted in the main text), was written after some criticism of this earlier book. Even in its title – *Mr. Plod and Little Noddy* – it is unique in having another character usurping Noddy's primacy. However, I have not been able to find reference to any

criticism. It should also be said that even here we hear of 'a few . . . [who] aren't very sorry' about Mr. Plod's accident (*N22*, p. 30).

6 The Famous Five: from Discursive Threads to Cultural Readings

1 Other Fives were serialized as follows: four in *Enid Blyton's Magazine: FGDTS* (no. 12), *FOST, FGTBH,* and *FGIF* (15–17). Three more in the girls' comic, *Princess: FOFF* (18); *FGTDR* (19) and the last, *FATA* (21). Some other, shorter pieces also appeared in magazines and elsewhere, since collected and published as *FHPT*.
2 George's 11 years is clearly flagged up in the first book, only to be mentioned one other time, in the third, *FRAT*, where all the children are said to be one-year-older (p. 10). Despite George's comment that 'Julian is in his 'teens already, and I soon shall be and so will Dick' (p. 27), ageing is not chronologically acknowledged again by Blyton – apart from once: 'Julian is sixteen now' (*FFIA*, p. 16). In the paperback version this has been amended to 'Julian is almost grown-up now'. However, *were* we counting, taking into account the seasons, George and Dick would be 23, Anne 22, Julian 24 and Timmy, very long in the tooth by the final adventure!
3 *Enid Blyton's Magazine*, 7, 10 June 1953, p. 45.
4 This is a recurring type, best represented by Cecil Dearlove in the Five (*FGOTC*). In *Six Cousins at Mistletoe Farm* (1948e) there is a similarly named Cyril, who's name, 'long hair and languid ways' amuse the main boys, though Cyril can see nothing wrong with his name:

   > 'No. That's just the trouble. . . . If you could, you'd jolly well get your hair cut as short as possible, you'd talk properly instead of in that namby-pamby fashion, and you wouldn't wear floppy bows and spout poetry!' (p. 39)

   Again, this is a stock type in children's fiction (commonly mocked, for example, in the 'William' stories), possibly originating in Burnett's *Little Lord Fauntleroy* (1886) who is lampooned by E. Nesbit in *The Story of the Treasure Seekers* (1899/1958).
5 The problem of smell affects many, including some champions of the working-class. For instance, the Independent Labour Party social reformer, Margaret McMillan, expresses similar concerns – see Steedman (1990, pp. 44–5).
6 Dixon says 'the names of foreigners are often German or Russian' (1974b, p. 55). In the Five this does not seem the case. I could only find Carlo and Emilio from *FHMTS* (Spanish?), Mr Wooh from *FATA* who 'spoke like a foreigner' (Chinese?), and Red Tower's henchman, Markhoff in *FFIA* (possibly Russian). If I were to count Gringo of Gringo's Circus (*FHPOF*), I might muster five.
7 Five books have none; five have inspectors; six have ordinary P.C.s; in the remaining five there is a mixture, adding up to one inspector, four sergeants and three P.C.s.

8 The maltreatment of animals has a long and established history in children's stories, from Mrs Trimmer's *Fabulous Histories*, or *The History of the Robins* (1786) which, with its baby robins, Robin, Dicksy, Pecksy and Flapsy, could easily have been Blyton creations. Blyton's stories are actually quite anodyne compared with many; for example, in Andersen's 'The girl who stepped on bread' (Andersen, 1974, pp. 606–13), the girl in question, who is unkind to animals, goes to hell for her actions!

9 This is not to dispute middle-class attempts to annex character:

> I want decent, fair, honest, citizen values, all the principles you were brought up with. You don't live up to the hilt of your income; if someone gets the bill wrong you tell them, you don't keep the extra change; you respect other people's property; you save; you believe in right and wrong; you support the police. . . . We were taught to help people in need ourselves, not stand about saying what the government should do. Personal initiative was pretty strong. You were actually taught to be clean and tidy, that cleanliness was next to Godliness. All these ideas have got saddled as middle class values, but they're eternal – Margaret Thatcher, *Sunday Times Colour Supplement* 20 August 1978.
>
> (quoted in Bromley, 1988, p. 140)

10 A similar moral dilemma is addressed in E. Nesbit's *Five Children and It* (1959) Chapter 4.

11 There are other intimate moments with Timmy, too, one of which Tucker cannot resist quoting, after a comment about bestiality: '"Dear Timmy," murmurs the androgynous George sleepily to her dog, settling down for the night in *FGTDR*, "I love you – but do keep your tongue to yourself"' (Tucker, 1970c). Needless to say, the Comic Strip reworked this line to good effect.

12 For anyone not in the know, this symbol – :-) – is a smiley, commonly used in email. The smiling face can be seen by tilting your head to the left. It is a common method of communicating good-humour, indicating that something is meant to be taken lightly.

13 Ironically, critics' own comments on Blyton are littered with food analogies, although I am less certain what to make of these. The following is but a small selection:

> books which . . . appeal to children in much the same way as do fish fingers and minced meat.
>
> (Capey and Maskell, p. 22)

> Just as we would think a parent very wrong who fed his children exclusively on jelly and shop cake, so I feel we are greatly to blame if we let our children grow up solely on formula stories.
>
> (Dodsworth, 1982, p. 27, quoting John Rowe Townsend)

> Enid Blyton's books are like baby food – nice and palatable but absolutely useless when it comes to needing a good diet.
>
> (Hindle, 1982)

> once the taste has been established it has an almost inexhaustible supply of food – the only problem is the number of spoons to be plunged into the same dish.
>
> (Hollindale, 1974, p. 153)

> Any success in popular culture will draw out a mixture of ready-to-hand substitute foods, brightly coloured, fatty sweet; and bad for you.
>
> (Inglis, p. 188)

Martin's analogies are strangely contradictory, calling Blyton's books both 'nauseatingly sugary' and 'veritable milk-and-water' (Martin, 1990, p. 27). But Barker's food analogy is even stranger, moving Blyton away from junk food analogies and into the healthy eating of the '90s:

> It is a pity indeed that we do not know the effects of popular reading on the recipient. Perhaps if we did, we could show a connection, however slight, in the recent growth of interest in health and whole foods and the descriptions of home-grown, home-baked, home-bottled food in Enid Blyton's books.
>
> (Barker, 1982, p. 11)

14 See Blyton (1948e; 1951b) for more pronounced examples of good and bad mothers; see also Barker (1982).

7 Sexism or Subversion? Querying Gender Relations in the Famous Five and Malory Towers

1 'Pour out the cocoa, Janet – and remember that we all like heaps of sugar' (Blyton, 1953b, p. 20). It continues, 'She poured out the cocoa, and Peter handed round the sandwiches' (p. 21).
2 It is interesting that in the 1957 film there is no mention of the island being passed down the female line. Also in the film, George's parents are referred to as Mr and Mrs Kirrin, suggesting that it is Quentin's name. In the books, surnames are avoided till number 16 in the series, *FGTBH* (1955), when we learn that George's cousins are also Kirrins, despite the link being through the females. However, in the very next book, *FGIF*, their surname is explicitly 'Barnard'! Despite some quite complex explanations of how this might be the case (Rudd, 1997b), Blyton herself admitted the error (Blyton, 1998).
3 Boys with feminine qualities are a different matter. 'Why doesn't he get his hair cut?' said Julian in disgust. 'Boys with long hair are just too sissy for words' (*FGOTC*, p. 110). This is the predictable reaction of the manly Julian to the rather soft Cecil Dearlove (see Chapter 6, note 4). However, Martin Curton in *FOKIA* is presented in a sensitive way, artistic temperament notwithstanding, despite crying, Anne supportively saying, 'Boys do cry sometimes'. In fact, Dick, we hear, 'had been a bit of a cry-baby' (*FOTI*, p. 31).
4 It is not mentioned by Ray (1982), Mullan (1987a) or Druce (1992). It is

worth noting that St. Rollo's is also a co-educational boarding school (see main text).

5 These anonymous sequels seem to draw on a wider tradition of school stories, including Elinor Brent-Dyer's 'Chalet School' series. In the latter, the protagonist, Joe Bettany, also returns to the school, marries, and has 11 children. Joe, like Darrell, also writes the Christmas plays and has aspirations to be a writer. She too has a temper.

There are also several parallels between these writers' lives – not least of which is their almost exact contemporaneity (1894–1969). Brent-Dyer came from a lower-middle class background too, and had a father who walked out on the family for another woman, which the young Brent-Dyer had to cover up. Finally, Brent-Dyer also trained as a teacher, though she practised far longer than did Blyton (see McClelland, 1986, 1989).

6 Imogen Smallwood relates that her stepfather, Kenneth Darrell Waters, was 'An absolutely punctual and reliable man himself, he had no tolerance at all for other people's more relaxed ways. Again and again, ready in the car to go to London, he would begin to hoot the horn if my mother delayed even for two minutes' (Smallwood, 1989, p. 102).

7 In some surviving notes for this story, Blyton has Gwen's father die; in the event, however, Blyton could not let this happen, even in fictional terms – see Chapter 10 for an explanation.

8 William Byrom Forbush, *A Guide Book to Childhood* (1921), quoted in Avery, 1991, p. 417.

9 In this I would disagree with Frith, who sees the series as representing a stage that must be grown out of. I would suggest that such a reading is warranted only by looking from the outside, diachronically. For the young reader there is simply a space opened up, in which the young reader, like Rachel, can wallow.

10 There is a clear double standard when it comes to classics, which are allowed to stay unrevised. Is this because they are for a more mature, immune audience? Thus in *Peter Pan* the 'picanniny' tribe lives on, and children can not only be heartless and ruthless, but 'gay' too (Barrie, 1986, p. 217). Peter Pan can even still say to Wendy, 'You are so queer' (ibid., p. 133). The period slang, 'wizard', 'gosh' and 'crikey' is cleared from popular authors but remains, say, in Golding's *Lord of the Flies* (1954); 'niggers' remain in E. Nesbit, though they have gone from Blyton and Richmal Crompton's 'William'.

8 Golliwogs, Racism and Blyton: from Preferred Readings to Cultural Effects

1 This is not in the original 1974(a) article, where Dixon himself uses personal anecdote, thus leaving himself more open to attack. Nevertheless, this style of argument is used by those on each side of the debate; for example Alibhai-Brown writes:

> 'The face has nasty gleaming eyes and it looked very dark. Perhaps it was a black man's face. Oh I was so frightened' . . . Incidentally the Blyton

> passage was pointed out to me by a mother of a young Black boy who had tried to rub off his skin with a brillo pad.
>
> (Alibhai-Brown, 1994, p. 66)

While it is always difficult to evaluate such personal statements, it is of note that the Blyton extract has not been causally linked to the boy's actions; in fact, it is not even clear that the boy had even read the passage. Be that as it may, I would again want to emphasize that Blyton regularly has faces appearing at windows; for instance, 'Dick saw him through the window – just a face, dim and wild-eyed, with a round bullet-like head' (*FOHT*, p. 55). In the extract that Alibhai-Brown quotes it turns out to be Jo's – a white, if unwashed, girl (*FFIA*).

2 In fact, some talk about storytellers using 'archetypes', Jung's term for what he considered to be universal figures who appear in myths and stories. Propp's paradigmatic analysis of Russian folk-tales also claimed to find universal types, though more schematically (Propp, 1968). However, there is always a problem of one person's archetypes being another's stereotypes.

3 'Blacks' have also been brown, of course – hence 'negro', 'brownie' (a word with a different connotation in Blyton) and 'nigger', the last now being one of the most offensive words in English (Cohn, 1988), though here too there has been some attempted reappropriation of the term in America. 'Black' too is now more frowned on, while the term 'Negro' is resurgent in some quarters (Crouch, 1997). Some Asians, too, have objected to the term 'Black', in that it categorizes them with African–Caribbeans:

> As many as 83 per cent of the West Indians and 43 per cent of the Indians and Pakistanis said they had most in common with the English. However, a further 31 per cent said that as far as they were concerned they had nothing in common with either. No more than 8 per cent of West Indian and 20 per cent of the Indians and Pakistanis felt that they had more in common with each other than with the English.
>
> (Daniel Lawrence's study in Nottingham, quoted in James, 1993, p. 267)

4 Rupert has also been criticized for featuring golliwogs, causing Express Newspapers problems with their facsimile editions. While the 1936–41 volumes are 'true facsimiles', the following ones are labelled 'reproduction annuals' because the text has been amended. In the 1942 volume 'wog' was erased from 'Golliwog', leaving gaps in the text; in the 1943 volume, 'Golly' is used as a replacement, avoiding gaps. When it came to the 1946 volume, which included 'Rupert on Coon Island', they obviously realized that such tweaking was impossible, so omitted this year entirely (together with the 1947 volume), moving from 1945 to 1948!

Generally, though, Rupert has attracted far less attention than Noddy. Alfred Bestall, the main artist and writer of 'Rupert', also illustrated Blyton's work, and some of Milne's, too, including some of the latter's incredibly popular children's verse. In Bestall's illustration to Milne's 'Forgotten', a precursor of Pooh stands next to a golliwog (Thwaite, 1992, p. 51); also, in Shepard's better known illustrations to the poem (Milne, 1965, pp. 95–8) there is what might be considered a suspect doll standing beside Pooh. It is fascinating to speculate on what might have been the fate of the 'Pooh' books had a golliwog lived in the Hundred-Acre Wood.

5 'They looked like golliwogs, like white people pretending to be black for the laughs they could get' as Kurt Vonnegut (1972, p. 105) puts it. This was certainly a common practice, expressing America's fear of the Negro – of the Other. It is interesting to note that cross-dressing – men dressing as women (and vice versa) – has been articulately theorized, using notions of transgression, but whites dressing as blacks, or blacks imitating whites, seems a far more taboo area.

6 The Working Group Against Racism in Children's Resources kindly provided me with a handout that has an illustration of what they claim is an 'anti-semitic Edwardian gollywog' [*sic*] (Racism Spotlight Group, 1984). It has a larger nose, but little else that signifies such a description, so I must presume that this labelling is based on some other knowledge.

7 The term 'dolly' is also used in the interpretation of James Robertson & Sons, the preserve manufacturers, who began using the golliwog in 1920 to promote their products. They claim that, just before World War I, on a visit to the backwoods of America, James Robertson's son noticed some children playing with some white-eyed, black, rag dolls. The doll was called a 'golly' by the children, their rendering of 'dolly'. Robertson thought it would make an appealing mascot. To make him more attractive, 'he was dressed in a very colorful [*sic*] suit' (Davis, 1992, p. 104, quoting Robertson's anniversary publication, *Fifty Golden Years – Robertson's Golly: 1920–1980*). Robertson's were forced to stop using their golly logo for a period in the 1980s, but now use it again.

8 The other text frequently mentioned is *The Three Golliwogs* (1944), nowadays unacceptable with its three heroes, Golly, Woggie and Nigger. It was amended in the late sixties to Wiggy, Waggy and Wolly, and, more recently, the book has appeared as *The Three Bold Pixies* (1994). However, at the time they were first written (1939), the original names were far more common – and, as with all Blyton's names, are deliberately basic, frequently based on the generic name: a goldfish is 'Goldie', a nodding man is 'Noddy', and a golly would be 'Golly' or 'Woggie'. The term 'Nigger', however, also common, is more revealing. Originally a term for a colour, it became closely linked with black people, making an association undeniable, if only at a subconscious level. Whether Blyton was more consciously aware of this is debatable, for she also has other characters with such names (for instance, some circus dogs are called 'Darky' and 'Nigger' – Blyton, 1938a).

Aside from the names, the humour of these golliwogs might also be considered offensive in that much of it is based on their being mistaken for each other – as other races are often portrayed ('they all look the same'). This could certainly be offensive, although again, mistaken identity is a common humorous device in Blyton. As Noddy laments in Toyland, 'all the Mr. Noahs look exactly alike' (*N9*, p. 34), and her interchangeable twins are legion.

9 *Snicker the Brownie and Other Stories* (1985) is, in effect, *Enid Blyton's Jolly Story Book* (1944b), without the offending 'The little black doll'. The only other change to this volume seems to be in 'The bad Cockyolly bird', where a prominent, quick-witted golliwog has been replaced by a 'baby doll'.

10 Linking blackness to monkeys is a particularly insidious move, textually unwarranted, yet discursively powerful. Surprisingly, George Greenfield, Blyton's literary agent, also gives voice to the erroneous view that 'her naughty characters were almost always black in hue' (1995, p. 113)!
11 'I shall run away', p. 55 (Blyton, 1965a, pp. 50–5; orig. *Sunny Stories*, 1949).
12 'The Odd little bird' (Blyton, 1974, pp. 84–90).
13 'Michael's Tail' (Blyton, 1964b, pp. 144–59; orig. *Sunny Stories*, 1945).
14 For other variants, see 'Cubby and the Cats' (Blyton, 1955), 'The white golliwog' (Blyton, 1948c, pp. 83–9; *Sunny Stories*, 122, 12 May 1939) and 'Old black face' (Blyton, 1950c). All show-up the bigoted nature of those who do the rejecting. It is an old theme. Blyton may well have picked it up from Struwwelpeter's 'The story of the inky boys' (1848 in English; 1845 in German), which Blyton certainly possessed.
15 This said, I am aware of an absence of African–Caribbeans in my sample. Only a few feature, simply because there are comparatively few in the Bolton area – unlike Manchester, where there is also far greater awareness of the discourse of racism. However, this also makes Blyton more taboo, and I was advised that I was unlikely to be allowed to speak to the children there so openly about the texts. (I should make it clear that I did not approach Manchester schools, following some 'insider' information advising me that it would not be well received. I had no official word on this, though.)
16 Dyer and Romalov (1995) point out that the rewrites of the 'Nancy Drew' books similarly excluded Blacks and other minorities. Likewise, it was insisted that no blacks appeared in Hergé's 'Tintin' stories in America, though they existed in the originals (Thompson, 1991).
17 The Burnage enquiry makes similar points (see Gillborn, 1995).
18 'Badness' is a vague word, but I looked for behaviour that was naughty or anti-social. 'Good' golliwogs were ones that either made some positive contribution (for example, helping others, suggesting ideas), or, ones who were simply named alongside other characters (that is, as part of the chorus).
19 This usage was also current earlier. Blyton has the following piece of dialogue in *FOHT* (1951), discussing – it should be noted – a white character:

> 'He looks like a gorilla or something with his broad hunched-up body. And WHY doesn't he cut his hair?' [Anne]
> 'His surname ought to be Golliwog. Or Tarzan.' [George] (p. 127)

Even earlier, James Joyce has the line 'Madcap Ciss with her golliwog curls' in *Ulysses* (Joyce, 1969, p. 351). Hair itself, though, is a potentially explosive topic. As I write (late 1998), there is currently controversy in America over the picture book *Nappy Hair* by Carolivia Herron (1997), which has resulted in a New York teacher being transferred.

9 The Mystery Explained (I): Writer of (and on) the Oral Stage

1 Arthur Mee's *Children's Encyclopædia* first appeared in fortnightly parts between 1908 and 1910, when Blyton would have been aged 11–13. We cer-

tainly know that she thought highly of his work, even annotating it (Stoney, 1974, p. 17), and that Mee wrote to her, encouraging her to write (ibid., p. 25). There seem to be several parallels in their approach, in that both wrote works in parts, maintaining regular contact with their readers (Mee also had a weekly *Children's Newspaper* and a monthly magazine); also, that their works unashamedly mix fact and fiction in what Crago (1989), speaking of Mee, terms an 'organic' way. Crago also notes that Mee believed that 'a child is largely its own teacher' (quoted p. 58), which Crago ties to the philosophy of John Dewey, but it was also very much the view of Froebel. Finally, Arthur Mee also liked to include his name in his titles (e.g. *Arthur Mee's Wonderful Day, Arthur Mee's Book of the Flag*).

2 In a *Guardian* interview (Ward, 1996), I drew parallels between 'Homer' and Blyton. The news that Blyton was 'Homeric' then exercised the media considerably. The *New Statesman & Society* held a competition challenging people to rewrite Homer in Blytonese, or retell Blyton in Homeric verse (Ross, 1996). However, Blyton was there first: she actually retold some of Homer's tales for young readers (Blyton, 1934a), though she did not rise to the classical levels reached by some of the competition winners:

> Recount, O Muse, the story of blue-helmeted Noddysseus,
> Who wand'ring far from Troyland's streets laments his silent hat.
> Behold the bearded Bigeus consoling his companion . . . etc. (later featuring the 'Cyclops Gollyphemus'!)
>
> (Silverman, 1996)

3 Bourdieu (1984) has usefully drawn attention to this traditional 'distinction' between popular culture's association with sensory gratification in contrast to high culture's respect for distance. It is captured in the double meaning of 'taste', which was initially something orally experienced, but later came to be a more value-laden term for the ability to discern quality at a distance.

4 For instance, several have commented on the closeness of *The Secret Mountain* to Rider Haggard's *King Solomon's Mines*; Druce (1992, p. 124) calls *The Circus of Adventure* almost identical to Dornford Yates' *Blood Royal* (1929).

5 'In *Sea of Adventure* (1948), Enid Blyton wrote a text so close to the text of *The Adventurous Four Again* (1947) that, had another author published it, the book could not have escaped the charge of plagiarism' (Druce, 1992, p. 125).

6 It is of note that many writers of children's fiction have worried about metaphorical language, fearing its profligacy, generating its own meanings in something of a quasi-sexual, reproductive way. Mrs Trimmer was of this opinion, as was Lewis Carroll, who, as Sewell (1952) powerfully argues, therefore sought to undo all figurative language by making things as literal as possible ('as mad as a hatter' = a real hatter, and so on); alternatively, he would construct lists of objects that could not possibly be run together, for instance, a bat 'Like a tea-tray in the sky', or 'shoes – and ships – and sealing-wax – / Of cabbages and kings': things completely non-transferable. Carroll, of course, even thought Bowdler's Shakespeare too suggestive, and wanted an expurgated version!

7 Notably, all of these activities, except writing, were more popular with yesterday's children – if the recollections of adults are trustworthy.

8 In her older fiction, this present-centredness is rendered through the dialogue, which also allows for more compressed and immediate storytelling.
9 She prefers this term because 'it places emphasis upon what the narrator is doing rather than upon what the character is thinking' (Wall, 1991, p. 191). In one way this is an unnecessary shift – as the term 'free indirect discourse' is suitably neutral – but in another way Wall's revision is most apposite, for it points to the notion of storytelling being a more personal activity, almost like daydreaming. The beauty of FID is that it is specifically neither narrator nor character that we hear, but both, and the term, 'free indirect discourse' seems to capture this neutrality. They seem to speak in a sort of compressed dialogism. 'Free indirect discourse' is often used as a general term for both the thoughts and the speech of characters, whereas 'free indirect speech' is used more specifically for the latter. There is some controversy over the term, however, especially as direct speech is taken to be the standard from which other forms deviate, whereas there is no such standard in the representation of thought (see Fludernik, 1993, for detail).
10 All of them date from the late 1920s, when Blyton was experimenting with narrative voice. Two animal stories, perhaps influenced by the example of *Black Beauty* ('The Adventures of Bobs', *Sunny Stories for Little Folks*, 19, April 1927 and 'Tibby's Adventures' *Sunny Stories*, 28, August 1927), two retellings about Swift's Gulliver (*Sunny Stories*, 4 and 20, August 1926 and April 1927) and a short story called 'The Secret Cave' (*Sunny Stories for Little Folks*, 61, January 1929, collected in Blyton, 1963a, pp. 68–81). There are also two full-length works: *Let's Pretend* (1928) and a recent find, *The Wonderful Adventure* (c1927).
11 Anne Wilson's (1983) notion of 'magical thinking' has many similarities.
12 One woman respondent bemoaned the fact that this never happened: 'I also joined the Famous Five club but I don't recall ever spotting anyone else wearing a similar fuzzy blue badge to whom I could claim instant friendship (as the club literature exhorted you to do I seem to remember)'. Perhaps she wasn't using Virginia's V-sign.

10 The Mystery Explained (II): Writer of Passages

1 *The Scotsman*, obviously following the same source, adds that the character has been 'expunged' (Anon, 1995), which was not true. He remains in print, then as now, which is fortunate for readers, amongst whom he is still popular (the twelfth most popular character, according to my research – albeit exclusively to females!). As one young girl expressed it, 'I liked the books of Mr Pink-Whistels books, he was a charactre that fixed everyones problems and helped them' [*sic*]. Older readers also remembered him with affection, if a little shamefacedly: 'I fantasized (a little embarrased here) that Mr. Pink-Whistle could one day come and save me from this horrible childhood of mine. I wanted to go where fairies lived and magic prevailed not this dump mundane world'(f).
2 A few others are: 'Cubby and the Cats' (Blyton, 1955), 'The Little Sugar-Mouse' (1941) (Blyton, 1964a, pp. 16–21); 'Hi, Feather-Tail!' (Blyton, 1965b,

pp. 7–16), which features a Big-Ears the goblin and Mr. Plod; 'Funny little Mankie' (*Enid Blyton's Stories for You* (1996a), pp. 48–65).

3 Otto Rank suggested that Freud spoke of the 'death instinct', a biological matter, in order to avoid explaining the 'death problem' (Becker, 1975).
4 In the Noddy passage quoted in Chapter 5 he even dreams that his friends are with him.
5 Perry Nodelman (1992) has argued that children's literature is often about 'Home and Away'. Basically, home is secure and cosy, but boring; away there is adventure, yet it is dangerous and insecure, hence the return home, and so on. Cawelti (1976) expresses a similar notion in terms of security and escape – see Rudd (1997c).
6 As Bloch notes, 'The might of giants is painted as one with a hole which the weak individual can get through victoriously' (quoted in Zipes, 1992, p. 122).
7 Personal communication. She goes on to say how the Famous Five stories developed this, she seeing herself 'merged with Georgina; not only did I begin to vocalize but actually organized the children from nearby into the famous five with myself as leader – the boys always holding a subordinate position'. However, unlike most middle-class readers, she records that 'The majority of people where we lived . . . were renowned for villainy, therefore, we assumed that we should have no problems rounding up a few', and relates how she got herself into trouble as a consequence!
8 Druce, although coming from a different perspective, makes a similar point about Blyton needing her audience, suggesting that the letters she received from children, 'were not merely of value to her in planning her future projects . . . but, far more important, they provided the existential confirmation she needed' (1992, p. 34).
9 Of course, Blyton could have been speaking metaphorically. It is a common authorial claim; Hergé, for example, said of his books, 'All are my children, of course' (Thompson, 1991).

11 Conclusion: Is Blyton Bad for You?

1 For example, Davis (1990) on Dickens' *A Christmas Carol*, or Bennett and Woollacott (1987) on James Bond. As the latter put it, 'there is no place – no cultural space – in which the individual texts of Bond can be stabilized as objects to be investigated 'in themselves', except by abstracting them from the shifting relations of inter-textuality through which their consumption has been regulated' (1987, p. 90).
2 Barker has written extensively about this topic, and his work has helped me think my way through the issue (see Barker, 1987, 1989).
3 This story, which also features Mr. Plod, is yet another about tails.
4 The recent Roehampton survey also found that children were less concerned with age, gender, ethnicity and so on than with personal relevance (Reynolds, 1996).
5 Umberto Eco (1979, pp. 144–74) seeks to argue for the innocence of 'blackness' amongst the villains of James Bond, too, but less successfully, I think, in that he ignores a psychoanalytical dimension.

6 Ernst Bloch spoke repeatedly of the hope expressed in popular cultural works, and this has been picked up by many others: Jameson (1979), Radway (1987), Modleski (1988), Geraghty (1991), Dyer (1992), and Zipes (1992).
7 This is what is unsatisfactory about Eales' (1989) critique, mentioned in Chapter 2: its target is awry, disempowering the already marginalized child, not the adult who tries to turn the fantasy into reality, hiding history in 'sunny stories'.
8 David Lane claims that Blyton herself 'wrote the golliwogs out of Noddy before she died; or at least started to do so. I have a manuscript in my possession that shows, in her own handwriting, she had started to do that' (Lane, 1996, p. 29). His backtracking from his initial statement is interesting, for certainly, in the last published Noddy volume, golliwogs still feature. But I'm also sure that this is what Blyton would have done had any child expressed concern or distaste.
9 In saying that Blyton does not 'stretch' the child I would not want to suggest that there is nothing of educational value in her work. Clearly, there is much natural history, there are the unusual words, and there is a great deal about how stories work. Also, Blyton seems to have been a very successful teacher, and many of her non-fictional works contain material that is still of value. However, my main point stands, I think.

References

Key Blyton texts

Famous five

(originally published in London by Hodder & Stoughton)

No.	Title	Abbreviation
1	*Five on a Treasure Island* (1942)	*FOTI*
2	*Five Go Adventuring Again* (1943)	*FGAA*
3	*Five Run Away Together* (1944)	*FRAT*
4	*Five Go to Smuggler's Top* (1945)	*FGTST*
5	*Five Go Off in a Caravan* (1946)	*FGOIC*
6	*Five on Kirrin Island Again* (1947)	*FOKIA*
7	*Five Go Off to Camp* (1948)	*FGOTC*
8	*Five Get into Trouble* (1949)	*FGIT*
9	*Five Fall into Adventure* (1950)	*FFIA*
10	*Five on a Hike Together* (1951)	*FOHT*
11	*Five Have a Wonderful Time* (1952)	*FHWT*
12	*Five Go Down to the Sea* (1953)	*FGDTS*
13	*Five Go to Mystery Moor* (1954)	*FGTMM*
14	*Five Have Plenty of Fun* (1955)	*FHPOF*
15	*Five on a Secret Trail* (1956)	*FOST*
16	*Five Go to Billycock Hill* (1957)	*FGTBH*
17	*Five Get into a Fix* (1958)	*FGIF*
18	*Five on Finniston Farm* (1960)	*FOFF*
19	*Five Go to Demon's Rocks* (1961)	*FGTDR*
20	*Five Have a Mystery to Solve* (1962)	*FHMTS*
21	*Five are Together Again* (1963)	*FATA*
–	*Five Have a Puzzling Time and Other Stories* (London: Red House, 1995)	*FHPT*

Malory towers

(originally published in London by Methuen)

No.	Title	Abbreviation
1	*First Term at Malory Towers* (1946)	*First*
2	*The Second Form at Malory Towers* (1947)	*Second*
3	*Third Year at Malory Towers* (1948)	*Third*
4	*The Upper Fourth at Malory Towers* (1949)	*Fourth*
5	*In the Fifth at Malory Towers* (1950)	*Fifth*
6	*Last Term at Malory Towers* (1951)	*Sixth*

Noddy

(originally published in London by Sampson Low)

No.	Title	Abbreviation
1	*Noddy Goes to Toyland* (1949)	*N1*
2	*Hurrah for Little Noddy* (1950)	*N2*
3	*Noddy and his Car* (1951)	*N3*
4	*Here Comes Noddy Again!* (1951)	*N4*
5	*Well Done Noddy!* (1952)	*N5*
6	*Noddy Goes to School* (1952)	*N6*
7	*Noddy at the Seaside* (1953)	*N7*
8	*Noddy Gets into Trouble* (1954)	*N8*
9	*Noddy and the Magic Rubber* (1954)	*N9*
10	*You Funny Little Noddy!* (1955)	*N10*
11	*Noddy Meets Father Christmas* (1955)	*N11*
12	*Noddy and Tessie Bear* (1956)	*N12*
13	*Be Brave, Little Noddy!* (1956)	*N13*
14	*Noddy and the Bumpy-Dog* (1957)	*N14*
15	*Do Look Out Noddy!* (1957)	*N15*
16	*You're a Good Friend Noddy!* (1958)	*N16*
17	*Noddy Has an Adventure* (1958)	*N17*
18	*Noddy Goes to Sea* (1959)	*N18*
19	*Noddy and the Bunkey* (1959)	*N19*
20	*Cheer Up, Little Noddy!* (1960)	*N20*
21	*Noddy Goes to the Fair* (1960)	*N21*
22	*Mr. Plod and Little Noddy* (1961)	*N22*
23	*Noddy and the Tootles* (1962)	*N23*
24	*Noddy and the Aeroplane* (1964)	*N24*

Secondary sources

Ahearne, Jeremy (1995), *Michel de Certeau: Interpretation and its Other*, Cambridge: Polity Press.

Ahlberg, Allan and Ahlberg, Janet (1991), *The Jolly Christmas Postman*, London: Heinemann.

Ahmed, Kamal (1997), 'What a jolly jape – the Malory gels are being updated', *The Guardian*, 14 October, p. 5.

Aitken, Ian (1991), 'Speaking clock PM in dire need of a good jokesmith', *The Guardian*, 28 June, p. 7.

Alcott, Louisa May (1953), *Little Women*, Harmondsworth: Penguin [orig. America, 1868].

Alderson, Brian W. (1969), 'The irrelevance of children to the children's book reviewer', *Children's Book News* 4, 1, p. 10.

Alderson, Brian (c1982), 'Knocking Noddy' [transcript of talk given on BBC World Service, reviewing Ray, 1982].

Alderson, Brian (1997), 'Putting Blyton in her place' [Chairman's comments], *Children's Books History Society Newsletter*, 59, November, pp. 7–8.

Alibhai-Brown, Yasmin (1994), 'The great backlash', in Sarah Dunant (ed.),

The War of the Words: the Political Correctness Debate, London: Virago, pp. 55–75.

Althusser, Louis (1971), *Lenin and Philosophy*, London: New Left Books.

Andersen, Hans Christian (1974), *The Complete Fairy Tales and Stories*, London: Gollancz.

Ang, Ien (1985), *Watching Dallas*, London: Methuen.

Anon. (n.d.), *Publicity Matter concerning Enid Blyton, Children's Author (for use either Abroad or at home)*, Publisher unknown.

Anon. (1943), [untitled review of *Seven O'Clock Tales*] *Times Literary Supplement* 5 June, p. 272.

Anon. (1958), *Focus on Enid Blyton: supplement to Games & Toys*, May.

Anon. (1966a), 'How does one wean 15-year-old girls from a diet of Enid Blyton?', *The Use of English*, 17, 3, 1966, p. 199.

Anon. (1966b), 'Problems', *The Use of English*, 18, 1, pp. 33–40.

Anon. (1986), 'The "loner", who hits headlines: profile of Conservative MP Harvey Proctor', *Sunday Times*, 2 November.

Anon. (1988), 'Criminologist Dr Cathy Currie chooses Noddy's Mr. Plod as the ideal local bobby', *Today*, 29 August.

Anon. (1993a), 'Cuckoo in Clubland', *The Independent on Sunday*, 7 February, p. 24.

Anon. (1993b), 'Noddy goes to Hollywood', *The Bookseller*, 23 April, p. 1.

Anon. (1995), 'Oh I say, still a spiffing read', *The Scotsman on Sunday*, 19 November.

Anon. (1996a), 'The Enid Blyton story' [letters], *Dunfermline Press*, 7 March.

Anon. (1996b), '"Send for Secret Seven"'[letters], *Dunfermline Press*, 22 March.

Anon. (1997), *UK Today 96: a television magazine* [feature on Enid Blyton, with Gillian Baverstock, Helen Cresswell and David Rudd] London: World Wide Pictures.

Armstrong, Judith (1982), 'In defence of adventure stories', *Children's Literature in Education*, 13, 3, pp. 115–21.

Ashworth, Andrea (1998), *Once in a House on Fire*, London: Picador.

Ashworth, Jon (1998), 'Noddy bound for lands of far beyond', *The Times*, 13 April, p. 44.

Atkinson, J. Maxwell and Heritage, John (eds) (1984), *Structures of Social Action: Studies in Conversation Analysis*. Cambridge: Cambridge University Press.

Attenborough, John (1975), *A Living Memory: Hodder and Stoughton Publishers, 1868–1975*, London: Hodder and Stoughton.

Attila the Stockbroker (1991), 'A Magna Carter for the nineties', *The Guardian*, 5 February, p. 32.

Auchmuty, Rosemary (1992), *The World of Girls*, London: Women's Press.

Auden, W.H. (1972), 'Today's "wonder-world" needs Alice', in Robert Phillips (ed.), *Aspects of Alice: Lewis Carroll's Dreamchild as Seen Through the Critics' Looking-Glasses, 1865–1971*, London: Gollancz, pp. 3–13 [orig. 1962].

Austin, J.L. (1962), *How to Do Things with Words*, Oxford: Oxford University Press.

Avery, Gillian (1975), *Childhood's Pattern: a Study of the Heroes and Heroines of Children's Fiction, 1770–1950*, London: Hodder and Stoughton.

Avery, Gillian (1991), *The Best Type of Girl: a History of Girls' Independent Schools*, London: André Deutsch.

Avery (1992), 'Home and family: English and American Ideals in the Nineteenth

Century', in Dennis Butts (ed.), *Stories and Society: Children's Literature in its Social Context*, London: Macmillan, pp. 37–49.
Bainbridge, Beryl (1974), 'I remember, I remember', *Times Literary Supplement*, 6 December, p. 1370.
Bakhtin, Mikhail M. (1981), *The Dialogic Imagination: Four Essays* (translated by Michael Holquist and Gary Emerson), Austin: University of Texas Press.
Banton, Michael (1980), 'The idiom of race: a critique of presentism', *Research in Race and Ethnic Relations*, 2, pp. 21–42.
Barker, Keith (1982), 'The use of food in Enid Blyton's fiction', *Children's Literature in Education*, 13, 1, Spring, pp. 4–12.
Barker, Martin (1987), 'Mass media studies and the question of ideology', *Radical Philosophy*, 46, pp. 27–33.
Barker, Martin (1989), *Comics: Ideology, Power and the Critics*, Manchester: Manchester University Press.
Barrie, J.M. (1986), *Peter Pan*, Harmondsworth: Penguin [orig. 1911 as *Peter and Wendy*].
Barthes, Roland (1973), 'The word of wrestling', in *Mythologies* (selected and translated by Annette Lavers), London: HarperCollins pp. 15–26 [orig. Paris, 1957].
Barthes, Roland (1977a), *Image, Music, Text: Essays* (selected and translated by Stephen Heath), London: Fontana.
Barthes, Roland (1977b), 'The death of the author', in *Image, Music, Text*, London: Fontana, pp. 142–8.
Barthes, Roland (1990), *S/Z*, Oxford: Blackwell [orig. Paris, 1973].
Barthes, Roland (1993), 'Authors and writers' [orig. 1960] in Susan Sontag (ed.), *A Barthes Reader*, London: Vintage, pp. 185–93.
Bates, Stephen (1987), 'Golliwogs lose their place in Noddy's tales', *Daily Telegraph*, 2 January.
Baverstock, Gillian (1989), 'Afterword', in Imogen Smallwood (1989a), pp. 154–5.
Baverstock, Gillian (1998a), 'The creation of the Riddle series', *The Enid Blyton Society Journal*, 6, pp. 14–16.
Baverstock, Gillian (1998b), 'The creation of the Riddle series', *The Enid Blyton Society Journal*, 7, pp. 32–5.
BBC (1994), *Pingu's Big Video*, London: BBC Enterprises.
Becker, Ernest (1975), *The Denial of Death*, London: Collier-Macmillan.
Belloc, Hilaire (1979), 'Frog', in Kaye Webb (ed.), *I Like this Poem: a Collection of Best-Loved Poems Chosen by Children for Other Children*, Harmondsworth: Penguin, p. 28.
Benjamin, Walter (1973), 'The Storyteller: Reflections on the Works of Nikolai Leskov', in *Illuminations*, London: Fontana, pp. 83–110.
Bennett, Tony and Woollacott, Janet (1987), *Bond and Beyond: the Political Career of a Popular Hero*, Basingstoke: Macmillan Education.
Bentley, Judith M. (1969), 'Enid Blyton – "What she meant to me": a student's view', *Lines*, 2, 7, pp. 6–8.
Benton, Michael (1978), *The First Two Rs: Essays on the Processes of Writing and Reading in Relation to the Teaching of Literature*, Southampton: University of Southampton, Dept. of Education.
Bergonzi, Bernard (1978), *Reading the Thirties*, Basingstoke: Macmillan.

Bernstein, Basil (1971), *Class, Codes and Control, Vol. 1* London: Routledge & Kegan Paul.
Bhabha, Homi K. (1994), *The Location of Culture*, London and New York: Routledge.
Billig, Michael (1996), *Arguing and Thinking: a Rhetorical Approach to Social Psychology*, 2nd edn, Cambridge: Cambridge University Press.
Billman, Carol (1984), 'The child reader as sleuth', *Children's Literature in Education*, 15, 1, pp. 30–41.
Blackman, Malorie (1991), *Elaine, You're a Brat*, London: Orchard.
Blakeslee, Thomas R. (1980), *The Right Brain: a New Understanding of the Unconscious Mind and its Creative Powers*, Basingstoke: Macmillan.
Bligh, Eric (1946), *Tooting Corner*, London: Secker & Warburg.
Blishen, Edward (1967), 'Who's afraid of Enid Blyton?', *Where*, 32, pp. 28–9 [reprinted with slight changes in Norman Culpan and Clifford Waite (eds), (1977), *Variety is King: Aspects of Fiction For Children*, London: School Library Association, pp. 79–82].
Blishen, Edward (1974), 'Life at Elfin Cottage: Enid Blyton as a case of arrested imagination', *Times Educational Supplement*, 27 September, p. 27.
Blyton, Enid (1922), *Child Whispers*, London: John Saville.
Blyton, Enid (1924), 'On pretending', *Teachers World*, 27 February [reproduced in Stoney (1974), pp. 189–90].
Blyton, Enid (ed.) (1926) *The Teacher's Treasury*, 3 vols, London: Newnes.
Blyton, Enid (1927), *The Wonderful Adventure*, London: Birn Bros.
Blyton, Enid (1928a), *The Animal Book*, London: Newnes.
Blyton, Enid (ed.) (1928b), *Modern Teaching*, 6 vols, London: Newnes.
Blyton, Enid (1928c), *Let's Pretend*, London: Nelson.
Blyton, Enid (ed.) (1930a), *Pictorial Knowledge*, 10 vols, London: Newnes.
Blyton, Enid (1930b), *Tales from the Arabian Nights*, London: Newnes.
Blyton, Enid (1931a), 'Tom Noddy', *Teachers World, Junior edition*, 26 August, xlv, 1474, p. 817.
Blyton, Enid (1931b), 'Hot roast chestnuts', *Teachers World, Junior edition*, 11 November, xlvi, 1485, p. 222.
Blyton, Enid (ed.) (1932), *Modern Teaching in the Infant School*, 4 vols, London: Newnes.
Blyton, Enid (1933), *Five Minute Tales: Sixty Short Stories for Children*, London: Methuen.
Blyton, Enid (1934a), *The Adventures of Odysseus: Stories from World History Retold*, London: Evans.
Blyton, Enid (1934b), *Ten Minute Tales*, London: Methuen.
Blyton, Enid (ed.) (1936), *Two Years in the Infant School*, 4 vols, London: Newnes.
Blyton, Enid (1937), *Adventures of the Wishing Chair*, London: Newnes.
Blyton, Enid (1938a), *Mr. Galliano's Circus*, London: Newnes.
Blyton, Enid (1938b), *The Secret Island*, Oxford: Blackwell.
Blyton, Enid (1939), *Naughty Amelia Jane!*, London: Newnes.
Blyton, Enid (1940), *The Naughtiest Girl in the School*, London: Newnes.
Blyton, Enid (1941a), *The Adventurous Four*, London: Newnes.
Blyton, Enid (1941b), *The Babar Story Book*, London: Methuen.
Blyton, Enid (1941c), *The Secret Mountain*, Oxford: Blackwell.
Blyton, Enid (1942a), *Circus Days Again*, London: Newnes.

Blyton, Enid (1942b), *Enid Blyton's Readers, Book 1*, Basingstoke: Macmillan.
Blyton, Enid (1942c), *Mary Mouse and the Dolls' House*, Leicester: Brockhampton Press.
Blyton, Enid (1943a), *The Children's Life of Christ*, London: Methuen.
Blyton, Enid (1943b), *The Magic Faraway Tree*, London: Newnes.
Blyton, Enid (1943c), *Seven O'Clock Tales*, London: Methuen.
Blyton, Enid (1943d), *Smuggler Ben*, London: Werner Laurie [orig. published under pseudonym Mary Pollock].
Blyton, Enid (1944a), *A Book of Naughty Children*, London: Methuen.
Blyton, Enid (1944b), *Enid Blyton's Jolly Story Book*, London: Hodder & Stoughton.
Blyton, Enid (1944c), *The Island of Adventure*, London: Macmillan.
Blyton, Enid (1944d), *The Three Golliwogs*, London: Newnes.
Blyton, Enid (1945a), *Hollow Tree House*, London: Lutterworth.
Blyton, Enid (1945b), *Round the Clock Stories*, London: National Magazine Company.
Blyton, Enid (1946), *The Castle of Adventure*, Basingstoke: Macmillan.
Blyton, Enid (1947a), *Before I Go to Sleep*, London: Latimer House.
Blyton, Enid (1947b), *Mischief at St. Rollo's*, London: Werner Laurie. [orig. published under pseudonym Mary Pollock].
Blyton, Enid (1947c), *More About Josie, Click and Bun*, London: Newnes.
Blyton, Enid (1947d), *The Mystery of the Missing Necklace*, London: Methuen.
Blyton, Enid (1948a), *The Little Girl at Capernaum*, London: Lutterworth Press.
Blyton, Enid (1948b), *Mister Icy-Cold*, Oxford: Shakespeare Head Press.
Blyton, Enid (1948c), *Now for a Story*, Newcastle upon Tyne: Harold Hill.
Blyton, Enid (1948d), *The Sea of Adventure*, Basingstoke: Macmillan.
Blyton, Enid (1948e), *Six Cousins at Mistletoe Farm*, London: Evans.
Blyton, Enid (1949a), *The Rockingdown Mystery*, London: Collins.
Blyton, Enid (1949b), *The Secret Seven*, Leicester: Brockhampton Press.
Blyton, Enid (1949c), *A Story Party at Green Hedges*, London: Hodder & Stoughton.
Blyton, Enid (1950a), 'A foreword from Enid Blyton', *A Complete List of Books by Enid Blyton*, London: John Menzies, pp. 1–4.
Blyton, Enid (1950b), *The Magic Knitting Needles and Other Stories*, Basingstoke: Macmillan.
Blyton, Enid (1950c), *Tales About Toys*, Leicester: Brockhampton.
Blyton, Enid (1951a), 'On writing for children', *The Writer*, December, pp. 4–5.
Blyton, Enid (1951b), *The Six Bad Boys*, London: Lutterworth.
Blyton, Enid (1951c), *Gay Street Book*, London: Latimer House.
Blyton, Enid (1952a), *The Circus of Adventure*, Basingstoke: Macmillan.
Blyton, Enid (1952b), *The Story Of My Life*, London: Pitkins [an 'edited', version published by Collins, 1986].
Blyton, Enid (1953a), 'Talk to the children', *The Writer*, 12, 5, November, pp. 4–5.
Blyton, Enid (1953b), *Go Ahead Secret Seven*, Leicester: Brockhampton.
Blyton, Enid (1955), *Mandy, Mops and Cubby and the Whitewash*, London: Sampson Low, Marston.
Blyton, Enid (1959a), *Secret Seven Fireworks*, Leicester: Brockhampton Press.
Blyton, Enid (1959b), 'Writing for children', *New Statesman*, 9 May, p. 649.
Blyton, Enid (1961), *The Mystery that Never Was*, London: Collins.
Blyton, Enid (1962), *Look Out Secret Seven*, Leicester: Brockhampton.

Blyton, Enid (1963a), *Enid Blyton's Chimney Corner Stories*, London: Dean [orig. 1946, National Magazine].
Blyton, Enid (1963b), *Tales of Toyland*, London: Dean [orig. Newnes, 1944].
Blyton, Enid (1964a), *Enid Blyton's Storytime Book*, London: Dean.
Blyton, Enid (1964b), *Fifth Tell-a-Story Book*, London: World Distributors.
Blyton, Enid (1965a), *Enid Blyton Easy Reader, Book 4*, London: Collins.
Blyton, Enid (1965b), *Enid Blyton's Sunshine Book*, London: Dean.
Blyton, Enid (1966a), *Enid Blyton's Stories for You*, London: Dean.
Blyton, Enid (1966b), *Fireside Tales*, London: Collins.
Blyton, Enid (1968), *The Children at Green Meadows*, London: Collins [orig. 1954, Lutterworth].
Blyton, Enid (1970a), *Bedtime Stories*, London: Purnell.
Blyton, Enid (1970b), *Enid Blyton's Happy Time Stories*, London: Purnell.
Blyton, Enid (1970c), *Sleepytime Tales*, London: Purnell.
Blyton, Enid (1971), *Little Animal Stories*, London: Purnell.
Blyton, Enid (1972), *Good Night Stories*, London: Purnell.
Blyton, Enid (1974), *The Three Naughty Children and Other Stories*, London: Granada [orig. 1950].
Blyton, Enid (1985), *Snicker the Brownie and Other Stories*, London: Award [orig. Blyton, 1944, minus 'The little black doll'].
Blyton, Enid (1991), *Enid Blyton's the Adventures of Mr Pink-Whistle*, London: Mammoth.
Blyton, Enid (1992), *The Secret Seven*, rev. edn, London: Hodder Headline.
Blyton, Enid (1994), *Three Bold Pixies, and Other Stories*, London: Award.
Blyton, Enid (1998), 'Letters from Enid: extracts from letters sent to Trevor J. Bolton by Enid Blyton', *The Enid Blyton Society Journal*, 7, Winter, pp. 24–5.
Bloch, Ernst (1988), *The Utopian Function of Art and Literature: Selected Essays* (translated by Jack Zipes and Frank Mecklenburg), Cambridge, Mass. and London: MIT Press.
Boshoff, Alison (1997), 'Noddy gets new image for £5m American adventure', *Daily Telegraph*, 18 March.
Bourdieu, Pierre (1986), *Distinction: a Social Critique of the Judgement of Taste*, London: Routledge.
Bourdieu, Pierre (1993), *The Field of Cultural Production: Essays on Art and Literature*, Cambridge: Polity.
Breuer, Josef and Freud, Sigmund (1974), *Studies on Hysteria*, London: Penguin [orig. in German, 1895].
Bromley, Roger (1988), *Lost Narratives: Popular Fictions, Politics and Recent History*, London: Routledge.
Brooks, Peter (1984), *Reading for the Plot: Design and Intention in Narrative*, Oxford: Clarendon Press.
Brooks, Peter (1994), *Psychoanalysis and Storytelling*, Oxford: Blackwell.
Brown, Maggie (1996), 'Golly – would Enid approve? – lashings of period detail or a radical updating?', *Daily Telegraph*, 1 July.
Buckingham, David (1987), *Public Secrets: EastEnders and its Audience*, London: British Film Institute.
Buckingham, David (ed.), (1993), *Reading Audiences: Young People and the Media*, Manchester: Manchester University Press.
Burnett, Frances Hodgson (1886), *Little Lord Fauntleroy*, London: F. Warne.

Cadogan, Mary (1982), 'Blight or blessing', *Literary Review*, October, p. 23.
Cadogan, Mary and Craig, Patricia (1976), *You're a Brick, Angela!* , London: Gollancz.
Campbell, Beatrix (1987), *The Iron Ladies: Why do Women Vote Tory?*, London: Virago.
Capey, A.C. and Maskell, Duke (1980), 'The ruder his words were, the more politely he spoke', *Haltwhistle Quarterly*, 9, Summer, pp. 21–7.
Carpenter, Humphrey (1994), 'The big unfriendly giant', *Sunday Times*, 20 March, section 7, p. 1.
Carpenter, John (1944), 'Talk of the Day' section, *The Evening News*, 16 November, p. 2.
Carroll, Lewis (1970), *Through the Looking-Glass and What Alice Found There* [orig. 1872] in Martin Gardner (ed.), *The Annotated Alice*, rev. edn, Harmondsworth: Penguin.
Cawelti, John G. (1976), *Adventure, Mystery, and Romance: Formula Stories as Art and Popular Culture*, Chicago and London: University of Chicago Press.
Chambers, Aidan (1969), *The Reluctant Reader*, London: Pergamon Press.
Chambers, Aidan (1975), 'From Blyton to Doetovsky (sic)', *School Bookshop News*, 3, October, pp. 18–19.
Chambers, Aidan (1985), 'The reader in the book', in *Booktalk: Occasional Writings on Literature and Children*, London: Bodley Head pp. 34–58 ['The reader in the book: notes from work in progress'; orig. *Signal* 23, May 1977, pp. 64–87]
Cherland, Meredith Rogers (1994), *Private Practices: Girls Reading Fiction and Constructing Identity*, London: Taylor & Francis.
Christian-Smith, Linda K. (1990), *Becoming a Woman through Romance*, London: Routledge.
Clark, Kenneth (1974), *Another Part of the Wood: a Self Portrait*, London: Murray.
Clark, Margaret M. (1976), *Young Fluent Readers*, London: Heinemann Educational.
Clifford, James (ed.) (1986), 'Introduction: partial truths', in James Clifford and George E. Marcus, *Writing Culture: the Politics and Poetics of Ethnography*, Berkeley: University of California Press, pp. 1–26.
Clive, [Lady] Mary (1964), *The Day of Reckoning*, Basingstoke: Macmillan.
Cohen, Morton N. (1995), *Lewis Carroll: a Biography*, Basingstoke: Macmillan.
Cohn, Dorrit (1978), *Transparent Minds: Narrative Modes for Presenting Consciousness in Fiction*, Princeton, NJ: Princeton University Press.
Cohn, Tessa (1988), 'Sambo – a study in name calling', in Elinor Kelly and Tessa Cohn, *Racism in Schools: New Research Evidence*, Hanley, Stoke-on Trent: Trentham Books, pp. 29–63.
Collodi, Carlo (1996), *The Adventures of Pinocchio* (translated by Ann Lawson Lucas), Oxford: Oxford University Press. [orig. in book form, Florence, Italy, 1883].
Colls, Robert and Dodd, Philip (eds) (1987), *Englishness: Politics and Culture 1880–1920*, London: Croom Helm.
Comic Strip (1982), *Five Go Mad in Dorset*, Channel 4.
Comic Strip (1983), *Five Go Mad on Mescalin*, Channel 4.
Connolly, Joseph (1990), 'Purged of prejudice: a Noddy for our times', *The Times*, 5 July, p. 18.

Corcoran, Bill and Evans, Emrys (eds), (1987), *Readers, Texts and Teachers*, Milton Keynes: Open University Press.
Coupland, Justine (1982), 'What's in a story: narrative structure and realisation in children's fiction', in Peter Hunt (ed.), *Further Approaches to Research in Children's Literature: Proceedings of the Second British Research Seminar in Children's Literature, Cardiff, September 1981*. Cardiff: Dept of English, UWIST, pp. 85–93.
Cowe, Roger (1996), 'Noddy ready to motor with new chums', *The Guardian*, 1 May.
Crago, Hugh (1989), 'The last days in the old home', *Signal*, 58, January, pp. 51–70.
Crago, Hugh (1990), 'Childhood reading revisited', *Papers: Explorations into Children's Literature*, 1, 3, pp. 99–115.
Crago, Hugh (1993), 'Why readers read what writers write', *Children's Literature in Education*, 24, 4, pp. 277–89.
Crago, Hugh (n.d.), 'Prior expectations of *Great Expectations*: how one child learned to read a classic', [mss. quoted; now published in *College English*, 58, No 6, October 1996, pp. 676–92].
Crompton, Richmal (1922), *Just William*, London: Newnes.
Crouch, Marcus (1962), *Treasure Seekers and Borrowers*, London: Library Association.
Crouch, Stanley (1997), *The All-American Skin Game, or, the Decoy of Race: the Long and the Short of it, 1990–1994*, New York and London: Vintage.
Culler, Jonathan (1981), *The Pursuit of Signs: Semiotics, Literature, Deconstruction*, London: Routledge & Kegan Paul.
Cullingford, Cedric (1979), 'Why children like Enid Blyton', *New Society*, 9 August, pp. 290–1.
Culpan, Norman and Waite, Clifford (eds), (1977), *Variety is King: Aspects of Fiction for Children*, Oxford: School Library Association.
Danks, Denise (1989), *The Pizza House Crash*, London: Futura.
Davies, Bronwyn (1989), *Frogs and Snails and Feminist Tales: Preschool Children and Gender*, Sydney: Allen & Unwin.
Davis, Norma A. (1992), *Lark Ascends: Florence Kate Upton, Artist and Illustrator*, London: Scarecrow Press.
Davis, Paul (1990), *The Lives and Times of Ebenezer Scrooge*, New Haven and London: Yale University Press.
Deane, Paul (1991), *Mirrors of American Culture: Children's Fiction Series in the Twentieth Century*, Metuchen, N.J. and London: Scarecrow Press.
Dinnerstein, Dorothy (1977), *The Mermaid and the Minotaur: Sexual Arrangements and Human Malaise*, New York: Harper Colophon [published in the UK as *The Rocking of the Cradle and the Ruling of the World*, London: Souvenir, 1978].
Dixon, Bob (1974a), 'All things white and beautiful', *Hard Cheese*, 3, pp. 70–90 [revised edn reprinted in Dixon (1977a), pp. 94–127].
Dixon, Bob (1974b), 'The nice, the naughty and the nasty: the tiny world of Enid Blyton', *Children's Literature in Education*, 15, November, pp. 43–61 [including editorial note by Kenneth Sterck, pp. 59–61]. [revised edn under the title 'Enid Blyton and her Sunny Stories', reprinted in Dixon (1977b), pp. 56–73].
Dixon, Bob (1977a), *Catching them Young, Vol. 1: Sex, Race and Class in Children's Fiction*, London: Pluto Press.

Dixon, Bob (1977b), *Catching them Young, Vol. 2: Political Ideas in Children's Fiction*, London: Pluto Press.

Dodsworth, Ruth E. (1982), 'The Blyton dilemma', *Review*, 10, 1, March, pp. 25–7.

Dohm, Janice (1955), 'Enid Blyton and others: an American view', *Journal of Education*, 87, August, pp. 358–61 [also as 'The Work of Enid Blyton', in Norman Culpan and Clifford Waite (eds), *Variety is King: Aspects of Fiction for Children*, Oxford: School Library Association, pp. 83–8; and in Boris Ford (ed.), (1963), *Young Writers, Young Readers: an Anthology of Children's Reading and Writing* rev. edn, London: Hutchinson pp. 99–106].

Donald, James (1992), *Sentimental Education: Schooling, Popular Culture and the Regulation of Liberty*, London: Verso.

Drotner, Kirsten (1988), *English Children and their Magazines, 1751–1945* Yale: Yale University Press.

Druce, Robert (1992), *This Day Our Daily Fictions: an Enquiry into the Multi-Million Bestseller Status of Enid Blyton and Ian Fleming*, Amsterdam–Atlanta: Rudopi BV.

Duffy, Maureen (1972), *The Erotic World of Faery*, London: Hodder and Stoughton.

Dusinberre, Juliet (1987), *Alice to the Lighthouse: Children's Books and Radical Experiments in Art*, Basingstoke: Macmillan.

Dyer, Carolyn Stewart and Romalov, Nancy Tillman (eds) (1995), *Rediscovering Nancy Drew*, Iowa City: University of Iowa Press.

Dyer, Christopher (1969), 'Anatomy of a Blyton', *Lines*, 2, 7, pp. 16–18.

Dyer, Richard (1981), 'Entertainment and utopia', in Rick Altman (ed.), *Genre: the Musical, a Reader*, London: Routledge & Kegan Paul.

Dyhouse, Carol (1981), *Girls Growing Up in Late Victorian and Edwardian England*, London: Routledge & Kegan Paul.

Eales, Derek (1989), 'Enid Blyton, Judy Blume, and cultural impossibilities', *Children's Literature in Education*, 20, 2, June, pp. 81–9.

Easthope, Antony (1985), 'The problem of polysemy and identity in the literary text', *British Journal of Aesthetics*, 25, 4, pp. 326–39.

Eco, Umberto (1979), *The Role of the Reader: Explorations in the Semiotics of Texts*, Bloomington: Indiana University Press.

Egoff, Sheila, Stubbs, E.T. and Ashley, L.F. (eds), (1980), *Only Connect: Readings on Children's Literature*, 2nd edn, Toronto: Oxford University Press.

Esrock, Ellen J. (1994), *The Reader's Eye: Visual Imaging as Reader Response*, Baltimore and London: Johns Hopkins University Press.

Ewbank, Tim (1990), 'Fusty! musty! dusty! what an adventure . . .', *TV Times*, 14–20 April, pp. 8, 10.

Eyre, Frank (1952), *20th Century Children's Books*, London: British Council by Longmans, Green & Co.

Eyre, Frank (1971), *British Children's Books in the Twentieth Century*, rev edn, London: Longman.

Fairclough, Norman (1992), *Discourse and Social Change*, Cambridge: Polity Press.

Faulks, Sebastian (1990), 'New man about Toytown', *The Independent on Sunday*, 5 August, p. 21.

Fish, Stanley (1980), *Is There a Text in this Class? the Authority of Interpretive Communities*, Cambridge, Mass.: Harvard University Press.

Fisher, Margery (1961), *Intent Upon Reading: a Critical Appraisal of Modern Fiction for Children*, Leicester: Brockhampton Press.

Fisher, Margery (1973), 'Motives for mysteries', *Growing Point*, 12, 4, October, pp. 2230–2.
Fisher, Margery (1983), 'A reputation reconsidered', *Growing Point*, 22, 2, July, pp. 4119–20.
Fisher, Margery (1986), *The Bright Face of Danger*, London: Hodder and Stoughton.
Fludernik, Monika (1993), *The Fictions of Language and the Languages of Fiction: the Linguistic Representation of Speech and Consciousness*, London: Routledge.
Follett, Ken (1994), 'Yes! Magazine' *Sunday People*, 28 August.
Forster, E.M. (1955), *A Room with a View*, Harmondsworth: Penguin [orig. 1908, published by Edward Arnold].
Foster, Aisling (1992), 'In an ideal world', *The Independent On Sunday, The Sunday Review* 8 November, p. 32.
Foucault, Michel (1972), *The Archaeology of Knowledge*, London: Tavistock [orig. 1969].
Foucault, Michel (1979), *Discipline and Punish*, Harmondsworth: Penguin [orig. 1975].
Foucault, Michel (1980), *Power/Knowledge: Selected Interviews and Other Writings, 1972–1977* (ed. by Colin Gordon), Brighton: Harvester Wheatsheaf.
Foucault, Michel (1981), *The History of Sexuality: an Introduction*, Penguin: Harmondsworth [orig. 1976].
Foucault, Michel (1986), 'What is an author?', *The Foucault Reader* (ed. by Paul Rabinow), London: Penguin, pp. 101–20.
Fox, Carol (1993), *At the Very Edge of the Forest: the Influence of Literature on Storytelling by Children*, London: Cassell.
Fox, Paula (1974), *The Slave Dancer*, London: Macmillan.
Fraser, Antonia (1966), *A History of Toys*, London: Weidenfeld & Nicolson.
Fraser, Antonia (ed.), (1992), *The Pleasures of Reading*, London: Bloomsbury.
Frazer, Elizabeth (1987), 'Teenage girls reading *Jackie*', *Media, Culture and Society*, 9, pp. 407–25 [edited version in Helen Baehr and Ann Gray (eds), (1996), *Turning It On: a Reader in Women and Media*, London: Arnold, pp. 130–7].
Frayn, Michael (1987), *Balmoral*, London: Methuen [orig. entitled *Liberty Hall*, 1980].
Freeman, Gillian (1969), *The Undergrowth of Literature*, London: Panther.
Freeman, Mark (1993), *Rewriting the Self: History, Memory, Narrative*, London: Routledge.
Freud, Sigmund (1959) 'Writers and day-dreaming', *The Standard Edition of the Complete Psychoanalytical Works of Sigmund Freud*, ix, London: Hogarth Press, pp. 143–53 [orig. 1908].
Freud, Sigmund (1961), *Beyond the Pleasure Principle* (translated by James Strachey), New York: Norton [orig. German, 1920].
Freud, Sigmund (1977), 'Family Romances', *On Sexuality: Three Essays on the Theory of Sexuality, and Other Works*, Harmondsworth: Penguin, pp. 221–5.
Freud, Sigmund (1985), 'The Uncanny', *Art and Literature: Jensen's Gradiva, Leonardo da Vinci and Other Works*, Harmondsworth: Penguin, pp. 339–76.
Frith, Gill (1985), '"The time of your life": the meaning of the school story', in Carolyn Steedman, Cathy Urwin and Valerie Walkderdine (eds), *Language, Gender and Childhood*, London: Routledge & Kegan Paul, pp. 113–36 [also in Gabby Weiner and Madeleine Arnot (eds), (1987), *Gender Under Scrutiny: New Inquiries in Education*, London: Hutchinson, pp. 118–33].

Fry, Donald (1985), *Children Talk About Books*, Milton Keynes: Open University Press.

Fryer, Peter (1989), *Black People in the British Empire: an Introduction*, London: Pluto Press.

Fuller, Roy (1976), 'The influence of children on books', *Children's Literature in Education*, 20, pp. 3–16.

Garner, Alan (1997) *The Voice that Thunders: Essays and Lectures*, London: Harvill Press.

Geraghty, Christine (1991), *Women and Soap Opera: a Study of Prime Time Soaps* Cambridge: Polity Press.

Geras, Adèle (1990), *The Tower Room* [Egerton Hall trilogy, part 1]London: Hamish Hamilton.

Geras, Adèle (1991), *Watching the Roses* [Egerton Hall trilogy, part 2] London: Hamish Hamilton.

Geras, Adèle (1992), *Pictures of the Night* [Egerton Hall trilogy, part 3], London: Hamish Hamilton.

Gillborn, David (1995), *Racism and Antiracism in Schools: Theory, Policy, Practice*, Milton Keynes: Open University Press.

Gilligan, Andrew (1995), 'Famous Five for grown-ups', *Sunday Telegraph*, 25 June.

Gilligan, Carol (1982), *In a Different Voice: Psychological Theory and Women's Development*, Harvard: Harvard University Press.

Gluck, Malcolm (1991), 'Superplonk: flush with the readies', *The Guardian*, 8 June, p. 19.

Godden, Rumer (1972), *The Diddakoi*, London: Macmillan.

Godfrey, Robert John (1996), [CD notes] *Anarchy on 45: Complete Singles Collection*, Mantella.

Golding, William (1954), *Lord of the Flies*, London: Faber and Faber.

Grahame, Kenneth (1908), *The Wind in the Willows*, London: Methuen.

Greene, Graham (1980), 'Beatrix Potter' in Sheila Egoff *et al.* (eds), *Only Connect: Readings on Children's Literature*, 2nd edn, Toronto: Oxford University Press, pp. 258–65 [orig. 1933].

Greenfield, George (1989), *Scribblers for Bread: Aspects of the English Novel since 1945*, London: Hodder and Stoughton.

Greenfield, George (1995), 'The famous one', in *A Smattering of Monsters: a Kind of Memoir*, London: Little, Brown & Co., pp. 110–33.

Grove, Valerie (1989), 'Snared by a Woolf woman', *Sunday Times*, 14 May.

Grove, Valerie (1993), 'Fitting the punishment to the victim', *The Times*, 12 February, p. 15.

Guillaumin, Colette (1995), *Racism, Sexism, Power and Ideology*, London: Routledge.

Gutteridge, Bernard (1982), 'Duffers and buffers', *London Magazine*, October, pp. 101–2.

Haggard, H. Rider (1885), *King Solomon's Mines*, London: Cassell.

Hall, Christine and Coles, Martin (1996), *The Children's Reading Choices Project, at the University of Nottingham sponsored by W H Smith plc: summary report*, Nottingham: University of Nottingham.

Hall, Stuart (1986), 'Introduction', in David Morley *Family Television: Cultural Power and Domestic Leisure*, London: Comedia, pp. 7–10.

Hammerton, Sir John (1946), *Child of Wonder: An Intimate Biography of Arthur Mee*, London: Hodder & Stoughton.

Harding, D.W. (1962), 'Psychological process in the reading of fiction', *British Journal of Aesthetics*, 2, 2, pp. 133–47 [reprinted in Margaret Meek, *et al.*, (1977), pp. 58–72].
Harrison, Tracey (1990), 'Strong charm of the law from the real Mr. Plod', *Daily Mail*, 17 November.
Havelock, Eric A. (1963), *Preface to Plato*, Cambridge, Mass. and London: Belknap Press/Harvard University Press.
Hebdidge, Dick (1982), 'Towards a cartography of taste, 1935–62', in Barry Waites, Tony Bennett and Graham Martin (eds), *Popular Culture – Past and Present: a Reader*, London: Croom Helm, pp. 194–218.
Heller, Joseph (1990), *Something Happened*, London: Transworld [orig. published in Great Britain by Cape, 1974].
Hennegan, Alison (1988), 'On Becoming a Lesbian Reader', in Susannah Radstone (ed.), *Sweet Dreams: Sexuality, Gender and Popular Fiction*, London: Lawrence and Wishart, pp. 165–90.
Herron, Carolivia (1997), *Nappy Hair*, New York: Knopf.
Hewison, Robert (1987), *The Heritage Industry: Britain in a Climate of Decline*, London: Methuen.
Hildick, Wallace (1970), *Children and Fiction: a Critical Study in Depth of the Artistic and Psychological Factors Involved in Writing Fiction for and about Children*, London: Evans Bros.
Hill, Susan (1982), 'Required reading', *Daily Telegraph*, 16 September.
Hincks-Edwards, Elaine (1982), 'Noddy in the space age', *Times Educational Supplement*, 16 April, p. 16.
Hindle, Christine (1982), 'How an overdose of Blyton can stunt your literary development', [letter] *The Guardian*, 5 April, p. 10.
Hobson, Dorothy (1982), *'Crossroads': the Drama of a Soap Opera*, London: Methuen.
Hobson, Margaret, Madden, Jennifer and Prytherch, Ray (1992), *Children's Fiction Sourcebook*, Aldershot: Ashgate.
Hodge, Robert and Tripp, David (1986), *Children and Television: a Semiotic Approach*, Cambridge: Polity Press.
Hoffman, Mary (1984), 'Growing up: a survey', *Children's Literature in Education*, 15, 3 Autumn, pp. 171–85.
Holbrook, David (1961), *English for Maturity*, Cambridge: Cambridge University Press.
Holbrook, David (1982), 'The Noddy safety harness', *Irish Press*, 2 September.
Hollindale, Peter (1974), *Choosing Books for Children*, London: Paul Elek.
Howard, Philip (1987), 'Political bywords: the wisdom of the double coalition', *The Times*, 25 May.
Howkins, Alan (1987), 'The Discovery of Rural England', in Robert Colls and Philip Dodd (eds), *Englishness: Politics and Culture 1880–1920*, London: Croom Helm, pp. 62–88.
Hughes, Colin (1991), 'Young readers rate Dahl above Blyton', *The Independent*, 17 July, p. 1.
Hulbert, Ann (1995), 'They won't grow up', *New York Times Book Review*, 12 November, pp. 46–7.
Hunt, Peter (1974), 'Criticism and children's literature', *Signal*, 15, September, pp. 117–30.
Hunt, Peter (1978), 'The cliché count: a practical aid for the selection of

books for children', *Children's Literature in Education*, 9, 3, Autumn, pp. 143–50.
Hunt, Peter (1981), 'Criticism and pseudo criticism', *Signal*, 34, pp. 14–21.
Hunt, Peter (1985), *A Step Off the Path*, London: Julia MacRae.
Hunt, Peter (1994), *An Introduction to Children's Literature*, Oxford: Oxford University Press.
Hunt, Peter (1995), 'How not to read a children's book', *Children's Literature in Education*, 26, 4, pp. 231–40.
Hunt, Peter (1996), 'Enid Blyton', in Donald Hettinga and Gary D. Schmidt (eds), *British Children's Writers, 1914–1960: Dictionary of Literary Biography, Vol. 160*, Detroit, MI: Gale Research, pp. 50–71.
Ingham, Jennie (1982), 'Middle school children's responses to Enid Blyton in "the Bradford Book Flood experiment" *Journal of Research in Reading*, 5, 1, 43–56.
Inglis, Fred (1983), *The Promise of Happiness*, Cambridge: Cambridge University Press.
Inglis, Fred (1997), 'Enid Blyton, Malcolm Saville and the good society', in Nicholas Tucker and Kimberley Reynolds (eds) *Enid Blyton: a Celebration and Reappraisal*, London: NCRCL, pp. 127–33.
Isaacs, Nathan (1952), 'Froebel's educational philosophy in 1952', in Evelyn Lawrence (ed.), *Friedrich Froebel and English Education*, London: Routledge & Kegan Paul, 1952, pp. 179–233.
Iser, Wolfgang (1974), *The Implied Reader: Patterns of Communication in Prose Fiction from Bunyan to Beckett*, London: Johns Hopkins University Press.
Iser, Wolfgang (1978), *The Act of Reading: a Theory of Aesthetic Response*, London: Routledge & Kegan Paul.
Jackson, Alan A. (1991), *The Middle Classes, 1900–1950*, Nairn, Scotland: David St John Thomas.
James, Winston (1993), 'Migration, racism and identity formation: the Caribbean experience in Britain', in Winston James and Clive Harris (eds), *Inside Babylon: the Caribbean Diaspora in Britain*, London: Verso, pp. 231–87.
Jameson, Fredric (1979), 'Reification and utopia in mass culture', *Social Text*, 1, pp. 130–48.
Jaynes, Julian (1976), *The Origins of Consciousness in the Breakdown of the Bicameral Mind*, London: Allen Lane.
Jeger, Lena (1966), 'In large print', *The Guardian*, 24 May, p. 18.
Jones, Alex I. (1991), 'Enid Blyton: the sources of creativity', *Papers: Explorations into Children's Literature*, 2, 2, August, pp. 65–74.
Jordin, Martin and Brunt, Rosalind (1988), 'Constituting the television audience: problem of method', in Phillip Drummond and Richard Paterson (eds), *Television and its Audience: International Research Perspectives*, London: BFI, pp. 231–49.
Josipovici, Gabriel (1997), 'Thirty-three variations on a theme of Graham Greene', in Philip Davis, *Real Voices on Reading*, London: Routledge, 1997, pp. 165–72.
Joyce, James (1969), *Ulysses*, Harmondsworth: Penguin [orig. Paris, 1922].
Katz, Wendy R. (1980), 'Some uses of food in children's literature', *Children's Literature in Education*, 11, 4, pp. 192–9.
Keller, Helen (1903), *The Story of My Life*, London: Hodder and Stoughton.

Kemp, Peter (1985), 'Outsider takes all: interview with Booker Prize winner Keri Hulme', *The Times*, 1 December.

Kimberley, Keith, Meek, Margaret and Miller, Jane (eds) (1992) *New Readings: Contributions to an Understanding of Literacy*, London: A. & C. Black.

King, Clive (1963), *Stig of the Dump*, Harmondsworth: Penguin.

Kington, Miles (1991), 'The life and times of the Famous One', *The Independent*, 10 May, p. 22.

Kirby, Heather (1992), 'Keeping radio's pot boiling: Pat McLoughlin', *The Times*, 13 May, p. 4.

Knight, G. Wilson (1940), *This Sceptred Isle: Shakespeare's Message for England at War*, Oxford: Basil Blackwell.

Knowles, Murray and Malmkjaer, Kirsten (1995), *Language and Control in Children's Literature*, London: Routledge.

Knowles, Stewart (1988), 'Noddy's adventures in the Big Apple', *TV Times*, 2–8 April, pp. 8–9, 18.

Kristeva, Julia (1982), *Powers of Horror: an Essay on Abjection*, New York: Columbia University Press.

Kristeva, Julia (1986), 'Word Dialogue and novel', in Toril Moi (ed.), *The Kristeva Reader*, Oxford: Blackwell, pp. 34–61.

Kristeva, Julia (1991), *Strangers to Ourselves*, New York: Columbia University Press.

Kuznets, Lois Rostow (1994), *When Toys Come Alive: Narratives of Animation, Metamorphosis, and Development*, New Haven and, London: Yale University Press.

Labov, William (1972), *Language in the Inner City*, Philadelphia: University of Philadelphia Press.

Lacan, Jacques (1977), *Écrits: a Selection* (translated by Alan Sheridan), London: Tavistock [orig. 1966, Paris].

Lambert, Angela (1993), 'Writers for children, please step forward', *The Independent*, 24 March, p. 19.

Lane, David (1996), 'Meet David Lane: managing director of Enid Blyton Ltd., interviewed by Norman Wright', *The Enid Blyton Literary Society Journal*, 1, Summer, pp. 28–30.

Laplanche, Jean and Pontalis, Jean-Bertrand (1986), 'Fantasy and the origins of sexuality', in Victor Burgin, James Donald and Cora Kaplan (eds), *Formations of Fantasy*, London: Routledge, pp. 5–34.

Lawrence, Elizabeth (1970), *The Origins and Growth of Modern Education*, Harmondsworth: Penguin.

Leeming, Jan (1982), [Interview with Sheila Ray on the *John Dunn Show*], BBC Radio 2, transmitted Monday, 23 August.

Leeson, Robert (1985), *Reading and Righting*, London: Collins.

Lehnert, Gertrud (1992), 'The training of the shrew: socialization and education of young women in children's literature', *Poetics Today*, 13, 1, Spring, pp. 109–22.

Leng, I.J. (1968), *Children in the Library: a Study of Children's Leisure-Reading Tastes and Habits*, Cardiff: University of Wales Press.

Lewis, C.S. (1950), *The Lion, the Witch and the Wardrobe*, London: Geoffrey Bles.

Lincoln, Yvonna S. and Guba, Egon G. (1985), *Naturalistic Inquiry*, London: Sage.

Lipman, Maureen (1995), 'Sunny Stories', in *You Can Read Me Like a Book*, London: Robson, pp. 94–102.

Lowe, Sue (1979), 'The effects of an overdose of Blyton: a case study', *Australian School Librarian*, 16, 4, Summer, pp. 107–9.
Lowry, Suzanne (1974), 'Behind the Green Hedges', *The Guardian*, 12 September, p. 11.
Lurie, Alison (1990), *Don't Tell the Grown-Ups: Subversive Children's Literature*, London: Bloomsbury [reprinted as *Not in Front of the Grown-Ups*, London: Cardinal, 1991].
Macaskill, Hilary (1991), 'Feminism and children's books', *Nursery World*, 12 September, pp. 20–1.
MacConnell, Mickey (c1993), 'Enid Blyton', *Peter Pan and Me* [CD], Rostrevor, Co. Down: Spring Records.
Macdonell, Diane (1986), *Theories of Discourse: an Introduction*, Oxford: Blackwell.
Mackenzie, Suzie (1997), 'Days of grace', *The Guardian*, 12 July, p. 25.
Macleod, Anne Scott (1994), *American Childhood: Essays on Children's Literature of the Nineteenth and Twentieth Centuries*, Athens and London: University of Georgia Press.
Maltby, Richard (ed.), (1989), *Dreams for Sale: Popular Culture in the Twentieth Century*, London: Harrap.
Mark, Jan (1993), 'Adlestrop and after', *Signal*, 71, May, pp. 94–102.
Martin, Constance (1970), 'South Sea Bubble', *Books*, 2, pp. 26–7.
Martin, Tony and Leather, Bob (1994), *Readers and Texts in the Primary Years*, Milton Keynes: Open University Press.
Mathieu-Colas, Marie-Pierre and Michel (1983), *Le Dossier Club des Cinq*, Paris: L'Ecole Magnard.
Matthews, Cindy (1984), [Letter] 'Well, golly bejabbers! three letters on racism and golliwogs', *The Guardian*, 12 May.
McAfee, Annalena (1994), 'Dreams, demons and a rare talent to disturb', *Financial Times*, 1 October, p. 21.
McClelland, Helen (1986), *Behind the Chalet School*, Bognor Regis: Anchor Publications.
McClelland, Helen (comp.), (1989), *Elinor Brent-Dyer*'s *Chalet School*, London: Collins.
McDowell, Myles (1972), 'Fiction for children and adults: some essential differences', *Children's Literature in Education*, 7, March, pp. 48–63 [also in Geoff Fox, Graham Hammond, Terry Jones, Frederic Smith and Kenneth Sterk (eds), (1976), *Writers, Critics and Children: Articles from Children's Literature in Education*, London: Heinemann Educational, pp. 140–56].
McKellar, Peter (1957), *Imagination and Thinking: a Psychological Analysis*, London: Cohen & West.
McKellar, Peter (1989), *Abnormal Psychology: its Experience and Behaviour*, London: Routledge.
McQuire, Elizabeth (1975), '"Home" versus "Dulce Domum"', *Children's Libraries Newsletter*, 11, 2, pp. 48–52.
Mee, Arthur (ed.), (1908–10), *The Children's Encyclopœdia*, 8 vols, London: Amalgamated Press.
Meek, Margaret, Warlow, Aidan and Barton, Griselda (eds), (1977), *The Cool Web: the Pattern of Children's Reading*, London: Bodley Head.
Meek, Margaret (1987), 'Symbolic outlining: the academic study of children's literature', *Signal*, 53, pp. 97–115.

Metz, Christian (1982), *The Imaginary Signifier: Psychoanalysis and the Cinema*, Bloomington In: Indiana University Press [orig. France, 1977].
Midgley, Carol (1998), 'Miss Marple starts a new life as she moves in with Noddy', *The Times*, 4 June, p. 1.
Miles, Robert (1989), *Racism*, London: Routledge.
Miles, Robert (1993), *Racism after 'Race Relations'*, London: Routledge.
Miller, Karl (1987), *Doubles: Studies in Literary History*, Oxford: Oxford University Press.
Millard, Elaine (1997), *Differently Literate: Boys, Girls and the Schooling of Literacy*, London/Washington, DC: Falmer Press.
Milne, A.A. (1926), *Winnie-the-Pooh*, London: Methuen.
Milne, A.A. (1928), *The House at Pooh Corner*, London: Methuen.
Milne, Christopher (1979), *The Path Through the Trees*, London: Eyre Methuen.
Modleski, Tania (1988), *Loving with a Vengeance: Mass-Produced Fantasies for Women*, London: Routledge [orig. Shoe String Press, 1982].
Moncrieff, Algy (1998), 'Bibliofile: Richard E. Grant', *The Sunday Times*, Books Section, 12 April, p. 11.
Montefiore, Jan (1993), 'The fourth form girls go camping: sexual identity and ambivalence in girls' school stories', in Judith Still and Michael Worton (eds), *Textuality and Sexuality: Reading Theories and Practices*, Manchester: Manchester University Press, pp. 173–92.
Morgan, Michaela (1994), *The Not So Famous Four*, London: Longman.
Morley, David (1980), *The Nationwide Audience: Structure and Decoding*, London: British Film Institute.
Morrison, Cathy (1984), 'Why PC Plod should come off the beat', *The Guardian*, 30 August, p. 8.
Morrison, Richard (1993), 'Grim scenes on the road to ruin', *The Times*, 22 March, p. 29.
Moss, Elaine (1974), 'The adult-eration of children's books', *Signal*, 14, May 1974, pp. 65–9 [reprinted in Margaret Meek *et al.* (eds), (1977), *The Cool Web: the Pattern of Children's Reading*, London: Bodley Head, pp. 333–7; also in Moss (1986), pp. 33–5].
Moss, Elaine (1977), 'The "Peppermint" lesson', in Margaret Meek *et al.* (eds), (1977), *The Cool Web: the Pattern of Children's Reading*, London: Bodley Head, pp. 140–2 [also in Moss (1986), pp. 113–8].
Moss, Elaine (1986), *Part of the Pattern: a Personal Journey through the World of Children's Books, 1960–1985*, London: Bodley Head.
Moss, Ernest (1970), 'Enid Blyton', [letter] *Times Literary Supplement*, 22 January, p. 85.
Moss, Gemma (1993), 'Girls tell the teen romance: four reading histories', in David Buckingham (ed.), *Reading Audiences: Young People and the Media*, Manchester: Manchester University Press, pp. 116–34.
Mourby, Adrian (1994), *Whatever Happened to the Famous Five?* Radio 4, 11 June.
Mourby, Adrian (1997), *Whatever Happened to . . . ? the Ultimate Sequels Book*, London: Souvenir.
Mullan, Bob (1987a), *The Enid Blyton Story*, London: Boxtree.
Mullan, Bob (1987b), *Are Mothers Really Necessary?* London: Boxtree.
Myers, Paul (1990), 'Toytown relief as Noddy and friends clean up their act', *The Guardian*, 1 August, p. 3.

Nash, Roy (1964), 'As Big Ears said to Noddy yesterday', *Daily Mail*, 7 February, p. 8.
Nell, Victor (1988), *Lost in a Book: the Psychology of Reading for Pleasure*, New Haven: Yale University Press.
Nelson, Clive (1993), 'Old golly has cost me my job', *Today*, 13 November.
Nesbit, E. (1959), *Five Children and It*, Harmondsworth: Penguin [orig. 1902].
Nesbit, E. (1958), *The Story of the Treasure Seekers*, Harmondsworth: Penguin [orig. 1899].
New Statesman (1980), 'Race, sex & class in children's books, parts 1–6, 14, 21, 28 November, 5, 12, 19/26 December.
Nodelman, Perry (1992), *The Pleasures of Children's Literature*, London: Longman.
Ochs, Elinor (1979), 'Transcription as theory', in Elinor Ochs and Bambi B. Schieffelin (eds), *Developmental Pragmatics*, New York: Academic Press, pp. 43–7.
Oliver, Paul, Davis, Ian and Bentley, Ian (1981), *Dunroamin: the Suburban Semi and its Enemies*, London: Barrie & Jenkins.
Opie, Iona and Opie, Peter (1959), *The Lore and Language of Schoolchildren*, Oxford: Clarendon Press.
Orton, Joe (1976), 'What the Butler Saw', in *The Complete Plays*, London: Eyre Methuen [first produced 1969].
Orwell, George (1954), *Nineteen Eighty-Four*, Harmondsworth: Penguin [orig. 1949, Secker & Warburg].
Orwell, George (1962), *The Road to Wigan Pier*, Harmondsworth: Penguin [orig. 1937, Victor Gollancz].
Osborne, Edgar (1948), 'The birth of Golliwog', [*sic*] *The Junior Bookshelf*, 12, 4, pp. 159–65.
OED (1989), Oxford English Dictionary 2nd edn, 20 vols, Oxford: Clarendon Press.
Palmer, Sue (1997), 'Enid Blyton – schoolmarm of the century', *The Sunday Times*, 12 January, p. 31.
Patten, Brian (1995), 'The secret pool', in *Green Hedges Magazine*, 15, p. 13.
Payne, Stewart (1993), 'Child-minder banned because of an old golly', *Evening Standard*, 12 November, p. 17.
Pearson, Allison (1992), 'Five talk dirty in Cornwall', *The Independent*, 8 March, p. 18.
Peelo, Moira (1994), *Helping Students with Study Problems*, Milton Keynes: Open University.
Peet, Hubert W. (1950), 'Birth of the Golliwogg', *John O'London's Weekly*, 22 December, p. 11.
Perkins, T.E. (1979), 'Rethinking stereotypes', in Michèle Barrett, Philip Corrigan, Annette Kuhn and Janet Wolff (eds), *Ideology and Cultural Production*, London: Croom Helm, pp. 135–59 [edited version in Helen Baehr and Ann Gray (eds) (1996), *Turning It On: a Reader in Women and Media*, London: Arnold, pp. 21–3].
Phillips, Judith L. (1992), 'Aussies go adventuring – readers in the making', *Orana*, 28, 4, November, pp. 272–8.
Pickering, Michael (1986), 'White skin, black masks: "nigger" Minstrelsy in Victorian England', in J.S. Bratton (ed.), *Music Hall: Performance and Style*, Milton Keynes: Open University Press, pp. 70–91.
Pieterse, Jan Nederveen (1992), *White on Black: Images of Africa and Blacks in Western Popular Culture*, New Haven and London: Yale University Press.

Plato (1955), *The Republic* (trans. by H.D.P. Lee), Harmondsworth: Penguin.
Powling, Chris (1983), *Roald Dahl*, London: Hamilton.
Preston, Ben (1993), 'County hall shuns Noddy and his pals', *The Times*, 14 September.
Propp, Vladimir (1968), *The Morphology of the Folktale*, 2nd edn, Austin: University of Texas Press [orig. Russia, 1928].
Quinn, Tim (1997), 'Mystery and suspense in the Land of Stupids, or: the mystery and suspense adventure', *The Enid Blyton Literary Society Journal*, 4, pp. 24–30.
Racism Spotlight Group (1984), *By Golly!! it's a happy nigger*, London: Racism Spotlight Group, Working Group Against Racism in Children's Resources.
Radway, Janice A. (1987), *Reading the Romance: Women, Patriarchy and Popular Culture*, London: Verso [orig. 1984, University of North Carolina Press].
Ray, Sheila G. (1982a), *The Blyton Phenomenon: the Controversy Surrounding the World's most successful Children's Author*, London: André Deutsch.
Renshaw, Heather (1980), 'Come back Enid', *The Times*, 5 March.
Reynolds, Kimberley (ed.) (1996), *Young People's Reading at the End of the Century*, London: Book Trust.
Richardson, Jean (1980), 'The Blyton case', *Birmingham Post*, 2 October, p. 4.
Robinson, Nigel (1997), *Enid Blyton's the Sea of Adventure: Screenplay Novelisation*, London: Collins 1997.
Root, Jane (1986), *Open the Box: About Television*, London: Comedia.
Rose, Jacqueline (1984), *The Case of Peter Pan, or, the Impossibility of Children's Fiction*, Basingstoke: Macmillan.
Ross, Gavin (1996), 'Endgames: weekend competition', *New Statesman & Society*, 9 February, p. 46; 1 March, p. 45.
Rowbotham, Judith (1989), *Good Girls Make Good Wives: Guidance for Girls in Victorian Fiction*, Oxford: Blackwell.
Rudd, David (1992), *A Communication Studies Approach to Children's Literature*, Sheffield: Pavic Press.
Rudd, David (1995a), 'Five have a Gender-ful time: Blyton, sexism and the infamous five', *Children's Literature in Education*, 26, 3, pp. 185–96.
Rudd, David (1995b), 'Noddy – his secret history', *Green Hedges Magazine*, 16, Autumn, pp. 3–10.
Rudd, David (1995c), 'Shirley, the bathwater, and definitions of children's literature', *Papers: Explorations into Children's Literature*, 5, 2–3, pp. 88–96.
Rudd, David (1996a), '"Malory Towers" – Enid Blyton's most popular series' [*sic*], *Folly*, 19, November, pp. 13–7 (see Rudd, 1997a).
Rudd, David (1996b), 'The mystery of the under-mind . . . a closer look at Enid's creativity – part I', *The Enid Blyton Book & Ephemera Collectors Society Newsletter*, 22, February, pp. 12–16.
Rudd, David (1996c), 'The mystery of the under-mind . . . a closer look at Enid's creativity – part II', *The Enid Blyton Book & Ephemera Collectors Society Newsletter*, 23, pp. 4–7.
Rudd, David (1997a), '"Malory Towers" – Enid Blyton's most popular school series – part II', *Folly*, 20, March, pp. 33–7.
Rudd, David (1997b), *The Famous Five: a Guide to the Characters Appearing in Enid Blyton's Series*, 2nd edn, Watford: Norman Wright [1st edn 1995].

Rudd, David (1997c), 'Enid Blyton and the paradox of children's literature', in Nicholas Tucker and Kimberley Reynolds (eds) *Enid Blyton: a Celebration and Reappraisal*, London: NCRCL, pp. 17–29.

Rudd, David (1997d) *Enid Blyton and the Mystery of Children's Literature*, PhD, Sheffield Hallam University.

Rushdie, Salman (1982), *Midnight's Children*, London: Pan.

Salinger, J.D. (1951), *The Catcher in the Rye*, London: Hamish Hamilton.

Sarland, Charles (1983a), [untitled review of Ray] *School Librarian*, 31, 1, March, p. 82.

Sarland, Charles (1983b), 'The Secret Seven vs The Twits: cultural clash or cosy combination?', *Signal*, 42, September pp. 155–71.

Sarland, Charles (1991), *Young People Reading: Culture and Response*, Milton Keynes: Open University Press.

Saunders, Kate (1995), 'Born on the wrong side of Toytown: Noddy and children's literature', *Sunday Times*, 16 April.

Savage, Juliet (1996), 'The Story of "Zwartz Piet"', *International Golliwog Collectors Club Newsletter*, 6 [http://columbia.digiweb.com/~brehm/golliwog/6gw2a.html].

Schneider, Elisabeth (1953), *Coleridge, Opium and 'Kubla Khan'*, Chicago: University of Chicago Press.

Schutz, Alfred J. (1962), *Collected Papers 1: the Problem of Social Reality*, The Hague: Martinus Nijhoff.

Sellers, Susan (1996), *Hélène Cixous: Authorship, Autobiography and Love*, Cambridge: Polity Press.

Selvon, Samuel (1979), *The Lonely Londoners*, London: Longman [orig. 1956].

Sewell, Elizabeth (1952), *The Field of Nonsense*, London: Chatto & Windus.

Shapiro, Michael Steven (1983), *Child's Garden: the Kindergarten Movement from Froebel to Dewey*, University Park and London: Pennsylvania State University Press.

Silverman, David (1996), 'Noddy loses his bell, by Homer', in 'Endgames', *New Statesman & Society*, 1 March, p. 45.

Sinclair, J.M. and Coulthard, R.M. (1975), *Towards an Analysis of Discourse*, Oxford: Oxford University Press.

Singer, Dorothy G. (1972), 'Piglet, Pooh, and Piaget', *Psychology Today*, June, pp. 71–4, 96.

Smallwood, Imogen (1989), *A Childhood at Green Hedges [a fragment of autobiography by Enid Blyton's daughter]*, London: Methuen.

Smith, Dennis (1987), 'English and the liberal inheritance after 1886', in Robert Colls and Philip Dodd (eds), *Englishness: Politics and Culture 1880–1920*, London: Croom Helm, pp. 254–82.

Smithers, Rebecca (1992), 'BBC buys Noddy and Big Ears', *The Guardian*, 6 March, p. 3.

Snoddy, Raymond (1996a), 'Noddy deal seeks big bucks from Big Ears', *Financial Times*, 1 May.

Soderbergh, Peter A. (1980), 'The Stratemeyer strain: educators and the juvenile series book, 1900–1980', in Sheila Egoff *et al.* (eds) (1980), pp. 63–73.

Speier, Matthew (1976), 'The Child as conversationalist: some culture contact features of conversational interactions between adults and children', in Martin Hammersley and Peter Woods (eds), *The Process of Schooling: a Sociological*

Reader, London: Routledge and Kegan Paul/Milton Keynes: Open University Press, pp. 98–103.
Spender, Dale (1990), *Man Made Language*, 3rd edn, London: Pandora.
Stainton Rogers, Rex and Stainton Rogers, Wendy (1992), *Stories of Childhood: Shifting Agendas of Child Concern*, London: Harvester Wheatsheaf.
Stallybrass, Peter and White, Allon (1986), *The Politics and Poetics of Transgression*, London: Methuen.
Steedman, Carolyn (1990), *Childhood, Culture and Class in Britain: Margaret McMillan, 1860–1931*, London: Virago.
Stephens, John (1992), *Language and Ideology in Children's Fiction*, London: Longman.
Stevenson, Robert Louis (1883), *Treasure Island*, London: Cassell.
Stones, Rosemary (1983), *'Pour out the Cocoa, Janet': Sexism in Children's Books*, London: Longman for the Schools Council.
Stoney, Barbara (1974), *Enid Blyton: a Biography*, London: Hodder and Stoughton.
Stoney, Barbara (1992), *Enid Blyton: a Biography*, rev. edn, London: Hodder and Stoughton.
Sullivan, Mary (1982), 'Land of Noddy', *The Sunday Telegraph*, 25 July.
Summerfield, Tony (1998), *Sunny Stories for Little Folks, 1926–1936: an Index*, Salisbury: Tony Summerfield.
Summerfield, Tony (1998), *A Comprehensive Bibliography of the Books of Enid Blyton, 1922–1970*, 3rd edn, Salisbury: Tony Summerfield.
Summerfield, Tony and Wright, Norman (1994), *Enid Blyton's Magazine, 1953–1959: an Index*, Watford: Norman Wright.
Summerfield, Tony and Wright, Norman (1995), *Sunny Stories, 1942–1953: an Index*, Watford: Norman Wright.
Summerfield, Tony and Wright, Norman (1996), *Enid Blyton's Sunny Stories, 1937–1941: an Index*, Watford: Norman Wright.
Sykes, Adam (1962), 'The books that children love' [an interview with Enid Blyton], *Time and Tide*, 43, 47, pp. 21–3.
Thatcher, Carol (1996), *Below the Parapet: the Biography of Denis Thatcher*, London: HarperCollins.
Thompson, Anthony Hugh (1975), 'The Enid Blyton affair', in *Censorship in Public Libraries in the United Kingdom During the Twentieth Century*, Epping: Bowker, pp. 137–57.
Thompson, Sarah (1987), 'Children love or hate Enid' *The Times*, 25 August 1987.
Thompson, David (1988), 'The genius of Enid Blyton', *Stamps and Printed Matters*, 9, 1, pp. 44–5.
Thompson, Harry (1991), *Tintin: Hergé and his Creation*, London: Hodder and Stoughton.
Thwaite, Ann (1992), *The Brilliant Career of Winnie-the-Pooh: the Story of A.A. Milne and his Writing for Children*, London: Methuen.
Tibet, David (1987), [Interview] *Option Magazine*, September/October [Internet edition].
Tolkien, J.R.R. (1937), *The Hobbit; or There and Back Again*, London: Allen & Unwin.
Tolkien, J.R.R. (1968), *The Lord of the Rings*, London: Allen & Unwin [orig. 1954–55].
Townsend, John Rowe (1976), *Written for Children*, Harmondsworth: Penguin.

Toynbee, Polly (1982), 'Noddy may be dead, but he won't lie down', *The Guardian*, 26 March, p. 11.
Trease, Geoffrey (1964), *Tales Out of School [a Survey of Children's Fiction]*, 2nd edn, London: Heinemann Educational [1st edn, 1949].
Trimmer, Mrs Sarah (1786), *Fabulous Histories, designed for the instruction of children, respecting their treatment of animals*, London: T. Longman & Co [later eds titled *The History of the Robins*].
Tucker, Nicholas (1970a), 'A glutton for punishment', *New Society*, 12 March, p. 446.
Tucker, Nicholas (1970b), 'All things Blyton beautiful', *Times Literary Supplement*, 16 April, p. 422.
Tucker, Nicholas (1970c), 'Family's Favourite', *New Society*, 20 August, p. 337.
Tucker, Nicholas (1976a), 'The Blyton enigma', *Children's Literature in Education*, 19 March pp. 191–7 [also in Norman Culpan and Clifford Waite (eds), *Variety is King: Aspects of Fiction for Children*, Oxford: School Library Association, pp. 72–8].
Tucker, Nicholas (ed.), (1976b), *Suitable for Children? Controversies in Children's Literature*, Sussex: Sussex University Press.
Tucker, Nicholas (1981), *The Child and the Book: a Psychological and Literary Exploration*, Cambridge: Cambridge University Press.
Upton, Florence K. and Upton, Bertha (1995), *The Adventures of two Dutch Dolls and a 'Golliwogg'*, London and New York: Longmans, Green & Co. [orig. 1895].
Upton, Florence K. and Upton, Bertha (1898), *The Golliwogg at the Sea-Side*, London: Longman & Co.
Valery, Anne (1991), *Talking About the War . . . [1939–45: a Personal View of the War in Britain]*, London: Michael Joseph.
Veeser, H. Aram (ed.) (1989), *The New Historicism*, London: Routledge.
Voilier, Claude (1987), *The Famous Five and the Z-rays* trans. by Anthea Bell, London: Knight [orig. *Les Cinq et Le Rayon Z*, 1977].
Voilier, Claude (1981), *The Famous Five Go On Television* trans. by Anthea Bell, London: Knight [orig. *Les Cinq à La Télévision*, 1973].
Vološinov, Valentin (1973), *Marxism and the Philosophy of Language*, New York: Seminar Press.
Vonnegut, Kurt (1972), *Slaughterhouse 5, or the Children's Crusade: a Duty-Dance with Death*, London: Panther.
Vygotsky, L.S. (1962), *Thought and Language*, Cambridge, Mass: MIT Press.
Wainwright Martin (1990), 'A telling story of children's TV celebrates 25 years', *The Guardian*, 27 December, p. 4.
Wainwright, Martin and King, Ian (1997), 'Butlin's spends £139 m sprucing up image', *The Guardian*, 4 September, p. 9.
Walker, Peter (1995), 'Flat earth: force of habit', *The Independent on Sunday*, 14 May, p. 18.
Walkerdine, Valerie (1986), 'Video replay: families, films and fantasy', in Victor Burgin, James Donald and Cora Kaplan (eds), *Formations of Fantasy*, London: Routledge, pp. 167–99.
Wall, Barbara (1991), *The Narrator's Voice: the Dilemma of Children's Fiction*, Basingstoke: Macmillan.
Walvin, James (1983), 'Black caricature: the roots of racialism', in Colin Husband (ed.), *'Race', in Britain: Continuity and Change*, London: Hutchinson, pp. 59–72.

Ward, David (1996), '"Sexist" Blyton turns feminist', *The Guardian*, 22 January, p. 7.
Warner, Marina (1994), *Managing Monsters: Six Myths of our Time*, London: Vintage.
Watson, Colin (1971), *Snobbery with Violence: Crime Stories and their Audience*, London: Eyre & Spottiswoode.
Watson, Ken (1987), 'Will Five run away with Biggles? – a series question', in Maurice Saxby and Gordon Winch (eds), *Give Them Wings: the Experience of Children's Literature*, South Melbourne: Macmillan, pp. 209–16.
Welch, Colin (1958), 'Dear little Noddy: a parent's lament', *Encounter*, 10, 1, pp. 18–23 [reprinted in *The Oddest Thing About the Colonel and Other Pieces*, London: Bellew, 1997].
Wells, H.G. (1895), *The Time Machine*, London: Heinemann.
Wheen, Francis (1997), 'Noddy in a spin', *The Guardian*, 3 December, p. 5.
Whitehead, Frank, Capey, A.C., Maddren, Wendy and Wellings, Alan (1977), *Children and their Books: Schools Council Research Project into Children's Reading Habits, 10–15*, Basingstoke: Macmillan Education.
Wilde, Oscar (1891), *The Picture of Dorian Gray*, London: Ward, Lock & Co.
Willey, Mason (1995), 'Sports and Games', *The Enid Blyton Book & Ephemera Collectors Society Newsletter*, 20, unpaged.
Wilson, Anne (1983), *Magical Thought in Creative Writing: the Distinctive Roles of Fantasy and Imagination in Fiction*, Stroud: Thimble Press.
Wilson, Jacqueline (1996), *Double Act*, London: Transworld.
Winder, Robert (1995), 'Noddy's off to Treasure Island . . .', *The Independent*, 18 November, p. 19.
Woodcock, John (1993), 'Tragedy of the schoolgirl from Malory Towers', *Daily Mail*, 16 December.
Woods, Frederick (1955), [Letter] *Journal of Education*, 87, p. 404.
Woods, M.S. (1969), 'The Blyton line: a psychologist's view', *Lines*, 2, 7, pp. 8–16.
Woods, M.S. (1974), 'The uses of Blyton', *New Society*, 19 September, pp. 731–3.
Wray, David and Lewis, Maureen (1993), 'The reading experiences and interests of junior school children', *Children's Literature in Education*, 24, 4, pp. 251–63.
Wright, Peter (1980), 'Five run away together – should we let them back?', *English in Education*, 14, 1, pp. 16–22.
Wyse, Barbara (ed.), (1996), *Guinness Book of Records, 1997*, London: Guinness.
Yates, Dornford (1929), *Blood Royal*, London: Hodder & Stoughton.
Zinsser, Hans (1935), *Rats, Lice and History*, London: Routledge.
Zipes, Jack (1992), *Breaking the Magic Spell: Radical Theories of Folk and Fairy Tales*, New York: Routledge [orig. University of Texas Press, 1979].

Index